Say What Your Longing Heart Desires

Say What Your Longing Heart Desires

Women, Prayer, and Poetry in Iran

NILOOFAR HAERI

Stanford University Press
Stanford, California

STANFORD UNIVERSITY PRESS
Stanford, California

Printed in the United States of America on acid-free,
archival-quality paper

Library of Congress Cataloging-in-Publication Data
Names: Haeri, Niloofar, 1958– author.
Title: Say what your longing heart desires : women, prayer,
and poetry in Iran / Niloofar Haeri.
Description: Stanford, California : Stanford University Press, 2020. |
Includes bibliographical references and index.
Identifiers: LCCN 2020025608 (print) | LCCN 2020025609 (ebook) |
ISBN 9781503601772 (cloth) | ISBN 9781503614246 (paperback) |
ISBN 9781503614253 (epub)
Subjects: LCSH: Muslim women—Iran—Intellectual life—21st century. |
Muslim women—Religious life—Iran. | Persian poetry—
747–1500—Appreciation. | Prayer—Islam.
Classification: LCC HQ1735.2 .H333 2020 (print) | LCC HQ1735.2
(ebook) | DDC 305.48/6970955—dc23
LC record available at https://lccn.loc.gov/2020025608
LC ebook record available at https://lccn.loc.gov/2020025609

Cover: *Sonnet III* by Jason Noushin

Book design: Kevin Barrett Kane

Typeset at Stanford University Press in 10/15 Sabon LT Pro

TO SHIRIN,
who made me think

TO MOHAMMAD-REZA,
for his luminous eyes

TO DANIYAL,
who was the answer to all my prayers

Contents

Note on Transliteration
and Translation

As a linguist who has studied Arabic and speaks Persian natively, I find the matter of transliteration particularly exasperating. Persian has countless borrowings from Arabic. These words are difficult to transliterate because Persian and Arabic phonologies are distinct, and one has to choose between making a word recognizable to Arabic speakers and reflecting the actual pronunciation in Persian. I have opted for the latter approach. I think the differences will not obscure the original Arabic. For example, *du'ā*, "prayer," is pronounced *do'ā* in Persian, where instead of the Arabic 'ayn, Persian speakers have a glottal stop, the hamza. I distinguish between the pharyngeal 'ayn (') and the glottal hamza (') *only* in the few instances where I quote some text in Arabic. Following the decision to use a transliteration system that reflects Persian phonology and pronunciation, no distinction is made between ayn and hamza because, in Persian, words derived from Arabic have their ayns transposed into hamzas.

I have tried to avoid excessive use of diacritics, to make the text more reader friendly. I have limited diacritics to the length marker (a macron, or bar, placed over a letter), because there are an overwhelming number of Persian words with long vowels. Rather than use two vowels—[*aa*], [*uu*], or [*ii*]—to indicate length, I use the aforementioned macron (ā, ū, or ī). Words with long vowels will appear in italics and with a length marker *the first time each word occurs in a chapter.* After that first time, the word will appear with one vowel, and will not be in italics. For example, *namāz* will be namaz after the first mention in each chapter. Two words that occur frequently in the text and are maintained in their Arabic transliteration are *sura* and *āya*. In Persian, they are *sureh* and *ayeh*, and I was not sure they would be recognized correctly by those who are familiar with the terms but not with Persian.

The spelling of Persian and Arabic words commonly found in English-language media has not been changed, in particular when it comes to proper names; hence, I use Saadi and Etesami instead of Sa'di and E'tesami. I use "Imam" in reference to Shi'i Imams but "imam(s)" when I am referring to someone who holds that position, say in a mosque.

In Persian, there is no pronominal gender in the third-person singular, or for that matter, any pronoun. In English, I am obliged to choose a gendered pronoun, and because it is accepted practice to use the masculine pronoun for God, I follow this tradition. Each time "He," "Him," or "His" appears, the reader is asked to remember that in Persian this designation is just a third-person singular pronoun.

All translations from Persian are mine unless otherwise indicated. Please refer to the glossary for guidance on the pronunciation of frequently occurring terms.

Preface

This book had its beginnings in a series of inquiries that sprang up unexpectedly while I was doing research several years ago in Tehran on a different subject. Having grown up in a religious family in Iran, with a rather well-known ayatollah as my grandfather, and having lived through the 1979 revolution, I spent many years of my life running the other way whenever the subject of religion came up. I was uninterested and at times even quietly hostile.

Then one summer evening in 2008, I went to visit a relative in Tehran. When the sound of the call to prayer came on the television, she went to her room to do the evening ritual prayers. When she returned, I noticed that she had a smile on her face and looked serene. She told me that her prayers that evening had "gone well" and that she had managed to feel close to God.

I was mystified. Could *ritual* prayers go well or badly? In all the years that I had spent in the company of women and men who prayed, I had assumed that they were basically uttering the same short *sūra*s (chapters) of the Qur'an while they went through the prescribed body postures and that the prayer session was finished once they had recited the very last sura and had completed the farewells to God and His messenger. That was all. So what could this woman mean when she said her prayers went well? Was she implying that prayers could also go badly?

Are rituals not authorless acts that are scripted, and believers just follow the script? And if so, then what could happen differently in the duration of their performance if every step was followed as the performer had been told to do it? Questions like these made me realize that in fact, I did not understand the most basic ritual that Muslims must perform every day. I had the sinking feeling of someone under whose nose whole worlds had existed and played out, while she had been running away.

But I don't think I was alone. The degree of intolerance that I witnessed on the part of secular Iranians toward their "religious" compatriots in the course of fieldwork for this book was an eye-opener. They often expressed cynicism and spoke of Islam as the source of "all of our problems." In one of my talks on prayer at a university in the United States, a number of Iranians in the audience accused me of engaging in propaganda in support of the Islamic republic because I did not express opposition to prayer but was instead doing research on it. I put the adjective *religious* in quotation marks earlier because I think we need to ask, and not take for granted that we know, what it means to be religious. This question became a major driver for the research that followed my experience with the woman who told me about her ritual prayer, her *namāz*. That research eventually led me to understand far better the significance of the questions that were being debated in the public sphere in Iran: What does it mean to be a Muslim? What kinds of Muslims are there in any given time and place? What kind of Islam is the true one? In this book, I explore the debates, doubts, imaginations, exchanges, ideas, and practices of a group of Shi'i Muslim women who aspire to find answers to those questions.

As a result of serendipitous conversations such as the one I just described, I fell in with a group of women who had been attending weekly Qur'an and classical poetry classes for years. The chapters that follow are based on exchanges with these women that took place between 2008 and 2016. I talked to several men as well—the women's Qur'an and poetry teachers and their male siblings—and also various other women and men that I ran into. These experiences led me to identify a few areas where there are marked gender differences. For example, women regularly organize various kinds of religious gatherings for which they go to great lengths in terms of time and expense. The frequency, size, and elaborateness of these gatherings depends on the organizer's class and education. I almost never heard of similar gatherings organized by men, at least not on a regular basis. In fact, during these kinds of ceremonies, the men in the house are generally asked to leave, although theoretically they could use a separate space in the house and have an event of their own. Another gendered practice is that many women use prayer books that aim to teach special rites for specific purposes and needs and that contain prayers said to be composed by the Imams, whereas these women also report that their fathers or brothers rarely show interest in such prayer books. I found that to be the case as well in my conversations with some of the men who became my interlocutors. Still, the type of searching and exploration of religion undertaken by the group of women with whom I worked can also be observed among men. For example, in poetry classes that are offered in neighborhood cultural centers, as well as in discussion groups organized at homes, there are usually as many men as women. The struggles to define the *kind of Islam* that one ought to pursue seem to me to be shared by women and men. In this book, however, I write almost entirely about the women I befriended. On the one hand, the rapport that I was able to build with them as well as my ease of access were determining factors leading me to limit my research to women. On the other hand, with a few exceptions, most of what has been written on Islam has focused on Muslim men, and we do need more studies of women.

Returning to my relative's living room on that night, I was so intrigued by what she said about prayer that I left the research project I had begun, and concentrated on namaz, the ritual and obligatory prayer of Muslims (*salāt* in Arabic) that must be performed five times per day. As I expanded my network and was able to engage in more in-depth conversations, the questions proliferated and led to others—for example, Muslims are routinely characterized by acts they are *required* to undertake, such as namaz, and not by those they engage in that are not compulsory—these are called *mostahabbāt* ("favored" acts). There are many of them. Muslims also do nonobligatory spontaneous prayers, called *do'ā*, at least as frequently as ritual prayers. And yet one rarely hears much about do'a—how, when, and why such prayer is performed. What do people say to God? Is God treated differently in a do'a than in ritual prayer? Is there anything to be learned from the fact that the namaz is in Arabic whereas the do'a that follows it is almost always in Persian?

As I began to accompany my interlocutors to their various weekly activities, I noticed that they all attended poetry classes as well—most for years if not decades (none of them writes poetry of her own as far as I could tell). The classes covered almost exclusively the work of classical poets: Hafez, Saadi, Mowlavi (Rumi), Nizami, and others. Was I to treat the women's commitment to poetry as something entirely different from their pursuit of Qur'an classes? What would we miss, both about their religiosity and about contemporary Iran, if we examined only what we perceive to be explicitly the domains of "religion" and of "Islam"— namaz, fasting, alms, pilgrimage to Mecca, and so on?

After participating in the weekly poetry classes, it became clear to me that poetry and prayer are companions in the lives of these women and, more broadly, in the cultural history of Iran over the last few centuries. They continue to exchange, argue, challenge, borrow, and glance at each other. Classical poetry, as others have pointed out, came to be synonymous with mystic poetry in Iran. And this poetry is simultaneously Islamic and a challenge to what some Iranians call "dry religion." More broadly, it has been the provocateur par excellence for posing theological and existential questions. As one of my interlocutors put it, "this poetry waters our religion." What does this companionship mean for forms of religiosity in Iran?

The women I write about came of age at the time of the 1979 revolution. They describe how the revolution prompted them to think more profoundly about Islam. They contrast their religiosity with that of their parents and grandparents, characterizing the latter's approach as "inherited"—that is, they relied on what they were told and were not sufficiently independent-minded. The stories and analyses of my interlocutors were an education for me, and I hope they will serve the reader in a similarly rewarding way. My overriding goal is to share these women's reflections.

I have tried to make this book, insofar as possible, free of jargon, having in mind, in addition to university students, a broadly educated readership. For this reason, I have avoided many theoretical lines of inquiry that I hope to pursue in other venues. In order to make it easier for the non-specialist reader to follow up on some of the discussions, I offer in the notes links to sources that are in English and easily accessible (such as entries in the *Encyclopædia Iranica*) in addition to scholarly references. I also include links to songs and recitations.

Acknowledgments

This book is the fruit of many exchanges in Iran, the United States, and Europe, over more years than I care to count. The earlier periods of fieldwork that I spent in Egypt are also in the background of some of these exchanges. Over years of my traveling to Tehran, the women who are the subject of this book gave me hours and hours of their time and attention and their profound reflections on my endless questions. I am immensely grateful for their generosity and openness. Without their enthusiastic involvement in my research, this book would not have come into existence.

In Iran and later on in the United States, several research assistants who are now scholars in their own right helped me at the National Library in Iran and located any number of articles, books, and websites: Leila Faghfouri-Azar, Fateme Bostani, Saeedeh Rahimzadeh, Paul Park, Victor Evangelista, and Jeffrey Culang. Natalie Stewart helped me with the formatting, bibliography, and an ever-present sense of humor. I thank the late Pouran Soltani, the director of the National Library, for her guidance.

Friends and scholars who inspired me and showed generosity in sharing ideas over the years are Behrooz Ghamari-Tabrizi, who often explained to me what I was really saying; Robert Orsi, whose encouragement and support as well as his own scholarship have been essential to the completion of this book; Fenella Cannell, to whom I am grateful for our exchanges and for her invitation to the workshop Comparative Ethnographies of Prayer in May 2014 at the London School of Economics, where I met Robert Orsi and also William Christian with whom I had the good fortune to discuss Catholicism and Islam; Michael Lambek, whose friendship and scholarship have nourished this book; Tanya

Luhrmann, who took an interest in my work on prayer and shared her own work; Kirin Narayan, who gave me both solid encouragement and her friendship; Michael Jackson, who offered graceful and perceptive comments on my chapter on poetry; Talal Asad, whose work has been a guiding light and who gave me helpful comments on my work on sincerity; Shahzad Bashir, with whom I have had great discussions about Islam and poetry; and Houchang Chehabi for his reading of some of the chapters and for his suggestions. I also thank Leslie Aiello and Danilyn Rutherford of the Wenner-Gren Foundation for their support and friendship.

Moving on to family, my sisters and brother gave me kind and unconditional support: Shahla Haeri, whose scholarship on Islam has been an inspiration; Shokoofeh Haeri, who made sure to check on me regularly to see if I had my wits about me; and Shirin and Mohammad-Reza Haeri, whose great enthusiasm for this research propelled me forward. Shirin was a singular source of great reflections on religion and prayer. I learned everything I know and did not know from Shirin, who gave me hours and weeks of her time. She is one of the women that I write about in this book, but she preferred to remain anonymous. My brother's knowledge of poetry and of Iranian cultural history were invaluable for my research. He located countless books and articles. Kioumars Mazandarni Haeri (aka Q) always made me think further about some of the arguments. My son, Daniyal Haeri Porteous, grew from a little boy to a teenager in the course of my writing, and never ceased to stop by my desk every few days and ask, "How many more pages do you have to write?" Pouné Saberi has been a solid pillar of support with her presence and smiles, giving me "strength of heart" across the years. I thank Catherine and Robin Porteous for sharing their views on Anglican prayers, Bible translation, and the history of Christianity. Ali Porteous read my work on prayer and gave me much encouragement. The friendship of Rebecca Porteous and Ali Fahmi has meant a great deal to me over the years. Tom Porteous listened patiently to my ideas as this research was taking shape. He read versions of the first few chapters and edited them for clearer prose. Let me here thank Kate Wahl of Stanford University Press for shepherding this book through publication with a warm, no-nonsense hand that I greatly appreciated.

The story of the beautiful cover of this book is worth sharing. After lengthy searches online, I came across the work of the Iranian-British artist Jason Noushin. I wrote to him asking if I could use his *Sonnet III* for my book cover. He could not have been more open and generous. We spent an hour on the phone reminiscing about Iran and life abroad. He not only let me use his painting but allowed us to make a mirror image of it. This latter was done with the help of Q. I thank Jason for being such a wonderful person and artist.

In Baltimore, I want to thank Linelle Smith and Tom Hall. Linelle read Chapters 1 and 3 and offered wonderfully insightful comments. I am grateful to Mae Thamer for one of the longest and warmest friendships I have ever experienced. Anand Pandian read early versions of my writing on prayer and made valuable suggestions. I thank our departmental staff Lexie Stafilatos and Clarissa Costley for their daily support. My colleagues Ryan Calder and Lawrence Principe at the Program for Islamic Studies at Johns Hopkins University generously took over the directorship of the program so that I could take advantage of my sabbatical leave in the 2015–16 academic year. In the course of the last few years, I lost three friends to early death: Pamela Neville-Sington who inspired me with her resolve not to be afraid of life, Bernard Bate, and Sonja Luehrmann, whose friendship I continue to miss.

Almost halfway through the writing process, I heard about Shahab Ahmed's seminal book *What Is Islam? The Importance of Being Islamic*. I learned a great deal from this work, but perhaps more importantly, I felt accompanied in what often feels like the rather discouraging task of writing about Islam for Western, non-Muslim publics. Shahab Ahmed died at a young age in 2015. I remain thankful to him for the extraordinary erudition and the amiable fearlessness with which he wrote his *magnum opus*.

I had the great fortune of receiving a generous Guggenheim fellowship and a Marta Sutton Weeks fellowship from the Stanford Humanities Center in 2015–16 that allowed me to pretend I was writing the whole time when I was often reading as much as I could. Having chosen a project that sat at the intersection of several fields, much reading was in order.

While at Stanford, I met a number of scholars who read and commented on various chapters of my book: Gabriella Safran, Rumee Ahmed, Kay Kaufman Shelemay, and Scott Bukatman. Caroline Winterer who was the center's director at the time, Lanier Anderson, a fellow, and the entire staff helped make our time at the center truly superb.

My parents, Behjatosadat Altoma Mousavi and Jamaleddin Mazandarani Haeri, have both passed away but they are ever present in my life and in every page of this book.

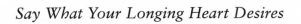

Say What Your Longing Heart Desires

Introduction

HOW DOES ONE AVOID LOOKING at the aftermaths of uprisings and revolutions and seeing them only in terms of failures and successes? Even when political failures may be obvious, developments in other spheres of life and culture also need to be carefully examined. The Iranian revolution of 1979 has had a transformative effect on matters of religion. Questions, doubts, ambivalences, and long-accepted divisions between "the secular" and "the religious" have become objects of debate on a wide scale, crossing class, gender, and ideological lines. The old distinction in Muslim-majority societies between the elite (scholars) and the laity has become increasingly blurred as non-clerics learn to engage in theological discussions. Given the eventual establishment of an *Islamic* republic, a series of fundamental questions having to do with Islam have come to preoccupy Iranians. The revolution is routinely characterized in Western media and by some in academia as one that made Iranian society "go backward." Yet, if we choose not to begin with the presumption of backwardness and absence of intellectual struggles, then we are open to discovering unexpected but crucial processes that have been set in motion.

A great deal of contemplation and reflection has emerged in Iran in relation to Islam, religion more broadly, ritual, divinity, worship, and mysticism. A vital question with high stakes that has come to be debated in the last few decades is, What *kind* of Islam is the true one and the one we should aspire to in the contemporary moment and in the wider world today? Given such a question, it is important to look at resources that laypeople use to find answers and to debate them.

There are Iranian Muslims, as there are followers of many other religions, who may be characterized as "blind followers" or at least as uninterested in intellectual inquiries. But there are also many others whose thinking on matters of religion has become far more informed and nuanced. For example, these days, even when an Iranian Muslim believes that doing an obligatory ritual without "presence of the heart" and sincerity is religiously valid and accepted, she or he *also knows* that many others, laypeople and clerics, are troubled by the idea of doing rituals if they are to be acceptable merely from the point of view of religious law. Hence, although it is the case that sincerity in ritual prayer, for example, is *not* required by religion (*vājeb*), lamenting its absence is a topic that routinely comes up in conversation and on radio and television. On many programs, hosts and guests offer suggestions on how to achieve a state of sincerity in worship. So well-known has the matter of the quality of ritual performance become that in some bookstores, one can easily approach a salesperson and ask, "Do you have a book on presence of the heart?"

Alongside widespread disenchantment and frustration with various postrevolutionary governments, a set of ferocious and high-stakes debates have been taking place in the public sphere. Iranians are grappling with increasingly difficult living conditions as a result of corruption, repression, and also extreme economic sanctions imposed by the United States, and at the same time they are wondering what ought to happen in terms of political solutions. Those who are believers see the question of what kind of Islam they ought to aim for as relevant to the other problems. In fact, all that has to do with religion has now become a matter of reflection and scrutiny—from the nature of God to how each believer ought to build a relationship with Him and also the role of rituals and the contradictions created by clergy who seek to participate in both the spiritual and the political spheres. What people encounter as "religion" and what they learn through family members, texts, teachers, art, sounds, experiences, and spaces form material that individuals *work with*. Once they interact with this material—for example, once they begin praying regularly—the prayer does not remain intact. The individual brings to the prayer her own background, body, imagination, thoughts, and past experiences, and also ideas from adjacent worlds such as poetry.

What I am interested in conveying in this book is what different individuals *do* with religion. That is, what is the content of their struggles? What are the means they use to advance their thinking? In the course of the following chapters, I offer an ethnography of a group of educated, middle-class women and of the ways in which they go about exchanging and debating matters of religion. Their attempts are carried out simultaneously on the individual and collective levels—they discuss their personal understandings and experiences with many others and engage in an ongoing back and forth. My interlocutors are not isolated individuals avoiding interaction with others. They talk to their friends and to people they meet in their weekly classes, participate in larger gatherings, read, have Facebook accounts, and send each other digital files featuring their favorite cleric, author, satirist, and politician. There is little about their deliberations, ideas, and practices that is "private." Agentive deliberation has become widespread. Their changing religiosity is a subject of complex interactions between the self and a community of believers.

Debates in the Public Sphere after the Revolution

Following the initial euphoria over the success of the 1979 revolution and the end of the Pahlavi monarchy—something no one in Iran expected to see in their lifetime—Iranians experienced several years of harsh repression in the 1980s and a devastating war with Iraq (1980–1988) that, in effect, consolidated the Islamist groups' hold on power. After the end of the war, as daily life began to become somewhat more predictable, Iranians' previous unidirectional interest in Euro-American history and culture was replaced by curiosity concerning all things Iranian—a shift that has been called the *reflexive turn*.[1] So much upheaval, hundreds of thousands of people killed and maimed in the war, cities showing enormous scars, so many families scattered all over the globe—all these outcomes and more brought on a sober mood mixed with curiosity about Iran and its inhabitants, its past and present, its cultures and religions. For instance, there appeared an ever-expanding number of gatherings and more formal classes (*kelās*) on the poetry of beloved poets such as Hafez Shirazi (1315–1390), Saadi Shirazi (1210–1291), and Jalal al-Din Muhammad Balkhi (1207–1273), referred to as Mawlana or Mowlavi in Iran (Rumi), and also classes on the Qur'an, Iranian classical music, architecture, and calligraphy. These were mixed in with even more classes in yoga, Carl Jung and other European thinkers, and also arts of self-improvement (*khod-sāzi*) and self-knowledge (*khod-shināsi*). The classes take place both in people's homes and in neighborhood cultural centers (*farhang-sarā*). One of the major initiatives of urban municipalities after the revolution was to build such cultural centers, particularly in poorer neighborhoods, to provide "healthy" and acceptable education and entertainment for youth.

Early in my fieldwork, I noticed that the question of what kind of Islam to pursue, posed in many forms, articulated or silently implied, exploratory or rhetorical, was ubiquitous. The Islamic republic set out to define its own kind of Islam and to produce, accordingly, citizens who would be *homo Islamicus*. But ideas about Islam, even among state institutions, were varied and changed depending on a variety of conditions, including the personalities of members of the top echelon, such as the Supreme Leader. Many institutions urgently set about re-evaluating practically all behavior, appearance, forms of worship, names of people and places (pre-Islamic vs. Islamic, or European names), relationships to the divine, and Iranian and Islamic culture(s), and determining how these re-evaluations ought to be propagated. As the state was busily engaged in these re-evaluations, practically everyone ended up with a stake in debating what is true Islam and who, if anyone, has the authority to define it. The state's claim on both the spiritual and the political realms, its coercive insistence on telling citizens how to dress, appear in public, pray, eat, drink, interpret verses of the Qur'an, and so on, made the debate an existential one. Either one had to conform, at least publicly, or learn to argue one's way out. Otherwise, one could potentially be punished, in many different ways.

The cooptation of the public sphere through the use of radio, television, newspapers, and the Internet and the coercive measures to form a Muslim citizenry could have resulted in a polarized population neatly divided into two camps: believers and nonbelievers, pro-Islam and anti-Islam, pro-regime and anti-regime. But instead, something more complex and varied has happened, a result less stark and black and white. There are, of course, people who have become allergic to the sound of and even the word *Islam* and all that goes with it. They simply cannot tolerate the Islamic republic's imposition everywhere they turn, and say so loudly in any place they can. It is not hard or dangerous to voice this dissatisfaction if one frames it in terms of "what is happening is not really Islam," a discourse deployed even by those who are not believers. But there are also many groups of women and men who have not ceded the grounds of religion to those in power. Instead, they have struggled to prevent the state's desired monopoly on the question of what kind(s) of Islam one ought to aspire to. They have done this, in part, by bringing religion to bear on matters that are of more recent concern, such as equality in marriage and divorce, ecology, natural resources, and water management. For example, in reaction to the everyday act of washing one's car on the street, it is common to hear neighbors ask rhetorically, "How can he be a real Muslim if he thinks nothing of wasting so much water when we have been in a drought for years?" Such commentary with this particular logic is ubiquitous these days.

Against the odds, the public sphere in Iran has become more vital and plural since the revolution.[2] This surprises most people outside the country and perhaps some inside, too. Given a form of government that claims to be Islamic and that expresses the desire to Islamize all acts, behavior, and institutions, the immediate questions became, what is Islamic? who decides? and on the basis of which traditions? As sociologist Behrooz Ghamari-Tabrizi explains, "By locating Islam in the public sphere," the religion itself was transformed "from an a priori source of legitimacy into a contested body of discourses." Wishing to Islamize Iranian society, Ghamari-Tabrizi continues, "the Islamizers had to struggle continuously over the meaning of Islam and its bearing on specific contemporary social, economic, and cultural issues."[3] Laypeople began formulating questions that had not been asked because the stakes were so low before the revolution—or that had been discussed only among clerics and intellectual elites. Such questions multiplied and extended far and wide, in large part in reaction to the efforts of state institutions to Islamize society from top to bottom. Piety had to be visible to the eyes and ears of the state. But many Iranians begged to differ, relying in part on the poets who continued to be widely recognized as the truest of Muslims.

It is not that these debates are new. Across the centuries, Muslim thinkers, philosophers, poets, theologians, and scientists have written on what it is to be *din-dar* (literally, to have religion or be with religion) and how to become *khoda-shinas* (a knower of God). What means, then, do ordinary

Iranians use to enter debates on religion, the ethics of being a true Muslim, and divinity? One of the most basic sources of ideas, concepts, and vocabulary is the vast body of mystical writing in Persian, and in particular, the classical poetry that Iranians have read or heard for centuries and continue to read today. This poetry is where, for example, the idea of praying with presence of the heart comes from—representing a kind of piety that is free of hypocrisy. One of the most consistent themes in this poetry is how to recognize religious hypocrisy. There are a surprising number of terms for insincerity in this poetry—a fact that shows the intense preoccupation with false piety. Among these terms are *riyā*, *salūs*, *tazvīr*, *nājins*, *nefāq*, and *zarq*, accompanied by the well-developed deceitful figures of the "piety-sellers," the sheikh, the frequent mosque-goer, and so on. As early as the tenth century, the poet Rudaki (d. 940) wrote:

> What God accepts from you are love's transports,
> But prayers said by rote He won't admit.[4]

The renowned translator of the Qur'an and literary historian Baha'eddin Khorramshahi has written extensively on Hafez, including a book-length monograph on the poet. In a section on Hafez's humor and doubts about what is held to be sacred (*moqaddasāt*), Khorramshahi writes:

> Given that *namāz*, fasting, praying and other sacred acts are important symbols and have high religious value, the question is why has Hafez tangled with such spiritual matters? Was there no other matter to go to combat against? The answer is that at the same time as recitation of the Qur'an and doing namaz and fasting and praying are sacred acts, unfortunately they are not always heartfelt, [done with] purity and sincerity. . . . Even the Qur'an itself rebukes those namaz-reciters who lack presence of the heart (Ma'un, 4:5): "Woe to namaz-reciters who are inattentive to their namaz." . . . The biggest threat [*āfat* (that which can act like a contagious disease)] to these kinds of worship and all that is sacred is insincerity and hypocrisy [*riyā*].[5]

One could say that all these poets and Hafez in particular were almost obsessed with the "disease" of hypocrisy and insincerity. As a casual exercise, I tried to count the number of verses in his divan that have to do with riya, but I soon lost count and gave up. Skepticism over coercive, visible, and legalistic religion has long been part and parcel of cultural and political discourse in Iran, even among clerics.[6] It is important to understand that what was new after the revolution was the reach and the high stakes of this discourse, partly owing to the flux of war, repression, a devastated economy, and long ration lines, but also owing to the uncertain excitement of a reflexive turn that posed questions such as should we pray out of love for God or out of fear. These questions gradually came to define the postrevolutionary and post–Iran-Iraq war moments.[7]

That laypeople engage in matters of theology has had the consequence of lightening the starkness of the long-standing historical distinction in Muslim societies between elites (*khawās*) and laity (*'avām*),[8] as was mentioned before. One factor, among many others, that has enabled the latter's participation is that they can read bilingual Qur'ans, in Arabic and Persian—most Iranians do not know Qur'anic Arabic.[9] Also, in weekly Qur'an classes, the availability of countless translations of the Qur'an results in participants' coming with many different translated editions. When each verse is read out loud, its Persian translation is shared by those whose versions differ. This immediately turns into a hermeneutic exercise in which lay Iranians can participate to various degrees. In the long debates that ensue, problems of translation and interpretation merge, so that the inadequacy of a word in Persian for a particular term in the original Arabic leads to further considerations that have to do with theological precedence, likelihood, and coherence. Some pull out various Arabic-Persian dictionaries to check their translations. In this way, even those without much knowledge of Islamic theology or of Qur'anic Arabic manage to participate in interpreting the Qur'an. Given Iran's high literacy rate today as compared to even a few decades ago, people's access to sources of knowledge, and the proliferation of colleges, universities, and seminaries, as well as publications and websites, that distinction has not only diminished but has become less acceptable and justifiable. Although one can still hear some impatience in the discourse of clerics and even, at times, educated secular Iranians, toward lay participants, it is not as taken for granted as it used to be.

In scholarly work, Islam is often represented as a uniquely legalistic religion whose adherents are always sure of what to do and what to think.[10] The late Shahab Ahmed refers to this approach as a "totalizing 'legal-supremacist' conceptualization of Islam as *law*, whereby the 'essence' of Islam as a phenomenon of prescription and proscription, induces, indeed *constrains* us to think of Muslims as subjects who are defined and constituted by and in a cult of regulation, restriction and control."[11] Muslims are routinely described in the media and in social scientific writing in terms of *obligatory* and required conduct—matters that are vajeb. But there is a large body of what are called *mostahabbāt*—acts that make one "favored" in God's eyes—and these are not vajeb, meaning that not doing them has no legally defined reprimand or punishment. I did not meet anyone who stayed away from such acts because they are not legally required. Examples are nonritual prayer (*do'ā*), visiting sick people, paying homage to elders, helping the poor, feeding the hungry, being good tempered, and even saying *salām* (hello). One could say that mostahabbat help clarify the *ethics* of being a Muslim. I include in this book two chapters devoted to acts that are *mostahabb*—spontaneous conversations with God and reciting Imams' prayers. The absence of systematic attention to favored as opposed to mandatory acts has made Muslims appear, for all times and in all places, as rigid, unbending, and without doubts or ambivalence about what it is they have to do to be a Muslim. One could be forgiven for thinking that Muslims have hardly any interiority and individuality.

At least since the thirteenth century, a great deal of mystical thought and theorization in Iran has been carried out in the form of poetry. Classical poets have elaborated on the nature of the divine, the path or journey toward God (*selk*), the conduct (*solūk*) through which one may seek a sincere relationship with Him that is out of profound love (*'eshq*) rather than fear, the quality of ritual performance, and the invisible heart (rather than public displays) as the true seat of religiosity. For many laypeople, it is this poetry that serves as the main source of ideas for exploring and making sense of what it is to be a true Muslim.

In the following pages, I examine the ways in which women's explorations of the kind of Muslim they strive to be involves, among other things, the centuries-old companionship and exchanges in Iranian cultural and intellectual history among mystical poetry and scriptural sources such as the Qur'an, the hadith, Imams' biographies, and more recent writings by clerical scholars and those who are referred to as "religious intellectuals." As I will show in the next chapter, this companionship is reproduced in women's daily lives. In addition to an ethnography of the place and role of poetry in the lives of my interlocutors, I will examine three kinds of prayers, each constituting a separate speech genre—spontaneous prayers called do'a, which are not mandatory, can be undertaken at any time, and are in Persian; ritual obligatory prayers called namaz (salāt in Arabic), whose verses come from the Qur'an and are therefore in Arabic; and finally prayers composed and passed down by various Shi'i Imams and gathered in prayer books edited and "updated" by well-known clergy. These are also in Arabic. In each chapter, I will attend to the contours of the coexistence of Persian and Arabic in the realm of religious acts and the implications of the contrasts in their historical and social lives. The doctrinal disagreements between Shi'a and Sunni Muslims are given much coverage in Western scholarship. But the contrasts between Arabic and Persian language ideologies and their implications for the choice of language of mass education, and the availability of bilingual Qur'ans in Iran, have had profound consequences for the participation of lay Iranians in theological debates. These and similar factors have little to do with denominational differences.[12]

My interlocutors for this study all read the Qur'an regularly. They have memorized many parts of it and attend Qur'an classes. But their reflections about who is a true Muslim are not limited to strictly religious or scriptural sources. In the course of the many conversations I had with them, it became clear to me that in order to understand their subjectivity as Muslims, it was not enough to examine how they performed ritual and non-ritual prayers and what ideas they held with regard to the underlying theology or philosophy of worship. Their attention to poetry, honed since childhood, was part and parcel of the same world. Scriptural sources and commentary on them on the one hand and mystic poetry and the vast literature on this poetry on the other are the major discursive traditions that have been in dialogue with each other over centuries, crisscrossing in different ways depending on sociopolitical conditions.[13] There are many historical and contemporary forces that shape Iranian society and the groups within it.[14] In this book I focus on the exchanges between mystical poetry and scriptural sources.

Using the grounds of prayer and poetry, I hope to illuminate the women's analyses, critiques, and disagreements. Almost all of them have been attending poetry classes with great commitment for at least a decade. They also organize their own gatherings where, among other things, poetry is shared. Historically, gatherings are the most popular form of socialization in Iran. There are many regular get-togethers. We have *dowrehs* (literally, cycle or periodicity—a regular gathering of people who, for example, went to the same school or worked in the same place), *mehmāni* (a generic term for "party"), *majles* (a get-together for poetry recitations and literary discussion; also meaning "parliament"), *sofreh* (a gathering for the purposes of a vow that has been made), and *rowzeh* (a mainly religious gathering where a reciter with a pleasant voice is invited and paid to recite *sūras*, prayers, and devotional poetry). Kelas (a class) can be added to such get-togethers regardless of where they take place. In classes, whether spontaneous or planned, it is common and even expected for various individuals to bring up particular poems to recite and discuss, or a paragraph from the writings of an author who has caught their attention and that they find somehow relevant to share; satirical writings on the political situation are also a regular part of gatherings, as are music and songs.

It is important to rethink the significance of the space of the home after the revolution in Iran. Under conditions where a variety of activities cannot easily find venues in more institutional settings, many events have moved indoors. The degree to which this movement to indoor space happens continues to vary depending on political conditions. The home has been transformed into a quasi-public space. People organize gatherings and sometimes even invite speakers—this can mean asking a friend or even a stranger they met somewhere to speak on a particular topic. These talks are followed by question and answer sessions and long discussions. Those who attend such gatherings do not all know each other; they may be invited by friends of friends of friends. People come prepared with material that for one reason or another they find relevant to share—a poem, a passage of prose, a joke or a literary satire, recent or old stories with punch lines.

They come with recommendations for books, CDs, and classes in another person's home or another cultural center. At times, television talk shows of various formats reflect the themes and questions raised in such home gatherings. Hence, making a sharp distinction between the public and the private would obscure the complexity of what has been happening.

Two of the most important terms used in this book are *mysticism* and *poetry*, but their associations in English, historical and contemporary, can lead readers astray. For *mysticism*, one can use *Sufism* in English. However, in Iran the preferred term is *'erfān,* derived from the Arabic root meaning "gnosis."[15] Although I will most often employ 'erfan, occasionally I will use "Sufi," "mystic," and "mysticism." In English, reading poetry is often deemed a rarified act reserved for a small group of highly educated, elite individuals who tend to read it silently, as a private activity. In Iran, the body of classical poetry that I discuss is shared and discussed most often in a group, congregationally. Poetry is recited and sung, offering a shared aesthetic pleasure, mediating group intimacy, and promoting debate about how one ought to behave, what an ethical life is, what use it is to pray if one lies and cheats, and other questions. Even more than with poetry, the term mysticism in English implies a domain of thought that is perceived to be far removed from the daily lives of ordinary people. This is not the case in Iran. 'Erfan is relevant everywhere, from mass media to music, everyday exchanges, textbooks, biographies of poets and Imams, and classes for adults.[16] It is broadly divided into "practical" (*'amali*) and "theoretical" (*nazari*). 'Erfan has become so popular that the term is now being used as a proper name for both boys and girls.

Let us examine in some detail the debates generated by one of the best-known and beloved versified stories of Rumi.[17] We can then see the place of 'erfan in contemporary Iran more clearly.

The Story of Moses and the Shepherd:
Grounds for (Self-)Exploration

During several summers spent in Tehran, I attended a class on Rumi that met once a week for two hours in one of the postrevolutionary neighborhood cultural centers funded by the Tehran municipality.[18] I was taken to this class by a woman who became one of my main interlocutors during the fieldwork for this book. The class met in the late afternoon in order to accommodate working adults—including the teacher, who had another day job. There were around fifty people in the class, ranging in age from the mid-twenties to the mid-seventies and more or less equally divided between men and women.

Every week, about four pages of text taken from Rumi's *Masnavi-e Ma'navi* (Couplets of true meaning) were distributed to each student. Rumi wrote the *Masnavi* toward the end of his life. It consists of hundreds of versified stories and has been published in six *daftar* (volumes). The *Masnavi* uses dialogue to tell its stories and represent different viewpoints. Rumi seems to favor this pedagogic form for elaborating his mystical ideas. The conversational form of address and the story genre give a certain simplicity to the language of the poems.[19]

The *Masnavi* is referred to by Iranians as "the Qur'an in Persian tongue" (*qur'ān-e fārsi*); it is considered by some to be the highest achievement of mystical thought.[20] One of the *Masnavi* stories read and discussed over several classes was the immensely popular *"Mūsa va Shabān"* (Moses and the Shepherd; Mūsa is pronounced "Moossa" in Persian).[21] It is perhaps the most famous of Rumi's dialogues. The story begins as Moses overhears a shepherd praying:

"O God, tell me where you are so that I may become your servant, stitch your shoes, rub your feet, wash your clothes, make your bed and kill your lice. . . . O, you to whom I sacrifice my goats."[22]

When Moses finds out that the shepherd is talking to God in such intimate ways, and as if God has a body, he tells him not to talk to God like that:

"Don't talk about shoes
and socks with God! And what's this with *Your little hands
And feet*? Such blasphemous familiarity sounds like
you're chatting with your uncles.
Only something that grows
needs milk. Only someone with feet needs shoes."[23]

The shepherd becomes despondent, tears his shirt, and runs into the desert.

God then sends a revelation to Moses:

> You have separated Me
> From one of my own. Did you come as a Prophet to unite,
> Or to sever?[24]
>
> . . .
>
> I have given each individual [kas] a nature [sirat]
> I have given each individual expression
>
> . . .
>
> Hindus praise Me in the Hindi tongue
> Sindhis praise Me in the Sindhi tongue
> I am not made pure by their remembrance [prayers]
> but pure, full of pearls, do they become[25]
>
> We have no regard for words or *qāl*
> We look at their spirit and *hāl*

The last verses end with the rhyming qal and hal. The former refers to language, or that which is expressed verbally, and the latter refers to one of the most central concepts in 'erfan. It is a complex term meant to capture a sudden, fleeting, and unpredictable change in one's emotional state, a moment when one feels an overwhelming sense of connection to the divine (to nature, to the universe)—a sense of ecstasy, joy, or even deep sorrow. It is this state that God tells Moses is important. The shepherd was in hal, the truest state. The qal does not matter.

The poem goes on to describe how Moses feels great turmoil after receiving this revelation: "He understood secrets that cannot be said; Truth found a home in his mind, he flew many times between eternities, he went through what cannot be put into words." Moses then runs after the shepherd and, catching up with him, tells him what God has revealed:

> Don't search for manners and rules
> say what your longing heart desires.[26]

This last verse has become a saying and the embodiment of the idea of the heart as the true and invisible place from which love toward God must emanate. It continues to be used in a variety of everyday contexts.[27]

Across the centuries, Moses and the Shepherd has been told and retold in many different forms, in songs, plays, comic strips, and even an opera.[28] It has served as a vehicle for calling attention to how each individual's particular approach to the divine may be different. As long as the hal is there, others should not interfere with the manner.

What has great implications for the continued presence of mystic poetry in Iran is that its language tends toward vernacular usage, shunning archaic and flowery styles. Peter Avery, a scholar and translator of Persian classical poetry, wrote about the appeal of Hafez, lasting over six centuries and continuing to the present:

> It should be noted that his diction is, in fact, ordinary colloquial Persian, with words and phrases that can be translated into such colloquialisms as the English "sure" and "OK"; but in Hāfiz it is colloquial Persian raised to the level of high literary diction. Yet, how far his usage consists of ordinary conversational Persian, as common today as it ever was, must not be forgotten. The Persian language has changed less since the death of the poet Rūdakī in 940–1 AD than has English since that of Chaucer in 1400; Chaucer, of course, was Hāfiz's contemporary.[29]

It is in fact the case that relative to many other languages, Persian has not changed as much in the same time periods and it remains for now somewhat of a puzzle why that should be the case. Similarly, historian of the Persian language John Perry believes that Rumi is a master of the "high colloquial . . . followed by Saadi and Hafez."[30] For an example of how Rumi viewed the matter of language, we should return once more to Moses and the Shepherd. Rumi was most certainly aware of the exalted status of Arabic, knew it, read it, wrote poetry in it, and mixed it in his Persian poems. Yet, he made in this poem one of the strongest statements against accepting the authority of a prophet to tell people how to talk to God and in what language. He seems to argue against the orthodoxy of language, formality, and a God-given sense of linguistic appropriateness more generally:

Hindus praise Me in the Hindu tongue
Sindhis praise Me in the Sindhi tongue

I am not made pure by their remembrance
but pure, full of pearls, do they become
We have no regard for words or language
We look for spirit and behavior
We see the heart and if that's humble
ignore the words used, brash or mumbled[31]

The language ideology exalting a form of vernacular Persian, albeit a "high colloquial" one, for the purposes of poetry in part explains how this centuries-old body of work continues to be accessible, to various degrees, to people with widely ranging levels of education. The form of Persian used in this poetry is largely a descendant of what is commonly called New Persian, developed after the conquest of Iran by Muslim armies in the seventh century.[32] New Persian emerged about two centuries after that conquest, a period chronicled by the cultural historian and critic Abdolhossein Zarrinkoub in a book called *Two Centuries of Silence*, a reference to the lack of material in Persian remaining for posterity from those centuries.[33] New Persian integrated a large number of lexical borrowings from Arabic, adapted Arabic orthography by adding new letters representing sounds that Arabic did not have, and eventually came to be used for administration, education, and literature. New Persian's lexicon, like that of other languages, has experienced additions, adaptations, extensions, and deletions over time, yet the poetic vocabulary continues to be taught at schools. Grammatically, New Persian has gone through a variety of changes, but as it is employed by the writers of classical poetry (for which syntax matters far less than it does for prose), it remains broadly accessible to contemporary readers in ways that a thirteenth-century poem in classical Latin or classical Arabic would not be to present day readers. Verses of Moses and the Shepherd and many other poems from the *Masnavi* at times sound startlingly contemporary.

The concept of hal has been central to continuing debates over piety, religiosity, sincerity in worship, and the unmediated relationship between the worshipper and God. Hal is a major contribution of Islamic mysticism to the understanding of metaphysical experience and divine presence.[34] It characterizes experiences that cannot be placed into binary categories of "religious" and "secular," or easily articulated discursively. An example of the occurrence of hal would be when, on a bright and sunny spring day, one is walking in a park and suddenly is filled with an unexpected and over-whelming joy—a sense of a connection to something larger than oneself. Hal is uncontrollable, unforeseeable, and cannot be honed. One cannot undertake certain practices or rituals so that it occurs more frequently or lasts longer. It does not depend on how often or how fervently one performs religious obligations. For these and similar reasons, the concept has, on the one hand, spawned a vast discursive tradition most eloquently expressed in poetry and also has, on the other hand, been a thorn in the side of official, legalistic religion, because hal, by definition, cannot be mediated by those who claim to possess more piety or a closer relationship to God.[35] As Rumi makes clear in his story, even a prophet cannot mediate it.

In May 2014, one of the Islamic republic's most ardent promoters ex-plained his opposition to this poem and to Rumi. Hojjat al-Islam Qara'ati has a large presence in the media, with his own show on television and an active website. He is also the head of the national prayer organization (Setad-e Iqam-e Namaz-e Keshvar).[36] In a television interview, he said that the story of Moses and the Shepherd clearly shows Rumi to be opposed to the whole idea of prophecy; Rumi is an "anti-prophet," and the poem is against the Qur'an: "I have critiqued this poem in my programs. This poem is wrong [ghalat]—its premise is wrong. It is not compatible with the Qur'an and our beliefs and hadis [hadith in Arabic; the Prophet's acts and sayings]."[37] The Hojjat al-Islam then referenced verse 19:90 in the Qur'an, where great wrath is expressed toward those who might assume that God has a body (jesm).

> Now some shepherd thinks that God has a body and says "where are you so I may comb your hair" and I don't know what. . . . Hazrat-e Musa [Moses the Prophet] tells the shepherd what are these things you are saying? This is polytheism [sherk]. But God then scolds Mo-ses and tells him, why have you separated us from our own.
>
> But . . . Prophets came in order to prevent such nonsense. The Prophet [Moses] is doing his job when he tells him don't talk to God

like that. But God says to him "you don't talk"! God should have said to Moses "Well done, bravo [*āfarin*]," but instead scolds him?

That last question was of course rhetorical. And as is the case in most discussions of literary stories, in particular in the body of classical poetry, the tale was treated as if it were a historical event. Hojjat al-Islam Qara'ati expressed strong disagreement with God and sided with Moses. Prophets must correct the ways of worshippers and mediate the relationship to the divine. Furthermore, the Hojjat al-Islam did not like the idea that there might be any kind of equivalence or simultaneous consideration between the Qur'an and the Prophetic *hadis*, which are guides to true Islam, on the one hand, and the work of Rumi, Saadi,[38] and Hafez[39] on the other. He reminded viewers of a hadis that says only the Qur'an and "my *sunna*" (my tradition) count. He concluded his attack on Rumi in this way: "No one says 'God's book and my sunna' AND *Masnavi* AND Saadi AND Hafez. Our poets, ulamā, and scientists are limited [*mahdūd*] and they may say things that are not correct."[40]

A few days later, when President Rouhani's special assistant on minority ethnic and religious affairs, Ayatollah Ali Younesi, paid a visit to a synagogue in Shiraz, he replied to the cleric, without naming him: "Worship ['*ebādat*] is the relationship of the individual [*fard*] to God [*khodā*]. It does not matter in what language and style. . . . Mowlavi [Rumi] wanted to illuminate one truth and that is the relationship between the human being [*ensān*] and God."[41] There were many reactions to Younesi on social media. In reply to the president's advisor, one right-wing website wrote: "If the language and expression of worship is not considered to be important, then essentially how can we prescribe to society any [religious rules]? . . . This tendency of Younesi is the opposite of the national policies of the republic with respect to questions of spirituality [*ma'naviyat*]."[42] Hojjat al-Islam Qara'ati also complained that mystic poems of the kind Rumi wrote are included in school textbooks. Indeed, in the Persian literature (*adabiyaat-e farsi*) textbook published in 2009 for the third year of middle school, an abridged version of Moses and the Shepherd appears. The paragraph-long introduction to the poem states that the *Masnavi* is an "ocean of '*erfan* knowledge, wisdom, and lessons" and ends by saying,

"Mowlana in this story has put the main condition for getting close to God and for his acceptance of our worship, a pure heart free of hypocrisy [bi-riyā]."[43] As can be seen, the Ministry of Education is implicated in the debates on who is a true Muslim. Persian language and literature textbooks have content from 'erfan sources and themes. Judging by the extent of the material on 'erfan, there must be a fair number of "'erfan-minded" people working on the content of the textbooks.[44] Perhaps one should not count on this state of affairs to remain unchanged, and when change comes to eliminate that content, it will be one of the most significant developments in the course of the revolution and the republic.

Both clerics, Hojjat al-Islam Qara'ati and Ayatollah Younesi, are deeply bound to the state in Iran, the former in his various capacities as a promoter of the republic and as a media figure, and the latter as a special assistant to the president. And yet, we can see a profound difference in their approach to religion and to what pleases God in relation to worshippers' attempts to get close to Him. This difference is widely reflected among Muslim Iranians. One might well ask why, if 'erfan thinking exposes such rifts and challenges "dry religion," should a major institution of the Republic propagate it through including it in teaching material? There are a number of factors at work here. 'Erfan is rooted in Islamic theology, history, cultures, and aesthetics; it is not foreign to or outside of the religion. Neither the poets (and thinkers) themselves nor their opponents have disavowed their identity as Muslims. Shunning 'erfan in Iran would mean having to put to one side what is considered to be one of the central crowning achievements of the Persian language and Iran's contribution to Islam across borders.[45]

The depth and breadth of the mystic tradition in Iran is such that it divides even individuals, groups, and institutions that are, to one degree or another, proponents of the Islamic republic. I offer two more examples. On the website of the Qom Seminary, the most august and prestigious institution of learning within Shi'i Islam, nonobligatory, spontaneous prayer (do'a) is defined as a "spiritual relationship between the creator and the created, and the thread of union [reshteh-ye peyvand] between the lover and the Beloved."[46] This is an arresting conception of the kind of prayer the shepherd was engaging in. The premier seminary of Shi'i Islam, which, in coordination with the seminary in Najaf, has trained the best-known ayatollahs—some of whom became leaders of the Islamic revolution, including Ayatollah Khomeini, refers to God just as Rumi does, as "the Beloved" and refers to the worshipper as "the lover." The seminary is not part of the state, and this is not to say that every single teacher or student at the seminary holds this view with respect to spontaneous prayer. There is routinely great disagreement among seminarians. And in fact, a fair number, though it is hard to tell the exact proportion, are against the republic. However, the website does officially represent, though admittedly homogenizes, the positions of some of its members.[47]

Let us move to another example. The state-owned and state-operated television network, National Iranian Sound and Image, has a channel, called Network 4, devoted to educational content. Several weekly talk shows, with somewhat distinct politics and approaches to religion, invite a variety of religious public intellectuals to appear, both clerics and non-clerics, or as some Iranians would say, turbaned and hatted.[48] The host of one of these programs, Ismail Mansouri Larijani, who has a doctorate in 'erfan from Azad University, was approached in 2008 by the director of Network 4 and asked to produce a program on the theme of "reason and love" ('aql o 'eshq). The choice of regular guests or co-organizers for the program was left to him. Eventually, a weekly program called Ma'refat (Gnosis) was produced, and one of the speakers regularly featured was the soft-spoken and elderly, retired professor of philosophy Gholamhossein Ebrahimi Dinani.[49] In one episode, Dr. Dinani spoke favorably of the mystical dance samā': "trees are in a dance, rocks, the sea, the mountains . . . the whole universe is in a dance . . . the 'ārif [mystic] experiences spiritual movement, his spirit is in motion. This spiritual internal dance also moves the body . . . it makes the body move in a harmonious way [mowzūn]."[50] He cited Qur'anic verse 27:88 in support of his position: "And you see the mountains, thinking them rigid, while they will pass [drift] as do the clouds."[51]

Judging by the number of websites that reported on this episode of the program, the number of comments each received, and the fact that one website contacted several major ayatollahs to get their opinion, Dr. Dinani's exuberant description of this centuries-old practice proved to be highly controversial. A large number of comments written on these sites were in agreement with him and cited all kinds of poetry by Hafez and Rumi and others to support their case. But most ayatollahs contacted said that dancing (*raqs*) is *harām* (religiously forbidden). Dr. Dinani was asked repeatedly on the same and other programs to explain himself.

All three of these examples demonstrate the ambivalence with regard to 'erfan of individuals and institutions across a spectrum of proximity to the state. Since the revolution, the historical practice of documenting and propagating the idea that the Qur'an has been the main inspiration for all of the mystic poets has become even more pronounced. There are many concordances showing, at times line by line, how, for example, Rumi's *Masnavi* is directly inspired by the Qur'an. But there is also a similar movement showing how the Imams were themselves major mystics ('arif). This is a way of laying claim to a national and historical poetic culture that continues to be reproduced generation after generation.[52] One could say that vis-à-vis this heritage, the state faces a central paradox. On the one hand, the state aims to define and impose visible signs of piety and to Islamize appearances, ideas, and practices, and it suppresses Sufi groups, especially after the death of Ayatollah Khomeini. But on the other hand, it also engages with the concepts and vocabulary of 'erfan—a discursive tradition that is highly skeptical about *mediated* piety.

I argue that poetry has been crucial in braiding 'erfan into various kinds of religiosity. One can hardly separate it from "Islam" in Iran, as is demonstrated by the three examples that we just examined. In my interview in the summer of 2015 with Mohammad Mujtahed Shabestari (b. 1936), one of the best-known, prolific, and original thinkers among the contemporary Muslim religious intellectuals (*roshanfekrān-e dini*), he said:

> After the revolution, there was a lot of *boghz* [pent up anger, grudge, rancor] but religious ideas came to be hotly debated. The time has passed when they would bring some [authority] and he would say this is the way things are and that would be it. The heart of our society has many diverse ideas . . . even in *sunnati* [traditional] groups.

[People] say, "Well, such and such ayatollah has said what he has said but that does not necessarily mean anything." . . . Ayatollah Khomeini himself changed the religion. He said that music is fine. He himself opened the way for religious discourse [goftār-i dini].[53]

Mujtahid Shabestari refers here to the highly controversial position that Ayatollah Khomeini once took against music, only to change his mind later.[54] I suggest that in contemporary Iran, what is true Islam continues to be debated and remains ultimately unresolved, notwithstanding the coercive powers of the state.[55]

What Does It Mean to Be Religious? The Use of *Hal* in Everyday Language

The discourse of hal permeates the classical poetry canon. But it is also present in the ideas and language of today's laypeople, including non-Muslim Iranians. Vernacular Persian contains many expressions constructed with hal. One hears, for example, "sometimes I go through periods where namaz does not give me any hal." The dictionary of contemporary vernacular Persian, *Ketab-e Kūcheh* (Book of the alley/street), lists more than thirty examples of phrases using hal, nine related meanings, and numerous infinitives (made with hal and a verb or hal and other nouns and a verb). Here are a few examples of expressions with hal, from my own fieldwork:

hal nemideh	does not give hal (said of praying in crowded mosques)
bā hal būd	it had hal (can be said of a performance, a gathering, a place, or a person: e.g., "she is ba hal")
hal kardan	to have a good time, to enjoy
hal-am jāā āāmad	[it] returned hal to me
sar-e hal būd	she or he was in good spirits
hal-esho gereft	she or he [or it] took away his or her hal (said of a bad experience)

There are also expressions such as *hālet chetowreh* (how is your hal), meaning "how are you?" And *hal o havā* (literally, "hal and air/desire,"), referring to, for example, a place or person that has good vibes. There are many more that I could list, but the point is that hal is a central concept in 'erfan that permeates ordinary, vernacular Persian.

It is noteworthy that such widely used expressions were not prevalent among the generation of the parents of the women I was meeting with. In past years, many of the expressions were strongly marked as lower class, male, street language, and slang, but this characterization has become less stark and/or less provocative, as the exponential increase in their use in the speech of the younger generations demonstrates. One of the most common ways hal is used is to give a positive characterization of a person or an event: for example, "she is very ba hal," meaning she is lively or has a good presence. Ordinary Iranians are, for the most part, familiar with the concept of hal, without necessarily having read some of the major thinkers of mysticism, such as Ibn Sina (Avicenna, 980–1037), al-Ghazali (1058–1111), Suhrawardi (1155–1191), Ibn Arabi (1165–1240),[56] or other more contemporary thinkers.

As I described in the preface, the idea that ritual prayers can "go well" or "badly" (see also Chapter 2) so puzzled and attracted me that I began to think more broadly about the question of what it means to be religious. That first conversation about namaz led in the ensuing summers to wider conversations and to other interlocutors. I met friends and friends of friends and people who were strangers to each other but whom I became acquainted with in various gatherings. I went to their classes and met more people to talk to, including the teachers. I noticed that one of the attractions of the classes for the people attending them was that they shared not just what they were reading but also their experiences, memories, dreams, inspirations, and imaginings to express what they were discovering and living through. Such networks of individuals who meet in each other's homes, in classes, in poetry reading gatherings, in lectures, and in celebrations are crucial to the vitality of daily life, at least in urban centers.

My Interlocutors in the Field
The number of people I talked to about the subjects of this book over the years likely exceeds sixty to seventy individuals. And I listened to many more. Among those I talked to over the several summers and also four

months in the winter of 2010 that I was able to spend in Tehran, I got to know twenty-five women more closely, most of them ranging in age from their mid-sixties to mid-seventies. A few were younger: two in their forties and one about fifty-five. Most of these women are retired public high school teachers and receive a pension from the state. At times, when I refer to them collectively, I say simply, "the women in our group." They told me how their own approach to religion had changed after the revolution by becoming far more reflective. Most of them had parents who were religious to various degrees, but as they explained to me, during the time they were growing up, religion was not something constantly being discussed or disputed everywhere. It was there, but "quietly" so. State institutions then, under Mohammad Reza Pahlavi, were at best ambivalent about Islam and often simply excluded it from consideration. There was in any case no coercion about conforming to particular practices in public. My interlocutors see their parents' approach to religion as a point of comparison to their own. For the most part, their parents were not as concerned with whether they had presence of the heart or felt hal once in a while when they prayed. It was a *taklīf* (duty) that they had to undertake because the namaz prayers are obligatory and so they performed them every day. The women implied that their parents may have thought of themselves as 'avam (laity).

With two exceptions, all the women in our group had lost their parents. But I was able to talk to three women who were in their early nineties and were family members of the younger women. I include my conversations with one of these older women, Aziz jan, in the following chapters. As is customary in Iran, due to her age she is referred to with respect and affection by attaching *jan* to her first name. In this context, it is a term of endearment that is hard to translate—a rough equivalent would be "dear," but literally it means "life" or "breath." Aziz jan finished ninth grade, called *sikl-e avval* (from French, *premier cycle*). She grew up in the holy city of Mashhad, and her husband was still alive. She continues to do charity work but was never able to hold a regular job due to lack of childcare. She has five children.

I met several of the twenty-five women who became my interlocutors in the various classes I began attending, and they introduced me to their friends and relatives. Some of them already knew each other to various degrees, being cousins or friends. They come from a range of middle-class backgrounds, with civil servant parents. Some suffer from large debts that they are repaying bit by bit out of their pensions, while a few are better off, with fathers and husbands who are businessmen. Their mothers finished ninth grade and some finished high school also. They themselves went on to college to study psychology, chemistry, mathematics, biology, English, and Persian literature. A few attended a teacher's training college. One has a master's degree from an American university in sociology and another a master's degree in English language from a university in Iran. Two worked in the Ministry of Culture under the previous regime, helping with the creation of a Persian dictionary. Although they all live in Tehran now, about half of them are from Shiraz, Isfahan, Yazd, or the Caspian Sea area. I have changed some of the details of their lives and used pseudonyms to protect their anonymity. In addition to this group of women, I interviewed their Qur'an and poetry teachers and a number of ayatollahs and other religious figures, as well as university professors, authors, journalists, and librarians.

In order to be able to communicate to the reader the level of ethnographic detail that I find necessary in relation to the questions pursued, I had to focus mostly on a subset of six of the twenty-five women, which means I do not write about all the women in equal detail, although what I describe for each religious act, for example, is based on everyone with whom I spoke. The older women in this group were both more available and seemed to have more to say about their life experiences. So, although I rely on my interviews with all of these women and I also draw on my experiences of growing up in Iran, the women with whom I spent more time appear more often in the following chapters, and I write about them at greater length. In each chapter, there are many details of their lives that emerge in their replies to my questions. Except for introducing the six women whom I talked to the most, I will leave those details to be discovered by the reader in the women's own voices instead of repeating them here. I was treated like a younger sister, and as such, there were certain questions that I did not broach. For example, I did not feel I should ask about their relationships with their husbands. And they showed no interest in talking about such matters. Of the women I mention by name, three have a living husband, though one of these men lives in another city and visits from time to time. The husbands of the others have passed away, and in two cases, my interlocutors had divorced their husbands before the revolution.

In almost all cases, I was invited to the women's homes and stayed for lunches and dinners, at times meeting them for breakfast instead when the day was going to be uncomfortably hot. In this way, I also met other members of their families—children who still lived with them or who came by, as well as other relatives. Each summer, I organized about three or four gatherings at my sister's home, and invited as many as I could for lunch. These gatherings often lasted for hours. Because the women are so used to taking classes in the Qur'an and poetry, and often share similar backgrounds in terms of their jobs, the gatherings proved highly successful in promoting long and detailed discussions.[57]

Let us learn a few more details about the women who figure prominently in the following chapters. Maryam, whose views on namaz encouraged my original interest in the themes pursued in this book, was in her early seventies when I talked to her. She is a retired high school teacher who majored in mathematics in high school and then went on to study psychology in college. She taught Persian grammar and literature in a girls' public high school in a poor neighborhood in south Tehran. She prepared herself for teaching grammar and literature by taking night courses in these subjects, since she had not specialized in them. The job opening was for a literature teacher and so she had to retool. Her mother had obtained a high school diploma and had also taught, but had to leave her job after a few years because she had no help with childcare. Her father was a civil servant who had gone to college. Both were from religious families and were themselves religious. They urged their daughters to go to university and become financially independent. Maryam did not feel that they saw any difference between her and her brothers in terms of aspirations and ability. She has grown children who live abroad. Her husband had passed away about a decade before I met her.

Parvin has a master's degree in sociology from an American university. She is the same age as Maryam. She went back to Iran after finishing her studies and began teaching social studies at a high school close to where Maryam was teaching. That was how they got to know each other. Parvin is the only one in this group who was sent to a private, religious elementary school; all the others went to regular public school. For her secondary education, Parvin, too, went to a public school and majored in physics. Her father, who was a civil servant, had a high school diploma while her mother had finished elementary school and never worked. Parvin married an artist from Tehran, whom she divorced when she was in her late fifties. She has three grown children.

Mina has a bachelor's degree in psychology and a master's degree in teaching English as a second language. She is in her early seventies. She taught social studies and history at the high school where she worked. She grew up in Shiraz before moving to Tehran. Her husband is a Sunni from the northwest of Iran. According to Mina, her parents prayed but were not very observant. Her father was an engineer. Her grandmother, who lived with them, was more observant, and she taught Mina how to pray. Mina has two grown children.

Pari is in her early seventies and has a bachelor's degree in chemistry. She taught the same subject. Before retiring about a decade ago, she became the director of her school for a few years. Her mother finished ninth grade and did not work. Her father was a civil servant. Her husband was a surgeon; they divorced when Pari was in her forties. She does extensive charity work searching for funding for families who cannot afford to send their children to good schools and colleges. She has one daughter.

Simin is about fifteen years younger than the others and did not go to college. In high school she majored in biology. Her father and husband are both well-to-do bazaar merchants, and this allows her not to work. She takes care of her three daughters' children while they work. She attends classes in *khod-shenāsi* (self-knowledge), Qur'an, poetry, and sports. As she herself explains (as reported in Chapter 1), her parents were not very observant, but they did teach her how to pray. Her mother finished elementary school.

Elaheh is in her mid-sixties and grew up in Qom and Tehran. After her children were grown, she went to college to study literature. However, the commute was too difficult for her, and she quit after two years. Her father, who is now deceased, was a religious scholar and a well-known translator of the Qur'an. Her mother finished elementary school and did not work outside the home. She has three grown children. Elaheh is invited on a weekly basis to give lectures in various Qur'an and poetry classes, where she teaches Saadi and Rumi. Her husband is a retired civil servant.

I begin in Chapter 1 with the place of poetry in the lives of these women, starting from their childhoods.

Where Do Ideas Come From?

An Education in Classical Poetry

In 1952, when Pari was about twelve years old, she won a prize at school for the recitation of a long poem by the female poet Parvin Etesami (1907–1941). It was one of Etesami's longest poems—more than fifty lines—and Pari was still proud that she had been able to deliver it in a school celebration in front of a large audience with great verve and without going blank. It is a beloved poem about Moses' mother fearing that her child will be in danger on the water and be forgotten by God. God replies to reassure her that her child will be taken care of. Pari's prize was a book of poetry by Etesami, which she has kept all her life.

During the summer of 2016, in one of the several gatherings my interlocutors and I shared, we discussed the presence of poetry in their childhoods, as they were growing up, and in the current moment. Pari said:

> My mother was very much into poetry and literature. The books of four poets were around us: Hafez, Saadi, Mowlana [Rumi], and Parvin Etesami. And there was also the Qur'an. These five books were always in front of our eyes. . . . My mother used to recite their poetry, often to herself, and just the sound of these poems in our house was very pleasing to us even when we did not really understand what the poems said.

Pari employed a widely used expression, *ahl-e* (fond of, into; literally, "a dweller of," "belonging to [the world of]"), to describe her mother's love of poetry. With this spatial expression, Pari described her mother as an inhabitant of the world of poetry. Speaking about her own encounter as a child of seven or eight with this kind of grown-up poetry, Pari explained that from some of the poets whose books were "in front of our eyes," she would pick up a few verses—those that she heard around her and was somehow able to relate to. For example, with Rumi, she found the lines of the poem at the very beginning of the *Masnavi* (lines universally known in Iran) particularly moving:

Song of the Reed (Beshno az Ney, or Neynameh)
Listen to this reed
Play out its plaint
unfold its tale
of separations[1]

She said that the verses "sat on my soul,"[2] as they spoke of the pain of the reed that had been torn off, separated from its bed, and made into a *ney*— a kind of flute. Any playing of the ney then brings out that "plaint . . . of separations."[3] Although at that age she found much of Rumi difficult to understand, her entry into his poetry began with just a few lines of this poem. The intellectual and emotional bonds that children make with poetry that is meant for adults often begin with a few lines whose rhymes and rhythms they find attractive. They hear the poem frequently, make a connection to it, and memorize and recite it, to the enchantment of themselves and the grown-ups around them. Even grown-ups, perhaps, do not fully "understand" all the poems and prayers that they enjoy, but that does not prevent them from reading and reciting them and making an effort to commit them to memory, especially when so many of these poems have become songs that can be hummed.

In this chapter, we explore the place of poetry in the lives of the women I came to know over several years, and how poetry, from their childhoods on, came to be a companion to the prayers they were be-ing taught. How were their encounters with these genres mediated—by what kinds of relationships, settings, texts, and neighboring art forms? What is significant about this companionship in the formation of religious subjectivities and imagination?[4] The ways in which religion is thought about, related to, and practiced do not depend just on what "the reli-gion" tells people to do. There are no hard and fast boundaries around a discreet object called "religion," as many scholars have pointed out.[5] Such boundaries are particularly absent in the lives of children. Familial relations, friendships at school, relationships with teachers, the contents of textbooks, and the ways in which adjacent worlds are described, explored, and valued join in constructing various understandings that last for some time and are then replaced by other tentative, new understandings as time goes by.

What is significant about growing up with classical poetry is that it is a complex and multidimensional kind of education. Much of this poetry is about religion, piety, divine and erotic love, hypocrisy (especially in matters of religion), and ethics. It offers a vocabulary, social types, paradoxical scenarios, and images—in sum, social analysis—through which one becomes tutored in the ways of religion and of the world.[6] This is why it is crucial to take note of classical poetry when seeking to understand contemporary Iranian culture (of course, a social *history* of poetry would be deeply illuminating and is much needed). More specifically, it is in part through this poetry that religion comes to be discovered, reflected on, and practiced. Given the dominance of mysticism in classical poetry, that approach to life becomes widely assimilated, to various degrees and depths.

Growing Up with Poetry and Prayer: Longtime Companions

Both of Maryam's parents were religious and "dwellers of poetry" (*ahl-e she'r*). In order to encourage his daughters, Maryam's father sometimes offered them rewards for memorizing poems, and also prayers from the Qur'an. When Maryam was about nine years old, her father told her that if she memorized Ayat al-Kursi, which is part of the Sura al-Baqara (the second chapter of the Qur'an) and a popular prayer across the Muslim world, he would give her ten *toman* (at the time, about the equivalent of a dollar). So, she set out to memorize it. On the day she was going to recite it for her father and get her reward, she became nervous. She asked a cousin to sit behind her father with the Qur'an open to that prayer. If she forgot something, he would mouth the correct word to remind her. She told him she would give him two of the ten toman. He took her up on the offer, but in the end she remembered the whole sura without faltering. "Did you get the reward?" I asked her. "Well, I can't remember," she said, laughing.

Together with their siblings, and with the help of their parents, uncles, and aunts, some of these women put together poetry notebooks meant to help them win in poetry contests, a *moshā'ereh*.[7] Poetry notebooks were (and still are) quite popular and came to be coveted objects accompanying the owners over a lifetime. In a *mosha'ereh*, the referee or one of the participants begins by reciting one or two lines of a poem, and the next person must offer lines that begin with the letter that ended the previous person's lines. The next participant must do the same and so it goes around. For example, if the first person recites, "Let us go then, you and I, / When the evening is spread out against the sky,"[8] the next person must start her recitation with lines beginning with a *y*. If she cannot, she will be given a few more chances, but if her inability continues, she will have to drop out. After many rounds, only two contestants will remain and one will win.

The poetry notebook belonging to Maryam and her sister contained many verses of poems, all ending in the letter *d*. That would force an opponent to repeatedly come up with verses starting with *d*. The hope was that the person would run out of such verses, and then one of the sisters would win. In this way, Maryam recalls, she and her sister beat their uncles and aunts—themselves formidable contestants—during a family gathering. Maryam still speaks of this event with glee.

National radio programming began in Iran in 1940.[9] Poetry contests were soon part of this programming, and they attracted large audiences. After television eventually came to Iran, in 1958, the contests were televised. I remember watching them with great interest in my own childhood—waiting anxiously, especially toward the end, when only two or three contestants (most of them between eleven and sixteen years old) remained and each was trying to "tie" the other to one single letter. I remember how astonished—and full of admiration—we were when, without missing a beat, participants would come up with verse after verse when it was their turn. The shows were so popular that the parents of the children who won could expect friends and relatives to drop by, or to call if they had a telephone, to congratulate them. Poetry contests still appear on television, though not as regularly as before, and although such programs now compete with countless others, especially with satellite television offering even more choices to viewers, they continue to be popular.[10]

The parents and grandparents of the women in our group were practicing Muslims, and they all prayed. But they do not seem to have taught their children much in the way of explicit religious doctrine. The one thing they insisted on was that the children learn the *namāz*, the obligatory ritual prayers that must be performed every day (see Chapter 2). Around age five, the children were taught to memorize the suras that make up the morning prayer, which is the shortest and hence easiest to learn. For example, they learned, in Arabic, suras such as al-Fatiha (the opening chapter of the Qur'an), which Iranians call al-Hamd; al-Ikhlas (Sincerity, Unity, Oneness), which is about the unity of God, and Iranians refer to it also as Towhid; al-Falaq (Daybreak), and other similarly short Qur'anic chapters (three to six lines).

Gradually, they were taught to put together the morning namaz—two suras in the first cycle, or part, and two in the second and last (they can be the same two in each cycle and usually are). Hence, the children's first encounter with the text of the Qur'an was not reading it but learning to recite it from memory. In time, they were taught the phrases that accompany the body postures of bending and placing hands on knees (*rokū'*) and of prostration, (*sojūd*). Next, it was time to learn the longer namaz that are to be performed at noon, afternoon, evening, and night. A widely shared experience was that their grandmothers had a role in teaching such suras—at times, standing in front and leading the prayer so their grandchildren could learn better. Many of the women in our group learned the namaz before nine—the age of *taklīf* (responsibility). After they reached that age or a bit later, their parents told them that from then on they had to pray regularly. They were routinely asked, "Have you done your namaz today?"

Beyond the emphasis on ritual prayer, as the earliest practice that teaches children what it means to be a Muslim, there does not seem to have been any systematic attention to teaching them religious *doctrine*. But the women remember that certain ideas were emphasized. For example, the line in the sura of Ikhlas that explains that God "has not given birth nor is He born" (Qur'an 112:3) was seen to be important in teaching them the difference between God and other beings—and also that there is only one God. They were told that the Prophet Muhammad is "our Prophet," and God sent with him a book called the Qur'an. They observed their parents handle their Qur'ans carefully and with respect; and when they finished reading from them, some lightly kissed them. Above all, as children they were told Qur'anic stories, for example, the story of Joseph, of Moses' infancy, and of Suleiman and David; and stories of the lives of the Imams, especially Hazrat-e Ali and Imam Hussein; but also stories from *Shahnameh* (*Epic of the Kings*), and *Amir Arsalan-e Namdar*, an adventure epic about a hero named Arsalan.[11] They grew up at a time when storytelling was still very popular.

Prayers and poetry seem to have been treated by their elders as kindred aesthetic and pedagogic activities that contributed to the cultivation of a literate, good, and moral person. Such a person would learn to be refined on the inside and the outside—embodying the concept of *adab*. A great deal has been written on adab. In the briefest definition, it is a highly valued cultural elaboration of cultivating one's character in ethics and aesthetics.[12] Prayers and poems were taught to be memorized and performed, without the use of written material. Once the girls were able to master a whole poem, they were asked to stand in front of family and friends and recite it as best they could—this was often a part of entertainment in gatherings. For the performance of poems, they were taught hand gestures, the elongation of the frequently occurring long vowel [aa] in Persian words, and correct intonation patterns. Such performances were (and still are) viewed as special accomplishments of children, putting on display her fluency, poise, voice, control, and memory, and demonstrating that she has arrived at a particular stage in the process of growing up in Iran in particular social milieus. In time, the poem comes to be embodied by the reciter.

For the child, the performance is an aesthetic experience—a pleasurable, if a somewhat nerve-wracking one, an occasion to stand tall in front of grown-ups, to enunciate words whose cumulative significance largely eludes her—something that adds to the charm of the occasion for grown-ups. These days, the Internet is full of videos of children (especially girls), between six and eight years old, reciting with verve long poems by Saadi, Hafez, and other poets. The closest parallel I can think of is when children learn to play pieces by Bach, Beethoven, and other musicians who composed for adults.

From the children's point of view, one may ask whether they distinguished between the recitation of poems and of the short prayers. The prayers were said in Arabic (though with heavily Persianized phonology), while the poems were in Persian. The women told me that they did distinguish between the two—they had no idea what the (Arabic) prayer said, but they knew at least some of the words in the poems. But at those young ages, neither the prayers nor the poetry had much semantic content for them. They were told in broad terms what the suras, in particular al-Fatiha and al-Ikhlas "meant," and as their reading abilities improved they could read the translations of the Arabic verses in Persian in bilingual Qur'ans and, at times, in their textbooks at school.

Today, even when one's parents or other family members are not ahl-e she'r, or dwellers of poetry, children across class and gender lines read and memorize poetry and songs as well as prayers at school and in other settings. The idea that literacy involves knowledge of both the Qur'an and classical poetry is shared at home and school—though the degree to which one or the other is emphasized changes from family to family. In the last several centuries, the ideal of literacy has been to have some familiarity with the Qur'an, and with Saadi's *Gulistan* and *Bustan*, in addition to Hafez and other poets.[13] The cleric mentioned in the Introduction, who objected to the inclusion of Rumi's poems in textbooks, also objected, in the same interview, to the idea that a Muslim must read the poets as well.

I found a number of the Persian language and literature textbooks that teachers used at the time many of the women in our group went to secondary school. While one cannot read too much into the content of textbooks (because the intentions behind the choice of texts are not all transparent, and what is taught is not necessarily received in all the intended ways by students), it is important to have an idea of how extensively schools relied on poems as teaching material. Let us take a look at a textbook for middle school, published in 1959, when these women were between thirteen and sixteen years old. This textbook has 192 pages with 130 lessons. Almost two-thirds of the lessons are poems. The very first lesson is "In Praise of God," a poem by Sana'i (early twelfth century), where the word that is used for God is *yazdān*—a Pahlavi word (a pre-Islamic language variety belonging to the Iranian language group). Among the poets represented, pieces from Saadi dominate. There are also single poems from Nizami (d. 1209), Anvari (d. 1189), Rudaki (d. 941), Onsori (d. 1039), and Farrokhi (d. 1037). (See Table 1.1.)

Along with lessons on grammar and the dos and don'ts of composition, the remainder of the textbook consists of various prose pieces. There are short pieces from literary journals such as *Yaghma*, and two pieces on Plato, one explaining who he was and what his works were about, and the other titled "Plato's Will (Final Words) for his Student Aristotle." A piece titled "Why We Should Love Iran," by Muhammad Ali Foroughi (1877–1942), a scholar and writer who also served as a parliamentarian and prime minister, appears twice. There are pieces by Khajeh Abdullah Ansari (d. 1088), whose book of *monājāt* (whispered prayers), written in Persian, contributed to making the Persian language an acceptable medium for devotional genres. One of the longest pieces, taken from *The Alchemy of Happiness* by the eminent Islamic philosopher Abu Hamed Imam Muhammad Ghazali (d. 1111), deals with educating children. Lessons about Islam have titles such as "Let Us Guard Our Religion as Long as We Have Life Left in Us," from the poet Fakhreddin Gorgani; "Translations [into Persian] of a Few Verses from the Qur'an," dating from the ninth century and taken from Tabari's *Tafsir,* one of the most respected

POETS	NUMBER OF WORKS
Saadi (d. 1291)	17 (from his Bustan and Gulistan)
Nasser Khosrow (d. 1088)	6
Jami (d. 1492)	5
Mowlavi (Rumi) (d. 1273)	4
Ferdowsi (d. 1020)	3
Parvin Etesami (d. 1941, female poet)	2
Iraj Mirza (d. 1926)	2

TABLE 1.1. Poetry in the Textbook for Persian Language and Grammar [*Qarā'at-e Farsi va Dastūr-e Zaban*], 1959 (Iranian year 1338).

tafasīr, "interpretations," of the Qur'an; "Gratitude and Admiration of the Prophet," from Nasihat al-Molūk's *Counsel for Kings* (twelfth century); and two pieces on the unity of God. Note that the authors of the lessons on religion and God are not clerics or holy figures. Again, there is not a great deal on the doctrinal foundations of Islam or even on Shi'i Islam. Textbooks for other years have similar content. The point of looking in some detail at the content of these textbooks is that it shows what a central place poetry occupied in Iranian education.

One might say it is likely that when the women in our group, as children, were told to stand and pray, a significant distinction between poetry and prayer emerged for them. The teaching of the bodily movements that go along with the namaz would make it clear that although for a while it was fine and even encouraged to stand in front of parents and recite a Qur'anic sura, they now had to learn to recite suras in correct order with correct body postures; and importantly, they must learn to address God with those words. They observed their parents pray every day and tried to follow them. These days, pictures and videos of very young children trying to do namaz as they stand next to their parents circulate widely online. I suggest that the suras and the poems began to diverge and to be embodied differently after the children were expected to do their prayers regularly, around the ages of nine and ten. And yet, something of the companionship of poetry and prayer and of their shared aesthetic pleasures remained with these women. They learned to embody and commit to memory *extra*-ordinary sounds.

Whether in childhood or later in life, reading poetry in Iran is largely a group activity—one could say a congregational act. One reads it or recites it, often from memory, in the company of others. People routinely look for occasions to deliver an apt line to fit the circumstances. This is a highly culturally valued act and delights listeners. Certainly, some people at times read poetry alone and in silence, but the unmarked use of poetry is in a gathering.

Parvin Etesami: A Woman in the Pantheon of Male Poets
One might ask, Who was the sole female poet whose poems were published in the 1959 textbook? (see Table 1.1). Parvin Etesami (1907–1941), who wrote the poem Pari recited in high school, seemed to have appeared

out of nowhere into the crowded scene of poets in Iran. For as long as the women in our group could remember, there had been Ferdowsi, Hafez, Saadi, Rumi, Nizami, and so on, but no woman, much less one who was a contemporary of their mothers and grandmothers, had come close to finding a place in their ranks. Etesami's father, who was a major figure in the literary life of the early twentieth century, published some of his daughter's poems in 1921 and 1922 in his literary magazine, and they were also published in other similar venues. Her first divan of poetry appeared in 1935, with 156 poems. After she died of an illness, her brother published her divan with more than 230 poems. Her poems were so well received that in a short time, her fame became almost universal in Iran. Women and men, young and old, were taken by the formal strengths of her poetry and by the tender themes she chose. Her poems were included in the textbooks for middle and high school when the women in our group went to school, and they still appear in school textbooks today, alongside all the major poets of the previous centuries. People speak of her poetry as deeply heartfelt, written on behalf of the downtrodden, the poor, the orphaned; she also wrote on behalf of Iranian women.[14] One of her most famous poems, one recited for me by several of the women because they remembered it from childhood, is called "Journey of a Teardrop." I offer a shortened version here to convey a sense of her style:

Journey of a Teardrop (Safar-e Ashk)
A teardrop welled up in an eye and departed
It rolled down softly, gently dropped, and departed

On the dark firmament of existence
It twinkled like a star and departed

It took its place in the sea of being,
Yet extracted only a drop of blood and departed

As I wept over heaven's cruelty,
It smiled at me and my weeping and departed

There was no ill-feeling between us;
No one knows why it was offended and departed

It crisscrossed through the mysteries of life,
Wrapped up its accounts and accounting, and departed

It fell on the scales of Providence
Would that its value had been weighed before it departed.[15]

Here, in an abridged version, is the poem that Pari recited in high school.

God's Kindness (Lotf-e Haqq)
When Moses' mother, Moses into the Nile threw,
For the glorious Lord had ordered her to,

From the riverside, with grief, she did stare;
"O, my little innocent babe," she did declare,

"If the Mercy of the Lord, you forget,
How will you be saved from this boat, pilotless?

"If the Immaculate God remembers you not,
The water will suddenly put you to nought."

Inspiration came, "What a wrong thought!
Our wayfarer already home We've brought.

"That which you threw, We caught;
The Hand of Truth you saw, but knew not.

"Within you is but motherly love and affection;
Justice and Kindness from Our direction.

"Don't lose your calm, jest is not God's way;
We will return that which We carried away."[16]

In a short while, Etesami became a larger-than-life figure whose poetry was published and praised in newspapers and journals. People offered her divan as a present to children and adults. Her poems were recited on the radio, and in ceremonies and gatherings. The best-known contemporary Iranian literary historian, critic, and poet, Shafi'i Kadkani, refers to her as a "miracle," both for her poetic abilities and for the fact that she came to appeal to men as well as women.

> Parvin is a member of one of the families of Persian poetry—the family whose fundamental values are respect [hormat], wisdom [kherad], morality [akhlāq] and human honor [sharaf-e insani]. . . . The father of this family is Ferdowsi and its elegant [rashīd; literally, tall] children are Nasser Khosrow, Nizami, Saadi and Ibn Yamin and Bahar, and its young daughter is Parvin Etesami.[17]

He goes on to assert that the "sudden appearance" of this poet after the constitutional revolution of 1906, "has been considered a great literary event," and many poets became inspired by her, wishing to write in her style.[18]

Etesami wrote many poems that were dialogues (monazereh): for example, between the comb and the mirror, the nightingale and the ant, the needle and the thread, the wolf and the dog. She wrote one mourning her lost cat. Readers found wonder in how well she represented multiple and opposing viewpoints. In the lifetime of these women and their mothers, she was the first woman ever to become so famous in the realm of poetry—a woman, moreover, who seemed more or less like themselves, educated, still a bit unsure of herself in public, but with lots to say. Maryam, Elaheh, Parvin, and others looked up to her with great admiration. So did their mothers and fathers. They asked their daughters to memorize her poems. Elaheh's father told her he would pay her a coin for every verse that she memorized, so she and her sister chose one of Etesami's longest poems. The language of Etesami's poetry was contemporary Persian as spoken by the urban middle classes. Given the wide variety of social themes about which she wrote, she enjoyed immense popularity.

When the mothers of these women were growing up, there were no women authors and poets as present in the public sphere as Parvin Etesami. But in these women's own generation, a fair number of women authors emerged. We had Parvin Dowlatabadi (1907–1941), who wrote poetry for children, and Forough Farrokhzad (1935–1967),[19] whose audacious poems on love, sexuality, and God's inadequacies made great waves among the literary and clerical elites. Simin Daneshvar (1921–2012) published a collection of short stories in 1948 and, in 1969, an extraordinary historical novel, titled *Savushun*, that has been translated into many languages. Moreover, at the schools our group attended, there were female principals, teachers, and headmistresses whose great competencies continue to be remembered fondly to this day. Hence, on the one hand, Iranian society continued to be patriarchal as these women were growing up, and on the other hand, it was a patriarchy in which women got educated, obtained jobs, received middle-class salaries, and became well-known headmistresses, teachers, poets, novelists, and founders of journals and various organizations. The role of women in society became a debate rather than an accepted fact.

Women's Presence in Public Life

The generation of women born in the 1940s is a special generation, and I argue that it has played a significant role in shaping contemporary Iranian society. Major changes were taking place in the 1950s and 1960s when these women were adolescents and young adults. Transformations that had begun decades before were accelerated.[20] Secondary public education had spread on a national scale in the 1920s and 1930s. And it expanded far more widely in the 1950s and 1960s. Teacher training colleges prepared women for all levels of teaching, and the University of Tehran opened its doors to them in 1937, three years after its founding.[21] There were coeducational schools as well as separate ones for girls and boys.[22] The women in our group—Maryam, Mina, Parvin, Pari, Elaheh, and others—all obtained their high school diplomas and went on to university. Their mothers had attended elementary schools, some finished middle school (seventh, eighth, and ninth grades) and some got their diplomas, but education was not as universal in their generation. A few of the mothers became teachers, but they had to leave their jobs when they had children, and rarely went back to work after that.

In the lifetime of their mothers, the first Pahlavi monarch, Reza Shah (1878–1944), had banned the wearing of turbans and robes for men in 1928 and the veil for women in 1937. Their parents and grandparents had had to appear in public with European hats and suits or skirts and jackets.[23] These forced measures caused great upheaval. The banning of the veil has been written about mostly with regard to Iranian Muslim women and the reaction of Muslim clerics. But at that time, Iranian women of other faiths, including Jews, Armenians, and Zoroastrians, also wore veils.[24] And men of most faiths were not used to wearing suits and hats. Hence, it was a more general disruption, affecting everyone's lives. Clerical authorities objected to such drastic changes, and in various protests people lost their lives.

By the time my interlocutors began going to school, the tumult of those years had long passed. Reza Shah had been replaced by his son, the second Pahlavi king, Mohammad Reza Pahlavi (1941–1979), who did not enforce the strict ban on veiling. Hence, the women in our group grew up seeing a whole variety of appearances in public: women with variously colored cotton veils (chador chiti), with scarves or hats, or with hair showing, and with modest suits and dresses. It must be emphasized that women wore many different kinds of styles of dress underneath their veils. However, because they were rarely photographed (and even when they were, such photographs would not circulate beyond their families), the image of women in public in Iran before the veil ban is that of vaguely identifiable individuals covered from head to toe.[25]

Most of the women remember, rather hazily, the 1953 coup d'état sponsored by the United States and the United Kingdom that toppled the democratically elected prime minister, Mohammad Mosaddeq. The coup marked a turning point in the relationship between the Pahlavi regime and the United States. The United States helped to reinstall the king and became a close ally and protector. Thousands of Americans traveled to Iran with their families and settled in major cities, and urban life became to one degree or another rather Americanized in those decades.

Reza Shah and his son were both dictatorial and repressive, and it was routine for citizens to go to prison or even be killed for speaking against the monarchy. But they also accelerated mass education and the entrance of women into public life. The world in which the women in our group were becoming adolescents and adults was opening up to them. They could go to school and continue through college. The first teacher training college for women having opened in 1919, they could apply for jobs as teachers and a few other professions and become financially independent, as historian Camron Amin's study of women in twentieth-century Iran shows.[26] Financial independence through a career outside the home had been largely unavailable as a prospect to their mothers. Almost all of these women got married and had children later than their mothers did—sometime in their early twenties. The sharp increase in the number of public schools at all levels resulted in an endless demand for teachers, and with a few exceptions, many of the women I write about became high school teachers. Similarly, as the state bureaucracy expanded, clerical positions became more available to women. Amin believes "a very basic change occurred in Iranian culture in the first half of the twentieth century. It became possible for Iranian women to imagine—publicly—a world in which they were not required to be obedient to the men in their lives."[27] My research with this group of women confirms such an assessment.[28] Many habits of consumption and cultural cultivation among the elites became possible for the newly expanding middle classes. As part of the same processes involved in forming the middle class in Iran, young women were finding their feet in society and in public life.[29] They became members of various school societies, delivered poems and speeches, and could participate in school plays.

At the time, schools met daily in two sessions, with a lunch break from noon to 2:00 p.m. Most students went home to eat lunch and rest before going back to school. Mina talked about how she and her friends decided to do their noon prayers at the local mosque in Isfahan. They got permission from their principal to pray at the mosque during their lunch break, rather than go home:

> At the mosque, the older women used to not let us stand in the first and second rows [for the congregational prayer] because they did not think that we were knowledgeable enough. One day I went to the mosque imam and complained to him: "We go through so much trouble getting permission from our school and then we come here and . . . " He said, "Go and unfold your *janamaz* [prayer cloth] where you want," and I said, "No they don't let us, they will throw

our janamaz somewhere else." He said, "Don't mind them; you go!"
We came out from behind the curtain [into the women's section],
and he went up on the pulpit and said: "From today onwards, these
school kids will be coming here. Instead of encouraging them you tell
them their namaz is not correct? How do you know that? These kids
are studying and know it well." So from then on, we stood in the first
row and prayed.

She spoke of this experience as one among those that gave her increasing
self-confidence to assert herself in public.

Circulation of Poetry through Songs:
Beloved Singers on the Radio

Poetry and song are of course inseparable. Poems spread far and wide
when they are made into songs and put to music. Radio further popularized classical poetry. Simin told us:

> My mother read some Parvin Etesami. She had a great voice and she
> sang at home. I became very interested and began to sing with her.
> My family on my mother's side were all into music [ahl-e musiqi],
> songs, and instruments. Then at school I became very attracted to
> literature; I actually specialized in the sciences but liked literature. I
> listened to the radio, to mosha'ereh, poetry competitions, and I used
> to tell myself, when I grow up and get married, I am going to have
> these kinds of gatherings at my house with poetry and so on. In any
> case, I sing a lot of poems.

Simin explained that she sang along with her mother, learning from her
and enjoying herself in doing so. It was a family activity, as her father and
uncles played various instruments and the cultural atmosphere of Isfahan
at the time encouraged many kinds of musical performances. On the radio
at that time, programs showcasing the two most beloved female singers
of the time, Marzieh (1924–2010)[30] and Delkash (1925–2004), aired at
least twice per week.[31]

Mina interrupted Simin to say how much she loved these singers as
well and how she tried to learn to sing like them:

I did not have the [same] talent as my mother with poetry or maybe I was not as interested, but when radio came and these singers began to sing, I loved that. I was a partisan [*tarafdar*] of Delkash.

Everyone laughed at this, because similar to long-standing arguments about whether Hafez or Saadi is the better poet, there were endless quarrels about Marzieh and Delkash. Mina went on:

Her songs were very beautiful. I got a notebook and began writing the lyrics. . . . And as Simin said, the whole atmosphere of Isfahan may also have had something to do with it. My grandmother who lived with us was very pious. She would say, "Girl, your voice is going to carry and that's not proper [*eyb*]." On the radio on Monday and Wednesday nights, I listened to these songs and never missed them.

Radio became phenomenally popular in Iran in a short time. Those who could not afford a radio set went to neighbors' or relatives' homes and listened. In 1956, a radio series devoted entirely to *'erfān* poetry put into song went on the air, and it became one of the most popular and enduring shows.[32] Titled *Golha* (Flowers), and composed of several separate programs with similar aims, it lasted until 1979 and gathered a huge listening public: "Modeled on the ages-old tradition of connoisseurs meeting in private homes (*majles*), the programs featured a judiciously balanced combination of mystical poetry (read and sung) and music, both solo and various sized ensembles . . . [they] cultivated the deep-seated Iranian values of adab and mysticism ('erfan)."[33] The *Golha* programs

exerted a tremendous influence in Persia and, to some extent, also in other Persian-speaking countries. First, they popularized Persian classical poetry and made a vogue of it, particularly among the middle class and the affluent social elite. They boosted appreciation of Persian poetry at a popular level to a degree never before achieved. Second, they brought masters of traditional music to public notice and bestowed on them the dignity that they deserved as artists. This should be seen against the background of earlier times, when musical performers were considered mere "entertainers" with a lowly rank in the social hierarchy (they were referred to as *motreb-ha*, often with a pejorative connotation).[34]

Radio and television became media of pedagogy and entertainment through songs, competitions, and recitations. Those who were not literate enough to read this poetry on their own or had been previously on its margins, became a part of that world with an increasing interest in popular songs. This is one of the most important reasons why Persian poetry, or at least love of this poetry, is not strictly limited to one particular social class or to those with a high level of education.

What Do Iranians Do with Poetry?

We can see that Iranians do a lot with poetry: they learn to think about certain ethical values, ways of being and conducting themselves; they become literate through it; they build friendships; they acquire performance skills and quick wittedness; they hone their skills in memorization; they use it to express their feelings; and, as I mentioned, they learn to think about religion in imaginative and paradoxical ways. They also use it to ease moments of tension both in close relationships and in dealing with strangers. Mina gave the example of her daughter's eighty-two-year-old father-in-law, who "has a poem for all occasions." Even when dealing with various bureaucracies, when he gets stuck, he resorts to reciting a few lines of poetry to "open the knot":

> He said recently, "This one poem saved me!" It was from Parvin Etesami. He was being given a hard time by some office manager and he recited a poem for him that was relevant to how he was being treated. He said that the guy at the office was rather boastful and he tried to answer with another poem. "I said, 'I am sorry but you are mistaken; you are not reading it right.' [*Everyone around our table laughed.*] The man took umbrage, but I began to recite his poem myself and people gathered around us, so he paused! But in the end, he relented and solved my problem."

Indeed, learning to recite the right kind of verse at the right time is the ultimate type of verbal persuasion into which Iranians become socialized.[35]

At times poems figure prominently in making, defining, and transforming relationships. Mina followed this story by talking about her husband and about how well-spoken he is. Maryam joined in to say:

> My parents liked each other but had very different personalities, and I could see that, at times, my father's being so disengaged from our daily lives made my mother lose her patience. But quite often around the dinner table or after dinner, for one reason or another, one of them would recite a line and others would follow, either reciting the rest of that very poem or reciting poems that had relevant themes. My father, who had hundreds of memorized verses up his sleeve, would keep coming back with his own poems, some of which he recited with a particular melody. My mother would join in, she would recite her favorite poems, often correct my father and others, and suddenly you could see that the expression on her face had completely changed. She had softened, had a lovely smile, and looked at my father with gentle admiration.

This is one of the most subtle and most substantial things that an exchange of poetry does—it transforms relationships. It illuminates dimensions of our interiority that, expressed through someone else's words, bring about the possibility to be bold in ways that are also considered aesthetically pleasing. Poetry is capable of shifting the established tone of a long-term relationship for a few moments, days, or weeks, or over a lifetime. Mina asks herself, "What role does speaking well play for me?" For her, "speaking well" includes poetry recitation, which her husband apparently did in abundance.

In her study of lyric poetry recited by Bedouin women in Jordan, Lila Abu-Lughod writes: "poetic discourse indexes social intimacy, reciting poems to particular individuals communicates, and even creates, closeness." She adds that the recitation of poetry is a "strategy for bridging social distance."[36]

The Poetry of (Self)-Exploration

Many of the classical poets who wrote in Persian were court poets. They wrote in a form called *qasideh*, in which they praised the kings and princes, their bravery, astuteness, good looks, and generosity, and at times composed advice for princes. These poems were to be recited and sung publicly. A form of love poetry that emerged out of the qasideh was the *ghazal*—often translated as "lyric poem." The ghazal gradually became an independent form, and poets used it for ruminations about life, worship, divine and erotic love, desires, piety, wine, music, sincerity, and hypocrisy.[37] As literary historians have pointed out, the ghazal came to serve largely as the vehicle for the expression of mystical world views. Speaking of the dominance of the ghazal form in mystical poetry, Dick Davis refers to a kind of "Sufi lingua franca" that saturated Persian poetry by the fifteenth century.[38]

In his extensive work on Hafez and that poet's "anticlericalism," the late Leonard Lewisohn translated many ghazals and couplets by him. To acquire an idea of the ghazal and of Hafez's thinking, let us read two of Lewisohn's translations:

> I am so disgusted in my heart by hypocrisy
> Of the Muslim abbey that if you were
> To wash me in wine, that would be a just thing.

> They say hypocrisy is kosher but the wineglass is prohibited?
> Which Sufi path is this? How great a government, what
> Purely Holy Canon Law, what fine Faith this all shows us![39]

It is in this poetry that *hāl* is conceptualized, that reciting namaz without presence of the heart is scorned, that visible piety is shunned, and that the wine bar is argued as more likely to be populated by sincere Muslims than a mosque full of men of religion. In this poetry, the poet explores emotions, experiences, reactions to events, and the ethics and aesthetics of living with others. The poet is the individual worshipper, facing God (or not), who struggles with the pitfalls of ostentatious religiosity.

I find a number of interesting similarities between the poetry I describe here and the sensibilities of the Chinese philosophers and poets described by Puett and Gross-Loh in their book *The Path*. Noting that memorization of a collection of poetry called *Book of Songs* was a necessity for anyone who wanted to become educated, the authors explain that

> the point wasn't to just memorize poems and passively recite them aloud. It was to draw actively upon one's knowledge of the poems

and one's reading of the real-life situation and rework them both in innovative ways. . . . Poetry became another important means of refining one's response to the world.[40]

In Iran, mystic poetry in ghazal form became the genre par excellence for self-exploration and individual expression. As Shahab Ahmed says:

> every ghazal is, in its social performance, a re-iteration and rehearsal of the centrality of the self in meaning-making. . . . Our received habits of conceptualizing Islam as discourses of prescription rather than as discourses of exploration have considerably obstructed us from recognizing the place of discourses of the Self as central to and constitutive of human and historical Islam.[41]

I argue that the poetic pedagogy in child rearing that I have been describing offers a stream of ideas with which one can grapple over a lifetime. It encourages the learner and the reciter to undertake, at one point or another, explorations of the self and of the various collectivities she interacts with; and it encourages pondering the qualities of her relationship to the divine. I follow this point further in the following section.

The Act of Reciting a Poem

We have already described the pleasure that Pari and others took in school performances, poetry competitions, their coveted notebooks, the family gatherings where everyone was expected to recite poetry, the prizes, the monetary incentives, and so on. Pari recalled:

> I liked memorizing poems so I could do mosha'ereh with other kids at school, and try to win. This was both hope and motivation. And then there was the childish [wish to] shine and stand out; of course, it was not out of any sophistication [*she laughed*] or deep thinking. . . . You know, you stand up somewhere in front of everyone and grab both sides of your skirt, like this, and recite a poem.

In the act of recitation, the voice of the reciter takes over that of the poet. We assume that the authorship of the poem remains entirely intact in that process, but I was repeatedly told that in the moment of recitation, "you are the author of those words." Mina said:

> At times, we do not find the right words, to convey how we feel inside; poetry does this for us. Poetry comes to our aid. Yes, it is true that when I recite this poetry, the poem is not mine, but I am the one who is expressing it [*bayānesh mikonam*]. And when I recite it on the right occasion, with good delivery, this really helps me express myself.

So, in the moment of recitation, the reciter is in a sense also the author. This is one of the major pleasures of poetry—one can feel able to express oneself with the most beautiful phrases and with the deepest, wisest, and most eternal of ideas. The term *vasf-ol-hal*[42] captures this momentary authorship. Vasf-ol-hal means, literally, "description of state [of feeling]." It is applied to poems (stories, sayings, and the like) that capture in an uncanny way one's life experiences, or exactly how one feels about something. People often seem stunned at just how precisely some poet has captured what they thought was unique to their life experiences. They seem almost ecstatic that someone like Hafez, for example, with his status, wisdom, and perceptiveness, has felt the way they do.

Simultaneously, poetry allows the reciter to hide behind its form and formality. Perhaps one could say that this is a property of all conventional forms—the user can claim that she is not the author—she is not the one who came up with the form and so is not fully responsible for it. Mina told us: "Whenever my mother was hurt by me, she found a poem to recite to me." In such cases, one is simultaneously claiming authorship and using the words of someone else to hide behind, as it were.

Poetry also offers the reciter a certain kind of audacity, perhaps related (though not necessarily) to the deniability that accompanies using the words of others. I have attended poetry nights where people who do not know each other get up one after another and recite extravagantly worded poetry that is parodic, erotic, satirical, political, or deeply personal. Almost four decades of the Islamic republic and its interventions into private life, along with political repression, have not discouraged this kind of public expression. On the contrary, people seem to relish the audacity that poetry allows. To hear one's own voice utter words that are apt, beautiful, hyperbolic, and surprising in what they convey or in how they are strung together, is an experience that many Iranians learn early in life, through poetry and songs.

The Conduct of Social and Ethical Life: "Saadi Is a Sociologist"

I had many individual conversations with the women in our group about poetry. As with the conversations about prayer, I followed these up with gatherings where we discussed similar questions. In one such gathering in the summer of 2015, we discussed the poets whom they read the most. We began with comparing the poets' comprehensibility. The women were unanimous in their ranking: Parvin Etesami was the easiest, then Saadi and Rumi, and then Hafez, though some people found Rumi to be both at times quite easy to follow and at other times not so much. Mina began by ranking the poets in terms of ease of language:

> MINA: After Parvin Etesami it is Saadi. Understanding Saadi is the easiest. All these books that have been coming out on Hafez, you read them and see that they say he has said things that are entirely different [from one's understanding]. [*She laughed.*]
>
> PARI: One enjoys Hafez but understanding him is something else.
>
> MINA: Saadi does not have so many metaphorical meanings. The same thing [scholarly criticism] is not done with Saadi, I find that books about him show the same understanding that I have.
>
> SIMIN: I think Saadi [shows] the realities of life, the way one must live, Saadi does not have such [fancy] interpretations. He tells you, for example, now that we are all sitting around a table, how should we behave, what should we be doing. How should we treat our friends, and so on.
>
> MINA: Saadi is a sociologist [*jāme'eh shenās*].
>
> SIMIN: Yes, exactly.
>
> MINA: Because he traveled a lot, he tried to understand the societies where he lived, and talked about these in verse.

A discussion ensued about how Saadi is full of thoughtful advice (*pand o nasihat*). He teaches us what to care about, how to live, how to understand friendships. He tells us to enjoy love and youth, speaks against being greedy, and shows how everyone including kings should treat others. He speaks about growing old with grace and gratitude. Saadi teaches us ethics (akhlaq: that is, how to behave); he teaches us how to live, in beautiful but simple prose and poetry. Simin said:

> I think that Saadi is all about guidance. Whoever wants to study literature should begin with Saadi—he is first a human being. He talks about how to live, how to be a friend, how to participate in a class even, [for example] you know, don't talk on your mobile if you are sitting in a class.

Parvin, who had studied sociology at the university, said, "You can see the social, political, and cultural conditions in Saadi's poems." She described how she uses his writings:

> For example, sometimes I reflect on this famous passage from Saadi, the one that we all memorized [in school]: "All praise to God! Obey Him and you draw near Him. Thank Him and His bounty is yours. In each breath you take there are two blessings: The air that fills your lungs prolongs your life. Giving that air back to the world refreshes your soul. For each of these blessings, each time you receive it, you must thank Him."

> But in whose words is there sufficient music
> in the work of whose hands sufficient grace,
> to satisfy the terms of this sweet debt?
> "O House of David, act and give thanks."
> But few among my creatures are thankful.
> Better to lie prostrate before God's throne,
> begging his forgiveness for our sin.[43]

Parvin went on:

> This is truly one of the do'as I do after namaz. I thank God and I say, "God I thank you for every second of my life," because it is now too late to go back and thank God for every single thing, so I say I am thankful for every second. In every breath, one must thank God, one that goes out and one that comes in, and it is this coming and going that makes it possible to continue life. And I am grateful for that.

Then she quoted the beginning of Saadi's introduction to *Gulistan* (Fragrant garden), which is quite long, but a selection has been appearing in textbooks for generations, and every Iranian schoolchild must memorize it. Parvin went on to say that, in fact, "many poems are like do'a. I have a friend who recites a few lines of Saadi in her *qonūt* (a nonobligatory part of ritual prayers described in the next chapter) when she does the namaz."

The Classical Poets as "True Muslims": Poetry Classes

Parvin also commented that Saadi "was a true Muslim [*mosalamāneh vāqe'i*]; no one cares whether he was Shafe'i, Hanbali, Hanafi [legal schools]. Even our mullahs don't care. His entire language is made of pearls [*dorr*]: human beings are the limbs of one body ['*bani ādam a'zāyeh yekdigarand'*].[44] He tells you what to watch out for in life." In fact, Shi'i Iranians virtually never comment on the fact that most of their beloved poets were Sunnis. So wholly are they identified as Iranian because they wrote in Persian that any other attributes—where they were born and raised, or their Sunni denomination—are seen as irrelevant. But Parvin later nuanced her assessment of clerics not caring:

> There are some clerics [mullahs]—I know some of them—who have not read *Masnavi* or Hafez, or they think that because Saadi was Sunni . . . or . . . whatever, they ought to look at him with prejudice . . . but the new [generation] of mullahs are more likely to be familiar with Mowlavi and you see them on television sometimes talking about him and relating his stories.

Elaheh, who is frequently asked to offer her own classes on the Qur'an and to give guest lectures in other people's classes, accepts such invitations on the condition that they spend part of the class time on one of the poets. I attended several such classes where she had the students read from Saadi's *Gulistan*. "These people [whose religion is dry] protest: 'Why do you say that Saadi is the same as Qur'an?' Well, God's manifestations are [of] many many kinds. . . . True Islam [*islameh vaqe'i*] can be learned from the interpretation [of the Qur'an] that [Rumi's] *Masnavi* provides, or from Saadi." She spoke of Rumi's *Masnavi* and repeated some famous lines about that work:

man nemīguyam keh ān *ālījenāb*
Hast peyghambar vali darad kitāb

I don't say that his highness [i.e., Rumi]
Is a Messenger [a Prophet] but he has a book [i.e., the *Masnavi*]

This is a reference to the view of the *Masnavi* as the "Qur'an in the Persian tongue." For Elaheh, and many other Iranians, it is hard to imagine that one can be *bā savād* (literate) and know not a word of this poetry. Elaheh related another story from a class to which she was invited in Isfahan:

> I was sitting in this class that was supposed to begin with the Qur'an and then go on to Saadi. One of the women there said something to the effect that there are four conditions for being truly pious. She went on to include a particular kind of jade ring, and how your pronunciation of Arabic words has to be perfect. She said, "If you don't know how to articulate the phrase *wala al-Daliin* well in the sura of al-Hamd, let me fix it for you." I said, "Do you really think that God cares about how you pronounce these words? This dry religiosity is what is really killing Islam." Everyone fell silent. I then went on and asked everyone to open their Saadi and start the lesson.

During a visit to Simin's house, I asked her to describe her various weekly classes. She said:

> I continue to go to many classes, where people recite, talk, critique. I like to be a listener. . . . I did not specialize in literature so it is not like I have a great deal of knowledge to impart, but, you know, for my own level, I do follow and understand and I'm happy about that. I think that Rumi is extraordinary. He is very deep and very simple and succeeds in making us understand his messages. But unfortunately some people try to take him to very faraway places where ordinary people can't reach, as if the farther he is from our reach, the better and the more bizarre, the better.[45]

She is referring here to what others were also saying about Hafez: that many of the articles and books about his poetry engage in complex hermeneutics of theoretical mysticism (*'erfan-e nazari*) as opposed to practical (*'erfan-e 'amali*).

I asked her what she thought of the idea that Iranians read too much poetry. I reported other Iranians (and non-Iranians) saying that "we are always going on about Rumi, Hafez, Saadi—it has become a joke that even our taxi drivers quote poetry." What do you think of that? She calmly replied,

> Well, those who do not want to read this poetry, don't have to read it. Those who have read it and understood it and think it has no more to offer them are welcome to stop reading it. But I keep reading it because I feel that there are things that I don't understand but that are important; and my understanding of these takes time. So, I keep going back to them.

She quoted a line from Hafez and then, linking poetry and religion, she went on to say that a poem "is not a matter of logic" (*manteq*). In poetry, "there is love and reason and feelings" and brevity:

> Poetry offers a subtleness [*letāfat;* also "tenderness"], so when I say, for example: "come back so that my life may come back / even though the spent arrow does not return" [lines from Hafez], well, I would have to speak for ten pages to convey this meaning. It is not necessary to study a lot [in order to understand these poems]. I think these [poems] sit delicately and subtly on our *rūh* [spirit, soul]. *It is like art; it seems to me religion is like art because it gives us that feeling that great art does, the gracefulness of a painting, or of a prayer. All of these give that hālat* [that is, hal].

I have emphasized her last few lines because I was struck by them. Note how she links poetry to prayer. She speaks of love, reason, and feelings—"but it is not a matter of logic." We are attracted to religion for the same reasons that we are attracted to art: a prayer, a poem, a painting can "sit on our soul"—it does so because it touches us in unexpected ways. It transforms our state and gives us that feeling of hal—connection with something larger than ourselves, with the universe and nature and, for some, God.

The scholar of Islam Navid Kermani has a similar view, expressed in the preface to his book *God is Beautiful*.[46] I quote him at length here to show the affinity between his thinking and Simin's statement:

> Religions have their aesthetics. Religions are not collections of logically reasoned norms, values, principles and doctrines. They speak in myths, in images, rarely in abstract terms. They bind their followers not so much by the logic of their arguments as by the aura of their proponents, the poetry of their texts, the appeal of their sounds, forms, rituals, even their interiors, colours and odors.

Kermani goes on to argue that people arrive at insights through sensory experience and insights that are "aesthetic rather than discursive in nature."[47]

Prayer and Poetry as Forms of Knowledge

In the daily lives of the women in our group, the worlds of prayer and poetry meet, mingle, challenge, argue, agree, question, and quote each other. The coexistence and mingling is due to shared worlds, language and concepts. And at the level of daily life, engaging with prayer and with poetry are kin activities—similar to how it was in their childhood. One engages with oneself and others in and out of gatherings and classes and seeks to make sense of the verses, referred to as *āya* for Qur'anic verses and *beyt* for poetry. These are individual and congregational acts of exploration, discussion, disagreement, and agreement. One of the most interesting similarities between prayer and poetry is that both involve "passes" over the same lines across long time spans. One reads the same poem over and over—at each pass, a potentially different interpretation becomes possible—different, more profound, less profound, more related to the reciter's life conditions, then related in a different way, to a different life, and so on.

Something similar happens with any given sura or aya in the reading of the Qur'an and the recitation of the namaz. I was told that, for example, al-Fatiha (The Opening) "does not always mean the same thing" to the reciter. Recited at twenty, it means something different than when recited at sixty. Its meaning changes with the world and with the reciter. Neither is the reading of Hafez or Rumi the same at different stages of one's life. Prayer and poetry are regarded by these women as inexhaustible sources, and one does not expect to understand any given poem from, say, Hafez once and for all and then never go back to it. One does not hear something like, "Okay, I finished reading Hafez, now I'll move on to Saadi."

Given these forms of knowledge that are read and recited over a lifetime, a purely semiotic approach would be insufficient in understanding the relationships that are forged with such texts. The recitation of prayer and poetry, at each iteration, looks back because there are traces of past encounters in it, and looks forward because a new iteration is being performed and what happens in the process of the present iteration is unpredictable. The events, people, and moments of life that such texts evoke are probably at least as cumulatively consequential in reaching new understandings as the semiotic meanings (admittedly themselves open to multiple formulations). I return to this point later in this chapter.

Two National Heroes: The Persian Language and Mystic Poetry

There is near universal agreement among Iranians that Persian is a powerful and beautiful language that has amply proven its pluck and vigor by having withstood the overwhelming force of Arabic when the Arabic-speaking Muslim armies conquered the Sasanian Empire in the seventh century. They speak proudly of how Persian survived, while in most other places, Arabic replaced the local language. In an interview in the summer of 2013 with two university professors of Persian literature who are not favorably inclined toward religion, one of them said: "In our classical poetry, we do not see a deep commitment to Islam. We do not say *sowm* [fasting] and *salāt*; we say *rūzeh* and namaz, from Zoroastrian times." As many others tend to do, they then went on to cite the eleventh-century *Shahnameh* (*Epic of the Kings*) by Ferdowsi as having "saved" the Persian language. The *Shahnameh* is a long epic poem of about fifty thousand verses. It retells the (mythic) stories of Persian kings from the sixth century BCE all the way to the Islamic conquest.

The 1959 textbook we examined earlier was edited by the well-known author, scholar, and cultural figure Saeed Nafisi (1896–1996), who was a secular, highly educated nationalist. In the introduction to the 1959 textbook, he addresses the children who were to use it. It is worth quoting the entire address to see some of the historical specificity with which the Persian language has been viewed.

Valued Offspring [Farzandan-e gerami]

The language of our fathers and mothers, whose beauty we have strived to show you in this book, is the most valued and lasting legacy [*yādegār pāydār*] of our great and respected ancestors. Nearly two thousand years ago, two languages appeared in two parts of Iran, both called Parsi. The language that was current in the east of our land was Parsi Dari and the one that was spoken in the west was called Parsi Pahlavi. The one we call today the language of Parsi is the same Parsi that across time has become sweeter [*shirin-tar*], easier [*āsān-tar*] and softer [*narm-tar*] and has become what it is from a thousand years ago.

Our language today is one of the most beautiful and most eloquent [*shivā-tarin*] of world languages, and its literary masterpieces, across the world, have been translated into many of the world's languages. Our poets [*sorayandegān*] and writers [*nevisandegān*] are some of the most famous in the world of literature. In times past, up to 500 million of the world's population spoke in our language and wrote and composed [poetry]. In spite of the fact that unfortunate [*nasāzgār*] events destroyed much of our prose and poetic masterpieces, our literature [*adabiyāt*] is still one of the most capacious and expansive [*vasi'-tarin*] literatures in the world.

The highest duty of us Iranians young and old and women and men is to love the language of our ancestors, which has all these qualities, with our hearts and souls. And strive to guard it and to learn it in the best way possible and to propagate and spread it.

Today in the world there is no more solid and clear symbol [*neshāneh*] for peoples [*mellat-hā*] of the world [than language]. *Language is the guardian of sovereignty* [*istiqlāl*] *and pride* [*sar bolandi*; literally, "head highness"] of each country. All peoples of the world strive to strengthen their mother tongue [*zabān-e mādari*] day by day. Let us fulfill this sacred [*muqaddas*] duty and try, night and day, until we become the worthiest and most accomplished children of our valued Iran.[48]

Proud of the literary heritage of the language, Nafisi also underlines what many Iranians are quite self-conscious about—that "language is the guardian of sovereignty." For an ancient society that has seen many conquests by those who are not Persian speakers, the survival and flourishing of Persian is seen as a supreme achievement. Although one could attribute the devotion to the Persian language and to mystic poetry as being entirely due to nationalism—and nationalism has certainly played an important role—I agree with Shahrokh Meskoob, a scholar of the cultural and linguistic history of Iran, that the matter should be looked at historically and with more nuance. In his study of the history of Persian prose and Iranian identity, Meskoob first notes:

> Gosticism ['erfan] is a sensual experience of the relationship between the higher world and the self. In the words of a friend, such a deep experience is rarely expressed in a language other than one's mother tongue. For example, it would be strange for an Iranian, Persian-speaking gnostic to sing of his excitement and proclaim the selflessness of love, the eagerness of union, and the pain of separation in Arabic, a language he learned at school.[49]

He goes on to add that "Iranian gnostics used the Persian language not because it was a national language, but because it was a native tongue. In fact, they did not turn to it, they were in its midst. Their link to the Persian language was . . . an existential connection."[50]

It is instructive to compare the contents of the textbook from the time my interlocutors went to school with a contemporary one. The Persian language and literature textbook published for the last year of high school in 2012 has 205 pages and thirty sections.[51] Each section contains more than one lesson, and one lesson may address only one poet or author while another lesson looks at three. Not counting lessons in prose that include lines of poetry, there are thirty-one poems. The introduction to this textbook begins with a line from Hafez, and the first lesson is Rumi's "Neynameh," which is more commonly referred to as "Beshno az Ney," the first few words of the poem. This is the poem that Pari learned in childhood. Here is an abridged version:

Listen to this reed
play out its plaint
unfold its tale
of separations:

Ever since they cut me
from my reedy bed,
     my cry
makes men and women
     weep
I like to keep my breast
fretted with loss
to convey
the pain of longing
     All those severed from their roots
     thirst to return to the source
. . .

In our sadness, time slides by listlessly
the days searing inside us as they pass.
But so what if the days may slip away?
so long as you, Uniquely Pure, abide.
. . .

Break off your chains
My son, be free!
How long enslaved
By silver, gold?
Pour the ocean
In a pitcher,
Can it hold more
Than one day's store?
. . .

He whom love runs ragged and haggard
Gets purged of all his faults and greed
Welcome, Love! Sweet salutary suffering,

physician-healer of our maladies!
Cure of our pride
Of our conceits,
Our Plato,
Our Galen!
By Love
Our earthly flesh
Ascends to heaven
Our mountains
are made supple,
moved to dance

> Love moved Mount Sinai, my love,
> and *it made Moses swoon.*[52]

The poems in the textbook are broken down in Table 1.2. Again, we see the extent of the use of poetry in teaching Persian language and literature, and also a certain pedagogy of 'erfan that is encouraged in textbooks published by the Ministry of Education of the Islamic Republic of Iran—a republic that also jails and silences those who self-identify as followers of one or another mystic order.

Some of the poems are pages long (such as those of Ferdowsi), and some are just couplets. In many of the prose pieces, as was just mentioned, the poetry of Hafez, Rumi, and Saadi in particular is quoted as well. There is a poem on Mansur al-Hallaj (tenth century), a central figure in the history of 'erfan. His most famous saying, "I am the Truth," which continues to be frequently quoted, cost him his life. Among the pieces by the twentieth-century poets who wrote "new poetry," there is this beloved poem by Sohrab Sepehri (1928–1980), a painter and poet whose modern free verse is considered to contain 'erfan themes and images:

The Sound of the Water's Footsteps
I am from Kashan
I am a Moslem
My Mecca is a red rose
my prayer-spread the stream, my holy clay the light

my prayer-rug the field
I do ablutions to the rhythm of the rain upon the
    Windowpane
In my prayer runs the moon, runs the light
The particles of my prayer have turned translucent
upon the minaret of the cypress tree
I say my prayer in the mosque of grass
and follow the sitting and rising of the wave.

The full poem is much longer, but this first part offers an idea of some of the thematic continuities between new and classical poetry—and of why this poem has become so popular. In this translation, "prayer" refers to namaz. In the textbook, a footnote to the last line given here states: "The poet sees all the elements of nature in his namaz. From the point of view of 'erfan, all phenomena are in the process of *tasbīh* [a kind of *zikr*, or prayer] and *ebādat* [worship]."

Secular Iranians often accuse religious institutions and individuals of Arabizing their language to add to their Islamic credentials—saying that, at times, some clerics in particular seem to compete with each other over how much Arabic they can fit into any one sentence. This is true of many clerics. Those who speak this way are stereotyped and made fun of. I searched for a potential contrast with modernist secular Iranians such as Nafisi, whose views continue to be represented by many intellectuals inside and outside of Iran today. Other than one or two well-known public intellectuals who have written against Persian classical poetry and the ineptitude of the Persian language for scientific purposes, (for example, Ahmad Kasravi, 1890–1946), I could not find opposing views on the heroic status of the language and the poetry. Following the widespread idea that more orthodox Muslims are against anything Iranian that does not have its origin in the history of Islam, I consulted the Qom Seminary website to see if it conveyed any ambivalence with respect to the Persian language and classical poetry.

As it turns out, I found a lengthy entry that begins by saying that "Farsi or Parsi" is the "language of speaking [*takallum*, an Arabic word] of a group of Iranians and some groups in Central Asia," and mentioning

POET	NUMBER OF WORKS
Tenth to Sixteenth Centuries	
Mowlana (Rumi)	2
Ferdowsi	2
Rabe'eh bint Ka'b (female poet)	1
Nizami	1
Saadi	2
Hafiz	1
Khayyam	1
Nasser Khosrow	1
Jami	1
Baba Taher	1
Vahshi Bafeqi	1
Twentieth Century	
Bidel Dehlavi*	1
Iraj Mirza	1
Iqbal Lahori**	1
Parvin Etesami (female poet)	1
Manuchehri Damghani	1
Bahar	1
Mehrdad Avesta	1
Salman Harati	1
Contemporary Ayatollahs	
Allameh Tabatai	1
Imam Khomeini	1
New Poetry (*she'r-e no*)	
Nima Yushij	1
Akhavan Sales	1
Twenty-First Century, Revolutionary Poets	
Qeysar Aminpoor	1
Hasan Husseini	1

TABLE 1.2. Poetry in the Textbook for Persian Language and Literature [*Zaban va Adabiyat-e Farsi*], (General [*Omūmi*] 1 and 2), 2012 (Iranian year 1390).
*Indian poet who wrote in Persian.
**Pakistani poet and philosopher who wrote in Urdu.

the fact that Persian is the native language of only slightly more than 50 percent of Iranians. Identifying the language with its literature, this commentary states:

> The *shīrīn* [eloquent, sweet] Persian language, whether in its ancient form on inscriptions . . . or in the form of Middle Persian and Pahlavi inscriptions, or in the form of Dari [New Persian] . . . contains the rich culture and productive literature after [the establishment of] Islam. It is everywhere the best national treasure [representing] Iranian identity. This precious gift [*amānat*, safe-keeping] is an inheritance [*mirās*] that has reached us from generation to generation and chest to chest [*sīneh beh sīneh*].[53]

Speaking of culture and language and the identity [*hoviyyat*] of Iranians in Iran and the world, and drawing an equation between Persian and classical poetry, the text goes on to claim that,

> [d]ue to the richness of its literature and having lofty [*boland*] concepts in *'erfan*, culture, and art at its heart, the Persian language has brought together vast possibilities of exchange on matters of science, literature, and history. It would be a matter of regret if this valuable wealth/capital [*sarmāyeh*] was allowed to suffer the attacks of colonialists, knowing enemies, and unaware and hapless friends.

The Persian language is cast as a victor that, against all odds, has not only survived but thrived and made all its speakers proud:

> What has this worthy heritage . . . not suffered in the course of its long history with its many ups and downs. It has put behind it rough encounters and events such as the invasions of Turan [in *Shahnameh* this refers to Turkish invaders], Yunan [Greeks], Mongols, and Tatars and the trickery of European colonialists, with even self-lost [*khodbākhteh*] Iranians; [yet] bringing to its [Persian language] eyebrows nary a frown.

The entry repeatedly makes the point that essentially, "without attention to the Persian language, one cannot have a wide and deep understanding of Islam and Islamic thinking." Note that, as an institution devoted to the study of Islam, Qom Seminary avoids making any mention of the Muslim conquest and the subsequent importance of Arabic. Persian, it makes clear, is simply crucial to Islamic civilization.

I have chosen to bring in the views of the Qom Seminary on the Persian language to show the widely shared view of Persian as shaping Islam in Iran and even beyond. It would be easy to demonstrate the attachment of countless nonreligious, unambiguously nationalist and secular poets, writers, and public figures to this language. But what I aim to show is that in this respect, there is little that divides religious and nonreligious Iranians. The Persian language has been the site of a major cultural and political convergence among Iranians over a wide spectrum of ideologies. It continues to be viewed as the vital organism that has withstood the mighty challenges of an Arabic divine language attached to the central text of the transnational Muslim community. What is more, the same consensus about Persian exists for 'erfan poetry and more generally for the vast body of writing representing different schools of mysticism that began centuries ago. The admiration for poetry and for the Persian language are inseparable. Secular Iranians see a certain open-minded modernity in 'erfan thought and religious Iranians see it as a vast reservoir of theological thinking. In Iran, mysticism troubles the binary of secular and religious. It allows and perhaps has always allowed an aesthetic and explorative space for those who are not pious but cannot be categorized as "secular" either.[54]

Presence, Meaning, and Memory

One might rightly wonder how it is that across centuries certain poems and prayers remain so beloved and continue to have such a strong sway in the cultural, social, and aesthetic life of Iranians. Certainly, what they "say" or what they mean must be an important factor in their longevity. Classical poems have been the subject of commentaries and hermeneutic labor for centuries, in particular because they have served as the main site for the elaboration and theorization of mystic concepts. Just as commentaries on the Qur'an and explanations of the significance of Qur'anic prayers (see Chapter 4) have been the subject of countless analyses. The hermeneutic work has been clearly important. It is hard to keep track of the number of books and articles devoted to the interpretations of such sources of discursive traditions as the poetry of Hafez, Rumi, Saadi, and others. And the formal features, sounds, rhyme, rhythm, alliteration, and so on that have helped these poems to lend themselves so well to being transformed into songs have also been studied in detail by Iranian and non-Iranian scholars.

The ethnography presented in this book shows that the various kinds of attachments, often lasting across lifetimes, to certain prayers, poems, and songs are not merely the results of what they mean or what they say or even what people "understand" from them. And in any case, these works are not manuals of instruction whose meanings are transparent and easy to follow. One might like a poem or prayer and recite it frequently without fully "understanding" it. Semiotic approaches that begin and end with analyzing linguistic components as various kinds of signs and their relations to cultural, political, or historical contexts do not fully explain these long-term attachments. I use the concept of "presence"—employed in different but overlapping senses within the tradition of mystic poetry by my interlocutors and by scholars such as Michel de Certeau, Robert Orsi, and Hans Ulrich Gumbrecht—in order to find a way of articulating what kinds of relationship individuals and collectives make with certain genres of language.

Meaning, relations between signs, semantic content, and interpretation do not exhaust the ways in which language affects us. Language has materiality—sounds, loudness, pitch, musicality, regional and class variations. Readers and reciters do not hear a disembodied voice when they return to beloved prayers and poems. [55] Over time, the voices of many people are carried in them—the voices of those who recited and performed them in previous times. Often, when we hear certain words, we also hear the ways in which specific people we have met utter them. Our bodies, ears, vocal tracts, chests, eyes, they all interact with what we hear (and of course what we say). We tend to be touched by certain voices, intonations, and pronunciations for one reason or another, and these stay with us. Prayers and poems, especially those that are repeatedly recited, bring forth different presences. We relate to them, are moved by them, and feel many emotions as we say them and hear them recited by others.

A number of scholars have used the idea of presence as distinct from meaning in different ways in their works. I would like to bring a few of these works together here and show their relevance to the study of poetry and prayer. A full exploration of the concept of presence in relation to language would require a book-length study.[56] Here, I aim to make a brief inroad. To begin, as we will see in detail in the next chapter, the ideal of a good namaz for my interlocutors is articulated as "creating a presence" in the act of performing it. What does it mean to create a presence in a scripted ritual? It means that in different ways, these women make the ritual their own—they tell God what they want or need to, they manage to concentrate and be in the ritual's sacred time-space, and they make a connection to the divine so that they may be co-present. There is also the centuries-old idea in mystic writings of having "presence of the heart" in any act of worship—a sincere state where the worshipper is fully focused and has no other motivation to do the worship other than to be in His presence.

Michel de Certeau speaks of a "presence" in the signifier.[57] That is, it is not just the sound image and the concept that defines the linguistic sign but the fact that people, memories, sounds, and events are often carried in language. One might hear different voices in various signifiers, as when one of the women says that she hears her father's voice every time she performs the morning prayer. Roland Barthes conceives of voice as "the very texture of memory."[58] Noting the overwhelming dominance of interpretive approaches in literary studies, Hans Ulrich Gumbrecht writes about "what meaning cannot convey."[59] Without discounting the necessity of semiotic approaches, he wants to make "present" that which is perceived as absent in what constitutes "meaning." Gumbrecht speaks of the "production of presence" in poetry: "Poetry is perhaps the most powerful example of the simultaneity of presence effects and meaning effects—for even the most overpowering institutional dominance of the hermeneutic dimension could never fully repress the presence effects of rhyme and alliteration, of verse and stanza."[60]

Hans Gumbrecht and Robert Orsi both write about the implications of the transformation of bread and wine in the Christian rite of the Eucharist into *symbolic* representations of the body and blood of Jesus following the Protestant Reformation: "Protestants deal in symbols, Catholics in the really real."[61] Gumbrecht traces the dominance of hermeneutic and semiotic approaches in literature to this transformation, and Orsi argues that it resulted in modernity being premised on absence: "The postulate of absence, along with the totalizing claims of discourse, make it diffi-cult *to work from inside the experience* of those who have encountered sacred presences outward toward the environment within which these experiences have their destiny, rather than the other way around."[62] Orsi speaks of "experiences of presence of God, gods, divine being, deceased ancestors." A great example of this is Maryam's description (in Chapter 2) of who is present when she performs the namaz imagining standing in front of the House of God in Mecca, where she conjures the presence of her parents standing with her (they have passed away), her siblings, and her children; and every fifteen days one of the Imams is there as well, beginning first with Prophet.

In response to the question posed by these and other scholars about how we are to analyze presence, my partial answer insofar as language is concerned is to recognize that semiotic signs in oral productions and exchanges are heard through specific voices. This makes the sign a more complex matter than a pairing of meaning and abstract sound image. The implications of this recognition would then have to be followed: for example, we are then more likely to pay attention to the possibility of accumulated presences in prayers and poems that become a part of their sounds. Methodologically, the route(s) through which these prayers and poems were learned and subsequent encounters and experiences become quite important. We need to develop a set of new questions to ask. Un-like semiotic material, such presences are not directly available for us to access. Exploring the importance of presence is particularly apt in the case of prayer and poetry in Iran, given the centrality of the concept of hal, the sensation that may transpire in the act of recitation. Little about the experience of hal can be captured through a semiotic approach alone. The momentary and unpredictable ecstasy that can happen in the course of praying, for example, cannot be captured through a semiotic analysis. But the experience has a profound effect on how one thinks of religion, ritual, and one's relationship to divinity. I argue that to understand the work of poetry and prayer—genres that are repeatedly read and recited, that are viewed as forms of eternal knowledge, and that embody extraordinary sounds, we need to develop concepts such as presence that add to semiotic analyses.

Conclusion

The companionship of prayer and poetry is created from childhood, both at home and at school. The companionship also characterizes more broadly the last several centuries of cultural history in Iran. Love for this poetry is often synonymous with reverence and admiration for the Persian language whose many attributes are seen to be in ample evidence in this poetry. After the revolution, the number of classes in poetry for adults increased exponentially. With few exceptions, most of the women in our group have been going to weekly poetry classes, where they read Ferdowsi, Hafez, Saadi, Rumi, and other poets. The late Iranian philosopher and scholar of Hinduism, Dariush Shayegan (1935–2018) wrote his last book on "five provinces of presence" and the "poeticity of Iranians." He devotes one chapter each to Ferdowsi, who wrote the *Epic of the Kings* in the eleventh century; Khayyam, whose chapter is called "Flashes of Moments of Presence"; Mowlavi; Saadi; and Hafez. Shayegan argues that each one of these poets continues to be *hayy o hāzer* (alive and present) for Iranians— they do not care who came first or last; these poets do not belong to the past, but are "eternal interlocutors."[63] Indeed, when Iranians quote from these poets, they never use the past tense—it is always such and such a poet "says." Poetry and songs provide the main conduits for the elaboration and spread of 'erfan and its reflections on religiosity. The concept of a "dry religion," or of those who practice it (*khoshkeh-mazhab*), comes up in relation to how this poetry "waters it."

CHAPTER TWO

Fixed Forms and the Play of Imagination
Everyday Ritual Prayers

In the aftermath of the revolution of 1979, debates about acts of worship became ever more intense. The obligatory ritual prayer, *namāz*, is one of the five "pillars of Islam," and it became enmeshed in broader contestations about how one ought to carry out any given religious ritual. If one *must* do the namaz every day, as all denominations and schools of Islamic jurisprudence have agreed, what kind of namaz should it be? Is it enough to utter the intention formula, recite the words of the Qur'anic verses, and go through the prescribed body movements five times a day? Or should the reciter aim for a connection with the divine, for "presence of the heart" and "sincerity"? How does legal validity weigh against the kind of experience that many reciters speak of where they manage to create a presence in the performance of these prayers? Many clerics, including major ayatollahs, believe that for laypeople (*'avām*), legal validity is good enough—they don't need that connection or presence of the heart for their namaz. During an interview that I carried out with Ayatollah Mohaqqeq-Damaad, he voiced this position, and called namaz "a duty that is to be carried out," *esqāt-e taklīf*, or, "getting the obligation done." But the first thing that the women I spoke to said about this prayer was that one must be able to have concentration (*tamarkoz*) during its performance, otherwise it will lack the basic prerequisite for a "good" namaz.[1]

These kinds of questions are ongoing and have contributed to robust and nuanced conceptions of religion among laypeople. Questions about any act, whether *vājeb* (required) or *mostahabb* (favored in the eyes of God but not mandatory) have resulted in an unplanned yet almost continuous education for ordinary people—in their thinking about the meanings of religion and its purposes, in imagining the relationship one ought to have with the divine, and in the question of who decides about the quality of that relationship. Before the revolution, few non-clerics were concerned with such inquiries. To be sure, there are Iranians who dismiss religion out of hand and engage in arguments only to prove that it is all a hoax and a way of fooling people. There are also those who accept the state's dominant version of Islam—legalistic, and mediated by clerics and mosques. But in between those views exists a wide spectrum of believers exploring and debating and trying to delve more deeply into what they care a great deal about and that is the *quality* of their religiosity and their relationship to the divine. Using Robert Orsi's formulation to characterize debates in Iran, the question of "how the human and the divine stand in relation to each other" came to be re-thought in large part because the state wanted to intervene and be present in that relation.[2]

Namaz is a *rokn*, a "pillar" of Islam, and it is at the center of what it means to be a Muslim.[3] It is what is called an *ebādat*, "worship," being a part of a series of *ebādāt* (plural) that Muslims engage in. Although there is only a partial overlap with the term *ritual* in English (because certain acts may be worship but not rituals), I will use the term ritual to refer to namaz. Namaz is the single most important ritual act that Muslims are required to undertake every day, five times a day. It is not uncommon to ask about a person one does not know well, "Is so and so a *namāz-khan* [a namaz-reciter]?"[4] in order to assess the basic but crucial quality of someone's religiosity. Considering all five pillars, this is the question that is asked first—one does not immediately ask whether someone has been to Mecca or pays alms or fasts, for example.

Western audiences are used to seeing images of Muslims performing congregational prayers in mosques around the world.[5] These are most often images of men in huge throngs who are rarely seen close up. The viewer does not find out about their individual lives and ideas. The default Muslim, based on such representations, comes across as an urban, lower-class, barely educated male of more or less unknown age. He is never shown praying on his own—and many people do pray on their own in mosques—and reflecting on his prayer. He does not appear to have much to say about his religion, as he is not asked about it, and seems never to experience doubts. These images, shown at times in the context of violent terrorist attacks, have made congregational namaz appear to be, among other things, a threatening act.[6] The unchanging image of congregational prayers, along with masses swirling around the House of God in Mecca, confirms the idea that Islam is uniquely a religion of rigid rituals carried out by those who have "submitted" and who therefore ask no questions. Muslim subjectivity is shown in broad strokes, with little depth and no hint of the existence of an interiority. I will discuss "submission" later at more length, but for now let us make a brief note that there is nothing transparent about the idea of submission and that various Muslims emphasize one or another dimension of this concept.

At mosques, both *namāz-e jamā'at* (congregational namaz), and *namāz-e foradā* (individual namaz) are performed. Because the latter is considered the unmarked or default form of namaz, it is referred to simply as namaz, whereas congregational prayers are specified by using *jom'eh* (Friday) or jamā'at as a qualifier. Those who like to pray in (neighborhood) mosques might have a favorite corner or a small arch or wide column that is a bit out of the way, with natural light or where the relative darkness offers more of a chance to gather one's thoughts and stand to pray alone. There are also many who do not like their closest mosques and avoid them. There is a fair amount of talk about how mosques have changed since the revolution, for the worse. I was told that the idea of a neighborhood mosque—one that was usually small and where familiarity with the imam, the custodian, and perhaps the azan reciter (if different from the imam) could be cultivated on a daily basis—is gone, at least in larger cities. At the moment, imams are usually appointed centrally and do not necessarily live in the neighborhood. Hence, they are not easily trusted. Also, mosques are no longer open all the time, and worshippers feel they may be being watched by the custodian or the imam. A number of the women in our group said that mosques used to be always open, and places of refuge, but they now have opening and closing hours.[7]

In any case, notwithstanding the ubiquity of images of crowded Friday prayers on Western televisions, over the course of each day and over their lifetimes, most Iranians, men and women do their prayers at home.[8] Depending on sociopolitical conditions, whether one likes the prayer leader, the state of one's neighborhood mosque, whether one's friends and family like to go there, and one's age and gender, mosque attendance goes up or down. The main congregational prayer in the Muslim world is the Friday noon prayer, and many make some effort to perform it in a mosque. Yet even for this namaz, many women stay home. When there are special occasions, such as the end of the month of Ramadan or remembrance of the martyrdom of Imam Hussein (described in Chapter 4), attendance goes up.

Why Muslims must pray and what the motivation for praying should be constitute the most frequently discussed questions on television, radio, and the Internet and among friends and strangers in Iran today. Should one pray out of love for God or out of fear? Who is one praying for: for God, to show off, or for oneself? Why, if namaz is supposed to teach one to be ethical and honest, if it is meant to bring about all the good qualities in Muslims—discipline, humility, a good temper, generosity—is there so much corruption and lying? Is a prayer valid even when our minds wander in the middle of it, or does its validity not depend on the concentration of the reciter? How should we think about a namaz where no connection to the divine is made, not even a momentary one? Can we pray in Persian, or does it have to be in Arabic?

Let us first develop an idea of what a namaz is before we move on to describing how the women in our group perform it and reflect on it.

Namaz: The Recitational Use of the Qur'an

The Qur'an has a number of recitational uses, and namaz is one of them. Recitational uses are different from readings whose purpose is to understand and interpret—an activity that some, though not all, believers engage in in various contexts, including gatherings and Qur'an classes. As mentioned before, in Arabic, the term for namaz is *salāt*. Salat and its derivatives occur frequently in the Qur'an, and the term has also been borrowed into the languages of societies that have converted to Islam. In Persian, the term namaz dates back to Zoroastrian times. Those who practiced Zoroastrianism used it to refer to their prayers, and it then continued to be used by Persian speakers who converted to Islam.[9]

The event that sets the preparations for namaz in motion is the call to prayer, the *azān*, that is timed in relation to the position of the sun. It is broadcast in Iran on all radio and television channels and from minarets, though in urban centers, in particular, almost all azan are prerecorded and broadcast; rarely does one hear a live azan coming from a minaret.[10] There are a handful of recorded *mu'ezzīn* (azan reciters) whose voices and styles are much loved, even by those who do not pray, are not believers, and are not Muslim. Some of these reciters have passed away, but their azan continues to be broadcast.[11] As a singularly powerful recitation that one hears from childhood several times a day, the azan comes to be inexorably linked to all kinds of images and memories—of childhood homes and neighborhoods, of the smell of food being prepared, of Ramadan dawns and the breaking of the fast, and of the people present in all such memories. Of course, once the performance of the noon and afternoon namaz was imposed by the state on all students and employees in public schools and offices, associations with namaz have likely become far more mixed and ambivalent.

Outside of public institutions where everyone is expected to go to the prayer room at the sound of the azan, some people begin preparations for the namaz as soon as they hear the azan. Some wait. It often depends on whether they are at home or not, or have guests or not. As mentioned in the previous chapter, *namāz-e sobh* (morning prayer) is the first one that children learn. In Arabic, this same prayer is called *salāt al-fajr* (dawn prayer). One must be ritually clean to pray, so one does *vūzū* (ablutions; Arabic *wūdū*). That is, the arms, hands, face, and feet are washed and dried.[12] Then one stands to pray in a clean spot. Some people, especially women, like to stand on their prayer rug (*sajjadeh*), though using such a rug is not a requirement. The prayer rug is generally made of velvet and is rectangular in shape. It is placed so one faces Mecca, the birthplace of the Prophet Muhammad. Thus, in Iran, one faces southwest. On top of the prayer rug, one spreads a smaller piece of cloth, called a *jā-namāz* (prayer cloth; literally, place of namaz) that contains a *mohr* (prayer stone). The rug is often colorful and may have a drawing of the House of God, the Kaaba. Some women and men like to throw rose or jasmine petals into their ja-namaz, along with their prayer beads. Women dress modestly, and most cover their hair for the duration of the prayer. Several women explained to me that a scarf or *chador* (veil) helps them to separate from their surroundings and takes them into "their own world." It helps their concentration. Elaheh said that she wears a scarf and brings it over her

eyes, because otherwise she gets distracted: "I suddenly see that a patch of the wall needs some paint or something like that. So, I like my scarf to cover my eyes since I just cannot keep them closed." Many wear long skirts or trousers instead of wearing a long veil. One woman told me that she puts on a bit of makeup because "God loves beauty and I want to look good when I talk to Him."

The namaz shows the recitational use of Qur'anic suras par excellence. The suras must be recited in their original Arabic, with care, and without hurry. To the best of the reciter's ability, the pronunciation of each verse, and each word within it, must be correct. Recall that the language of the Qur'an is the most refined *classical* Arabic, and that Persian speakers on the whole do not have knowledge of this language. Hence, they *must learn* correct pronunciation. I often heard a certain level of self-consciousness when the women described their attempts to muster good Arabic pronunciations; some had taken a few classes to learn, in particular, the pharyngeals (the famous 'ayn, for example) and the interdental sounds (such as "th" in *these* and "th" in *nothing*) that are absent in Persian. The two languages have distinct phonologies, and when Persian speakers pronounce Arabic words, they are often unrecognizable to Arabic speakers. Such matters are a staple of jokes among Iranians.

Here are the details of the morning prayer. The morning prayer, which is the shortest, has two *rak'ats* (prayer cycles). The noon and afternoon prayers have four cycles; the evening prayer three, and the night prayer four. Altogether, they comprise seventeen prayer cycles per day.

Morning Prayer

namāz-e sobh (namaz of morning, in order of acts).

niyyāt (intention): One says, "I pray two rak'ats for the morning prayer, required, to get close to God." The niyyat may be said silently as well.[13]

takbīr (declaring that God is great): "Allaho akbar."

Hands are raised toward the ears, and then brought down, hanging on the sides of the body.

Rak'at-e avval (First cycle, or part)

One recites two suras; this is referred to as "doing the *hamd o sūreh*."

Rokū' (hands on knees): In this posture, one says, for example, "*sobhan allah* [Praise be to God]."

One stands up.

Sojūd (prostration): In roku' and sojud, one generally recites similar phrases; for example, *sobhan allah* (Praise be to God) three times.

After prostration, one stands up. This completes one rak'at, or prayer cycle. Each time one stands up after prostrating, one prayer cycle has been completed.[14]

Rak'at-e dovvom (Second cycle, or part)

One recites the first and second sura (*hamd o sureh*), followed by:

qonūt (extra or voluntary prayer): This is not an obligatory part of namaz; it is mostahabb. One's hands are held close together so that the palms meet, and are raised toward the heavens, and a brief prayer (usually) is recited. Various choices may be made as to what to say during the qonut.

One does roku' and sojud, as before.

tashahhod (testimony of faith): While one is sitting down, one says, "I bear witness that there is no god but God and no partner to Him, and I bear witness that Muhammad is His servant and His prophet. O God bestow blessings upon Muhammad and the household of Muhammad."

salām (recitation of farewell greetings): In this last part of namaz, one can say the following or a similar version: "Peace be upon you, O Prophet, and God's mercy and blessings of peace on us and on the honorable servants of God."

Once the salam is recited, namaz is finished, and the reciter then often sits on the prayer rug cross-legged and speaks to God in Persian (see Chapter Three); and/or does *zikr* (remembrance). There are many different kinds of zikr. One kind consists of phrases that one says a certain number of times in order to remember God: for example, *bism allah al-rahman al-rahim*, said nineteen times or in several rounds of nineteen times while using *tasbīh* (prayer beads; also a kind of prayer). Another zikr is to recite all the names of God.

The sound of the azan can begin to mediate the ideal detachment from one's surroundings and everyday tasks that leads to directing one's attention to the performance of namaz. As can be seen, any given namaz is part of a sequence consisting of the call to prayer, ritual washing, utterance of intention, recitation of namaz, and then optional *do'ā*. Again, one does not simply get up and pray after hearing the azan. What is called by Iranian Muslims *hamd o sūreh*, in reference to what one recites in namaz, is made up of the very first sura of the Qur'an. It is called al-Fatiha in Arabic, but Iranians commonly call it al-Hamd because the first word after the formulaic "In the name of God the Compassionate the Merciful" is al-hamd.[15] This is the only sura that must be recited in each namaz. After its recitation, theoretically any other sura can be chosen. Al-Fatiha is viewed as the "key" (*kelīd*) that allows the reciter to enter the hoped-for, sacred time-space of the namaz. Referring to its first verse, "In the name of God, the Compassionate the Merciful," Elaheh said:

> "Bism-allah al-rahman al-rahim" is a code [*ramz*] for entering the namaz. When we stand to pray that means that we are trying to be honest with You [God] and we don't stand on formalities, and through the back of our hands that face the world, we leave that world behind and enter. [We utter] "allaho akbar" and then we leave everything that is important and dear to us behind, property and status and children and cooking—we put them behind.

Al-Fatiha is a sura that is also used on many different occasions—to ward off harm, to keep away bad thoughts or to calm oneself at bedtime, to ask for the healing of those who are ill, and so on. It has ceremonial functions—it is recited upon first entering a new home or wearing new clothes, by officials at various events, and at business transactions; at times of bereavement, for the peaceful resting of those who have departed this world; and at times of travel. It is the sura most commented on by the women in our group and one to which they have strong emotional bonds. It is also, perhaps, the sura most written about in Western scholarship. According to historian of religion Michael Sells, "Because of its eloquent statement of devotion and the manner in which it pervades religious life, The Opening has been called the Islamic equivalent of the Lord's Prayer in Christianity."[16] Angelika Neuwirth, another scholar of Islam, characterizes al-Fatiha as a "solemn recitation" that is "given to the Muslim community, of publicly staged communication between God and man."[17]

Al-Fatiha (The Opening)
In the name of God
    the Compassionate the Caring
Praise be to God
    lord sustainer of the worlds
the Compassionate the Caring
master of the day of reckoning
To you we turn to worship
    and to you we turn in time of need
Guide us along the road straight
    the road of those to whom you are giving
    not those with anger upon them
    not those who have lost their way[18]

The Opening is followed by short suras that have come to be standard choices: for example, sura 112, al-Ikhlas (or Towhid: Sincerity, Oneness, Unity). This is one of the shortest suras in the Qur'an, but it affirms one of the most significant concepts for Muslims—namely, the unity of God.

Al-Ikhlas (Sincerity)
Say, he is God, one
God the refuge
Not begetting, unbegotten,
    And having as an equal none[19]

One can perform the cycle four times, exactly as just explained, for the noon, afternoon, and night prayers and three times for the evening prayer. After the Opening, one can choose several other suras, as I will elaborate on shortly. The structure of namaz is similar to that of a narrative in that it has a beginning, a middle, and an ending salutation (the salam). It is, therefore, not simply a recitation of a string of suras that begin and end suddenly. Another crucial aspect of namaz is the time it takes from beginning to end, approximately three to six minutes for each cycle, depending on one's speed and concentration. This span of time is central to how it is experienced.

In the previous chapter, I described some of the routes for learning about religion. The namaz was learned by the women in our group in childhood, at home, and from parents and grandparents, as is the case for many people. This route inevitably teaches variation. The kind of pedagogic process that one experiences—involving family, friends' families, teachers, classes, manuals, books, and combinations thereof—can make a fundamental difference both in the ways rituals come to be embodied and in people's ideas about the legitimacy of variation and the role of sources of authority.[20] To learn to pray from a kinship network is to learn variability because inevitably there are individual differences that are explicitly commented on. One hears many stories, such as, "my grandmother told me: 'I like to say *sobhan allah* three times when I go to *sojud* but your grandfather preferred *ya latif.'"*[21]

Depending on the personal context of each reciter, a number of less frequently used suras may be chosen for the namaz by the women. In place of al-Ikhlas, for example, if one is seeking refuge in God in times of distress, al-Falaq (The Dawn, sura 113) and al-Nās (The People, 114) are preferred; when one is feeling light and in a good relation with God, having been given what one asked for, al-Nasr (The Victory, 110) may be recited; when one needs to be patient, one might choose al-'Asr (The Time, 103); and "for when you need to be reminded that after every period of hardship comes a period of ease and comfort," there is al-Sharh (The Relief, 94). In these suras (the longest is six verses), the women see something personal being expressed that can be related to their life conditions. These are the examples mentioned most frequently, but the choice can be any chapter of the Qur'an.[22]

The section of the namaz called the qonut illustrates this kind of variability well. It can be included after the recitation of the *hamd o sureh* of the second prayer cycle. The idea of the qonut is articulated by both laypeople and clerics in these terms: "the qonut is there for you to express something that is left to say to God beyond what the suras already say." A few women told me that they rarely change what they say, and they seemed to treat the qonut as a rather fixed part of the prayer,[23] whereas others recite a line of poetry from Hafez or Rumi or another poet in Persian, or choose additional brief verses from the Qur'an. At times, the women did not know the exact source of a phrase or even a one- or two-line do'a that they used, but they had learned it from their father or mother, or some relative or friend. In choosing to recite it, they memorialized the person and their relationship to him or her in their namaz. The qonut offers a chance to create variation in what is recited.

Religious leaders have their own websites these days, revealing differences of opinion among them about, for example, whether it is acceptable to recite either the whole namaz or the qonut in Persian rather than in Arabic. Insofar as the qonut is concerned, a few ayatollahs state that Persian is allowed. Most recommend Arabic then add that the use of Persian does not render the namaz invalid.[24] The use of Arabic is spoken of as taking caution (*ehtiyāt*) to be sure that any given performance is a legally valid one (as discussed further later).

Congregational and Individual Prayer

Now that we have an idea of a whole namaz, we can delve more deeply into its many dimensions. There is no religious requirement that every prayer be performed in a mosque, not even Friday prayers, but since the revolution in Iran, there has been an upsurge in promoting mosque prayers.[25] Many clerics encourage performing Friday prayers at the mosque, though often this is an ambiguous suggestion with regard to women. In the Qur'an, in verse 9 of the sura of Jom'a (Friday), believers (in particular, it seems, shopkeepers) are told to leave their shops and go to the mosque to pray on Fridays when they hear the call to prayer to remember God. This is followed by the verse, "That is better for you, if you only knew." Two verses further on (62:11) we read about what it is that is "better": "But when they saw a diversion or transaction (O Muhammad), they rushed to it and left you standing. Say, 'What is with Allah is better than diversion and a transaction, and Allah is the best of Providers.'" Hence, what is better is to pray when it is time to do so and "be with Allah." The "better" is not referring to praying in the mosque, at least not transparently.

The Qom Seminary website offers separate entries for *namaz* and for *congregational namaz*. After praising the latter, it goes on to explain that there is disagreement among the schools of jurisprudence on whether it is vajeb (required) or mostahabb (favored) to do all prayers congregationally. It concludes that in the legal opinion of Shi'as, Hanafis, and Malekis, only the Friday prayer must be performed in a congregation. For all the others, that is mostahabb, not vajeb.[26] Whether praying at the mosque has a special status and is a requirement is caught up in the long-standing, explicit, and eloquent dislike of ostentation (*tazāhor*) in piety. This old discourse has been renewed with vigor after the revolution. Besides countless poems against "piety sellers," even clerics who are opposed to the regime point out that the state is in effect saying to citizens that it is permissible *to pretend* one is a believer if one is forced to pray. Nationwide, mosques must close for Friday prayers so that congregants can go only where the national government wants them to. In Tehran, one can go only to the long-in-completion Musalla (opened in 2012), and before that, for years, everyone had to go to the grounds of the University of Tehran, where multiple cameras belonging to state media live streamed or otherwise broadcast many parts of the Friday prayers.

In mosques, congregational prayer sessions appear to the observer as indistinguishable from one another, and the experience of the praying individual and collective is often left unexplored. What do individuals experience when they perform the daily prayers? What are they aiming for?

(Not) Being Satisfied with One's Namaz: Experiences of Ritual Prayer

As I began talking to individual women about their experience of doing the namaz, I also learned vocabulary and concepts that kept coming up: "concentration" (*tamarkoz*), "presence of the heart" (*hozūr-e qalb*), "sincerity" (*kholūs*), and "presence" (*hozur*) both in the namaz and in the company of the divine, and still others. I was interested to know when the women had begun to pray regularly. To answer that question, many said that they had gone through periods when they had stopped praying. They became interested in doing their namaz regularly (*morattab*) and taking up the Qur'an "seriously" (*betowr-eh jeddi*) a few years into their fourth decade of life, that is, after the revolution. I expected a series of doctrinal answers, such as how it is incumbent on any Muslim to do the namaz every day and that the Prophet and the Imams have urged all to pray and so on. But while the importance of namaz for Muslims was mentioned, the answers were at times surprising. Parvin said:

> We used to go to the public bath in our neighborhood for years but in my 20s, we were finally able to build a shower in our home, and for the first time I felt that I could be sure to be *pāk* [clean] whenever I want to pray. You know, this kind of cleanliness is very important for women.

Hence, having a shower at home—a fact that could not be further from a doctrinal matter—can play a major role in one's commitment to this ritual. Indeed, many of the women spoke of being able to shower at home as instrumental in their regular praying. Another important factor was the characterization of doing regular namaz as an act that would catch God's attention, as Maryam explained:

> Every time I would complain about something in my life, my father would say, "Do your namaz and it will work out. God will pay attention to you." He just kept encouraging me in this way.

But most important was the revolution:

> When I was thirty-six, the revolution happened. It turned our attention to religious matters.

I heard variations from many people on how the revolution played a central role in their returning to and reflecting on religion.

One can detect a general "mistrust of the experiential" on the part of some social scientists, and especially in the study of Islam.[27] An aim of this chapter is to describe experiences of the namaz that were conveyed to me by these women. In several group discussions that I held in March 2011 on different experiences of namaz, Pari said:

> For me to do namaz, the most important thing is silence [*sokūt*]. I had this experience at the shrine of Imam Reza in Mashhad] yesterday—

it was too crowded and there was the voice of this person who was chanting some kinds of prayer. . . . [That was distracting.] For me, silence is important and also my own mood.

In that same trip to the holy city of Mashhad, she also prayed in the Gowharshad Mosque that is part of the shrine complex. She had gone to Mashhad on a field trip organized by her high school, taking a group of students. But she lost track of time in praying:

In the courtyard of the Gowharshad Mosque, one evening, it was raining lightly. I went to pray under one of the arched ceilings that still allows you to be outside, smelling the rain. You know, namaz becomes shorter when one is traveling, but I stayed in the qonut for so long that I lost track of time. We had taken seventeen, eighteen high school girls with us and they were my responsibility . . . anyway, it was very intense. I was able to make this beautiful and celestial connection. The huge expanse of the sky [*Several of the women listening say together, "and the rain . . . "*], yes, and the rain. . . .

Pari does not express a strong preference for home or mosque as a place for her namaz, but she mentions silence as being key to her experience. What is interesting about what she describes is that in two quite similar public contexts, she had very different experiences while praying by herself.

The other women mostly expressed a preference for praying at home, in their own rooms or in a space where they can be alone. Maryam compared praying at home and in a mosque in this way:

There is a big difference. I don't like praying with a prayer leader [*pishnamaz*] at all. It does not put me in the right state of mind. First of all, women can't even *see* the prayer leader, and so there is the *mokabbir*, who is usually a young boy, who repeats what the prayer leader is saying loud enough to help the women know what is going on, like "*qad qāmat il-salat*," so you know that you have to stand up at that point. And then for other prayers they don't even recite them out loud, so you don't hear anything in addition to not seeing anything. They really don't think about women.

Praying in crowded areas such as a mosque was spoken of as not being conducive to concentration, which is necessary for a good namaz but a state that is hard to achieve and a constant struggle. At prayer times, some women go to their rooms, lower the lights, draw the curtains, close the door, and stand to pray. Others pray next to a window or a balcony for the natural light. Those who pray are left alone, and people hold off on telephone calls at prayer times. A few of the women pray aloud because this allows them to concentrate better. This is in spite of the fact that it is men who are generally encouraged and allowed to recite out loud, in particular for the morning prayer. Women can do so if there are no men present, similar to the conditions under which they can lead prayers. For most prayers, they said, they whisper, and in my experience their whispering is audible.

Given a prayer leader, one must follow his exact choices and movements while standing behind him. This is not a struggle that the women in our group have explicitly taken on, but at the same time, it is one of the reasons they do not like praying at mosques.[28] In the many all-women gatherings that they organize in various homes, some of them do lead prayers. The implication behind the idea that the prayer leader must be a man—even if he is not religiously very literate and/or even if he is younger—is that no matter who he is, he can lead women. This is not acceptable to the women in our group. They told me that many prayer leaders do not necessarily have their respect in matters of religion or politics.

A Ritual Is a Ritual Is a Ritual?

When one prays alone, the mood, the choice of suras, and the speed depend on one's own conditions and preferences. One may make a number of choices based on considerations unrelated to what a prayer leader is doing or to the group with whom one is praying. One might think that a ritual is a ritual is a ritual, a copy of a copy. But it is crucial to realize that even with a script, *the reciter cannot know in advance* when she starts the prayer how that performance will turn out. Hence, if we grant the unknowability of how iterative acts may turn out—if we acknowledge the crucial role that time plays in the unfolding of rituals—then our well-entrenched ideas about their rote eventuality are fundamentally challenged. The realization of this fact about the namaz (and other rituals) is crucial. It is enough to think about practically any other kind of scripted act to realize its importance. A pianist who has played the same piece over and over cannot know *in advance* how a particular performance will unfold as she goes through the piece. It is only to a degree that practice can determine the quality and flow. One can stumble even after much practice, or surprise oneself by the smoothness of the performance. Similarly, the reciter of namaz cannot be sure in advance whether during any particular iteration of this ritual, she will be able to make a connection and prevent her mind from wandering.

There is good reason to analyze what happens in the performance of namaz as practice rather than as repetition. A practice as an iterable act is necessarily open-ended each time it is undertaken. The possibility that at each turn, the performer may arrive at a new understanding, a different way of making a connection with God (or not), of finding new things to say, of using a chapter of the Qur'an that she has never recited before, and so on, all this makes "submission" a complex concept that has multiple dimensions. There is, in a repeated act, a trace, a memory, but at the same time, each iteration of the act is open. Each practice of prayer looks back (since it has been done before many times), and it also looks forward to what is happening. This is similar to the recitation of memorized poetry as well. The open-endedness of iterable acts means that when we say that for Muslims namaz is an act of submission (*taslīm*), we do not quite know what it entails insofar as the reciter is concerned. I was told that taslim means trust in God and deference to Him. What the reciter experiences in taslim, the analyst cannot fully access.[29]

I wanted to know if namaz is viewed as a form of communication with God. There was general surprise almost each time I asked the question. Parvin told me:

> What else am I doing? Of course I am communicating with God but I tell Him different things depending on what is happening in my life. I do not immediately begin to pray as soon as I stand on my sajjadeh. I pause and gather my thoughts. Then I try to concentrate on each word that I am saying and while doing that I am also telling God what I need, what I am afraid of, I ask for guidance. *Al-Hamd [al-Fatiha] does not always have the same meaning.*

Note the last assertion of this reply. How can the most recited sura of the Qur'an "not always have the same meaning"? It seems that the unchanging *forms* of the verses recited (the actual words) do not limit what is conveyed to God. What many of these women explained effectively meant that they use God's chosen words to tell Him what *they* want to share: requests, gratitude, questions, anxieties, and remembrance of a person who is ill or has passed away, or wordless thoughts and feelings. I asked, "Are you saying that in reciting the same sura, you say *different things* to God?" She replied, rather emphatically, "you say *a thousand things* to God. Over the course of a day and throughout your life there is so much that comes up that you want to tell Him." This was explained to me repeatedly by my interlocutors—that "things happen," "things come up," and you need to talk to God about them.

I posed the same question to Maryam about whether doing namaz is a form of communication: "Well, I am not choosing the words of the sura," she said, "but I concentrate on pronouncing them well, not hurrying through them, and I try to learn to tell God what I want to." She gave the following example to explain what is happening in her prayers (at least at times) when she is reciting al-Hamd. (This is a different translation from the one by Michael Sells that I used earlier.)

In the first four *ayāt* [verses], you are praising God and God is in the third person—you feel that He is rather far from you.

1. In the Name of God, the Beneficent, the Merciful

2. All Praise be to God, Lord of the Worlds

3. The Most Beneficent, the Most Merciful

4. Sovereign of the Day of Resurrection

But suddenly in the next verse you address God directly and you feel closer to Him; you say:

5. It is You we Worship and You we Ask for Help

These words you say very slowly and calmly because now you have reached a station [*jāygāh*][30] where you are talking to God *directly*, you are addressing him. Here you are saying that "I seek your aid. Only yours." Now you say what it is you want, what is in your heart. You seek his aid on behalf of yourself, say if your child is sick, or on behalf of a friend who needs help.

Although I had heard previously that "you tell God what is on your mind" while enunciating the words of the sura, this was the first time someone offered such a detailed description of how that can happen. Perhaps the simultaneity is possible precisely because these words are utterly familiar to the reciter. Yet familiarity is clearly not leading inexorably to roteness.

Having said that you tell God what you have in mind, she went on:

Then, at this point, while you are still addressing God directly, you go on to say:

6. Guide us to the Straight Path

7. The Path of Those you have Blessed, not Those who Have

Provoked Your Anger and Those who Have Gone Astray.

Now this is the path of God but you don't know exactly what that means: does that just mean you pray and you fast? One constantly asks God and oneself this question: What path is that? What is it you have to do to be on that path?

In her experience, even though for years the words of this sura have been repeated over and over, they have not only not become meaningless or rote, but on the contrary, they have served as vehicles for intimate conversation with God—telling Him of concerns and worries and posing questions. Maryam continued:

There is a certain answer to that: it says the path of those that you have blessed. But who are the ones God has blessed? I think it is those that God never leaves alone, never forgets. We ask God not to leave us to ourselves even for a second because without that overseeing, we would be lost, be without protection. So even if we can't or don't know what it means to be "blessed," we ask God simply not to forget us.

As we will see in the next chapter, being forgotten by God is one of the biggest concerns that figures into these women's relationship with the divine.[31] When one is able to have this kind of communication in the namaz, it means that one has been able to perform it with hozur-e qalb (presence of the heart) and kholus (sincerity). These terms are centuries old, but they continue to be used routinely in discussing the performance of the five daily prayers.[32] They figure in many prayer books and appear in lengthy discussions of namaz in the writings of scholars. At their heart, lies the anxiety of praying yet simultaneously acting unethically, so that the words of God and the act of praying result in just moving one's lips and body without sincerity.[33] Continuing with our analogy to a pianist (or to the player of any other instrument or any kind of sports for that matter), we would never conceive of what a pianist does as mindless repetition when she practices the same piece over and over again. Indeed, what happens gradually is that she creates a presence in what she plays, so that listeners can distinguish one player's rendition of a particular sonata, for example, from another's. Similarly, the reciter of namaz strives to create a space of co-presence by using God's words to tell Him what the reciter wants. She comes to coexist with the divine in the very words that belong to Him.

Parvin also answered the question about namaz as communication with God and my inquiry about different meanings of al-Hamd:

It is definitely a conversation for me, I mean that I am talking to God. I begin with Hamd. . . . I think this is a kind of summary of the whole of Qur'an. It is the only sura in the namaz where you are actually addressing God. Here you are talking to someone who has both a general kindness and a specific one (for you)—a God that is like this, a God that is like that. And then you say "God [khodaya] guide me . . . to a path where there is no hate, there is no wickedness."

She went on:

If you pay attention, every day when you recite this you find something new. In my opinion, this is like the Qur'an. Now you in this situation under these conditions understand this sura in this way.

You then go further and you might understand it in a different way, because your thinking and knowledge have moved further.

It seems as though the same sura is approached differently depending on whether it is being recited in the course of namaz or it is being read to be interpreted. This difference underlines the slippery nature of conceiving of *one* ultimate meaning underlying Qur'anic verses. The women do not express anxiety about the fact that the meanings can change all the time, while also noting that what is changing is their understanding or circumstances. Zahra, a friend of some of these women, who joined the group discussion on that day,[34] echoed the point that this sura does not always mean the same thing by offering this example: "today, the phrase 'those who have gone astray' for me means Mubarak [the former President of Egypt]; tomorrow, it may be someone else." This interview took place during the antigovernment protests in Egypt in January 2011. Pari said that in her experience, "If you leave the doors open, the meaning of *al-hamd li-allah rabb al-'alamīn* [Praise be to God, Lord of the Worlds] changes every day." I asked her to explain what she meant.

> Today my namaz will most certainly change because of what I have heard in this gathering. When I think [later] of what was said here, I take something from all of it. And one day, if I enter [the namaz] with anger, it will be different. One day I enter in joy, my namaz changes. It means that my emotional state is 100% in motion and growing and that impacts my namaz.[35]

Such observations recall Jonathan Culler's insight that meaning is "context-bound but context is boundless."[36]

As can be seen, the question of meaning and understanding in the case of the namaz and, more generally, sacred and poetic texts is exceedingly complex. It is clearly the case that in namaz, there is *no constant, necessary*, and predictable relation between form and meaning. This may be a consequence of regularly and frequently recited texts. It is also a consequence of the fact that the text is being recited for the purposes of a ritual and is not being approached and read hermeneutically.

In the case of Persian speakers, most of whom do not know Qur'anic Arabic, a discussion of meaning may be puzzling, not just when the Qur'an is being read and pondered over by a non-Arabic speaker but also in recitational and liturgical contexts such as the namaz. In the former context, in any given Qur'an class, for example, participants come with different editions and translations, as was mentioned in the Introduction. When the teacher or one of the students reads a verse out loud and then reads its translation, quite frequently those whose Qur'ans have different translations raise their hands and read theirs. The simultaneity of so many translations inevitably leads to lengthy hermeneutic discussions—are any of the Persian versions apt, has the translator really understood the meaning or is the translation misleading, why has he dropped an entire word, and so on. Even when the readers are Arabic speakers of any of the modern national vernaculars, the Arabic of the Qur'an is fundamentally different, in particular in its grammatical rules, and so it takes some effort even for them to understand the Qur'anic Arabic. Within the Arab world, there are no translations of the Qur'an into vernacular Arabic. Even so, through a variety of means including schools, special classes, radio and television, adult classes, and so on, the verses come to be learned to various degrees, debated, and deciphered in vernacular Arabic. The absence of translation does not render the meaning of the verses fixed. Only conceptions of scripture premised on the idea that scriptural language is like any other and that the relationship of the believer to this text is based *mainly on the meaning* of the verses would lead one to conclude that a translation is necessary for there to be a strong attachment to any given sacred text.

In the case of the recitation of suras for the purposes of namaz, even if the reciter is not Arabic speaking and even when she may not know the meanings of each word, there is neither an absence of meaning—what secular Iranians seem to believe is the case—nor any fixity to meaning.[37] The forms are fixed, but the daily acts of recitation in so many different contexts, and the play of imagination, keep the meaning from becoming fixed and unchanging. But this "meaning" is not the same as semantic content, though the latter might contribute to it. Once more, this complicates the form-content relationship.

What happens to meaning over time is that a relationship develops between the reciter and the text and the act of namaz that includes past memories, present expectations, the state of her relationship to God, and a network of other important figures in her life—family members, friends, Imams, and of course God. All these factors result in the emergence and *proliferation* of meaning, rather than a fixing and fading of it.[38] Any given verse can have indexical significance that might correspond to the particularities of the life of the reciter in the moment of the performance. And as those particularities change, the indexical significance can change as well. Elaborating on Robert Orsi's idea that religion is "a network of relationships between heaven and earth involving humans of all ages and many different sacred figures together,"[39] I would say that prayers, psalms, hymns, songs, and poetry are a means through which those in the network become alternately present.

Dolla rāst: Namaz without Sincerity

A namaz without presence of the heart has a name, one that is a common expression in everyday usage. The antithesis of a namaz that is done with kholus (sincerity) and has the potential to arrive, however briefly, at hal, is described disparagingly as *dolla rāst*. Dolla rast literally means mindlessly bending and straightening (while rushing through the words of the verses). A frequent example brought up by the women was that of "jumping up to pray" at the sound of the azan when one is a guest at someone's home. This is what some clerics refer to as esqat-e taklif, as I mentioned earlier—just getting the obligation done. But to pray "in front of others" risks ostentation, and so, even though by the time they would get home a particular prayer time might have passed, most of my interlocutors preferred waiting to praying in someone else's house where they would lack privacy. Anxieties about how one can go through the motions of worship for a lifetime yet continue to be dishonest and hypocritical are centuries old.[40]

In the first conversations I had with my interlocutors about the namaz, almost all told me that they were "not satisfied with their praying." They would explain this by saying that they find concentration quite a challenge and their minds often wander. They added that at times certain conditions in their lives were very distracting. For example, Simin told me about the time right after her father had passed away. He had asked in his will for his children (grown sons and daughters) to pay someone to do namaz on his behalf in case he had missed any. She was so troubled by this request of her father's that, she said, "I asked myself did I even know my father." Her father had been a decent person and had prayed all his life. What could have been going through his mind? She explained that after this event she could not concentrate for a long while when she prayed. While one has been used to reading and hearing religious scholars and clerics speak of concentration, sincerity, and presence of the heart for their own namaz, these same qualities are now defining a "good namaz" for some laypeople after the revolution. Simin does not appear to think that because she is not a religious scholar, she should be satisfied with just getting the obligation done.

The tradition of 'erfān mysticism, as expressed through poetic articulations of ostentatious namaz, encourages profound reflection on the intention to pray and the quality of the performance. Does one pray to put one's piety on display, to avoid hellfire, or for the love of God? Do we do the namaz to get something in return from God? Are we doing business (tejārat) with Him? Is namaz performed as wishing simply to fulfill an obligation, or do we undertake it to build ourselves and make a connection to the divine? In classical poetry, the number of verses about namaz are countless. One could write at least one book on the many classical poets who wrote against insincere namaz. Here are only three examples from Saadi's *Gulistan* (1258):

> When I was a child, all I cared about was proving my piety, and so I became addicted to prayer and abstinence, often keeping vigil through the night. One night, I was sitting with my father, holding the Qur'an in my lap, watching the people around us as they slept. "These people are sleeping," I said, "but they might as well be dead. Not one of them has roused himself to offer prayer."
>
> My father replied, "My son, it would be better for you too to sleep than to spend these hours criticizing others."

One of Saadi's most famous poems ends with this caution:

> It is the key to the gate of hell that namaz
> That you perform in front of others[41]

Much has been written in Persian and English on Hafez's repudiation of hypocrisy in religion. Returning to the study of Hafez's "anti-clericalism," the late scholar of Sufism and Persian literature Leonard Lewisohn discusses how Hafez ironically "contrast[s] . . . the conceited self-esteem of the ascetic engaged in ritual 'prayers' [*namaz*] to his own drunkenness [*masti*] and poverty of spirit [*niyaz*]."[42] Here are a couplet and then an abridged longer poem from Hafez, showing his antipathy toward hypocrisy in religion.

> Kiss only the lips of the lover and the wine cup
> Mistake to kiss the hands of piety-sellers

Of Pulpit Piety
> Act in a wholly different way
>   When no one's there to see.

> This is my question for the wise—
>   How is it those who teach
> Repentance are so rarely found
>   To practice what they preach?

> You'd think they'd no belief in God
>   Or in His Judgement Day,
> Given their frauds done in His name,
>   The pious tricks they play.

> My master reigns among the ruins,
>   And the poor whom he
> Attracts know needing nothing's wealth,
>   And pride's humility.[43]

It is not only the classical poets who urge reflection and warn against ostentation and mindlessness. The Qom Seminary's website offers the following interpretation of the Qur'anic verse (23:2): "Those who have humility in their prayer."

This is an allusion to the fact that their [the believers'] namaz is not just phrases and movements that lack soul and meaning. On the contrary, while doing namaz, they pay such attention to God that they detach from anything other than Him and join Him. They sink so deeply into reflection, presence, and *rāz o niyāz* [intimate prayer; literally, secrets and needs] that it affects every particle of their being. They see themselves as a speck facing an infinite being, and a drop facing an infinite ocean.[44]

Hence, even the Qom Seminary does not treat this central ritual as a straightforward matter of esqat-e taklif, "fulfilling the obligation."

The teacher of Maryam, Simin, and Parvin's Qur'an class, who was in his mid-fifties at the time of my interview in 2011,[45] was against the idea of simply fulfilling the obligation:

If someone does namaz and it has no effect on him [*ta'sir nadareh*], that's not namaz. . . . The Qur'an says over and over, "*Construct your prayer*"—build your prayer, from sand, from plaster. Namaz must be built in its spiritual and holy dimensions, so that when it is finished, the structure actually stays. For example, if you walk out of a mosque and see a woman who has no hijab and you judge her, your namaz is lost because you know nothing about her. She may be far more pious and a far better human being than you are.

Because namaz is widely articulated as that which leads us toward a more ethical life, disappointment combined with incredulity that one can spend a lifetime praying but still end up as an insincere hypocrite is expressed quite frequently. The regular television broadcast of the Friday namaz elicits a variety of comments from viewers. One of the most common skeptical reactions to the visible piety of state officials, displayed in the way they perform the namaz, is, "Look, you can pray all your life without becoming a true Muslim." Some routinely assert that while praying is a necessary condition for becoming a true Muslim, it is not sufficient, as the examples of many officials demonstrate. Television and the easy availability of images on social media have only increased the antipathy toward outwardly displaying one's piety.

The ethical benefits of performing the namaz were articulated by several of the women in our group. They emphasized that God wants people to pray so that they become better human beings, stay away from lies, and learn to be more compassionate and less hypocritical. But he "does not *need* our prayers." Simin summarized the women's views well:

> You go forward with namaz. I go through some periods when I don't do namaz. But then I miss it and I go back to it. It does not stay one thing . . . its meanings little by little become deeper and find a place in our hearts. It helps us to become better persons; I mean it should do that, but if it does not, well, among millions we have one Prophet, one Edison, one Hafez. . . . So among thousands who do namaz, we have one [who becomes a better person]. I try not to judge anyone anymore; I want to gain self-knowledge—this is an important stage in one's life if one reaches it.

Imagination and Techniques of Concentration

The basic condition for a good namaz, as was mentioned earlier, is when the reciter manages to have concentration.[46] Concentration was described by everyone as difficult to achieve but also as necessary for namaz to feel not like *ādat* (habit) but like 'ebadat (worship). Simin said:

> Sometimes the most ordinary matters destroy my namaz. I try to convince myself that God is standing in front of me and looking at me. God is simple [*sādeh*] and in front of God I am doing roku' and sojud. One of the ways I use to gain concentration is that I recite namaz out loud and I try to enunciate every single word. This way you feel the presence of God better.

I asked whether there are techniques for achieving concentration. Maryam replied that she had one she had never told anyone about, based on her experience of going on pilgrimage to Mecca. The first time she went, she was in her late thirties. She had a transformative experience while doing the various required acts. Each time she performed namaz there, it turned out to be special. For example, she prayed where Hazrat-e Hajar (her Holiness Hagar) is buried, in a section called Hejr-e Ismail by Iranians. It is shaped like a half-moon and located close to but not attached to the Kaaba (some describe this section as the "skirt" of Hagar). Here, Maryam explained:

> Ibrahim left Hajar and Ismail in a desert where there was no water. And no one to help them. Ismail was thirsty and Hajar left him to go find water. She went seven times between the Safa and Marva mountains and did not find any. Finally, when she had lost hope, she went back to her son and saw that water was bubbling up from under his feet.

She finds this story particularly moving, and added: "Knowing that close to the Kaaba, there is a slave woman who is buried, a brave and strong woman, really affected me. So when I prayed in her skirt, it was an extraordinary experience."

She then went on to describe her technique:

> In order to achieve complete presence in my prayer, I do a *tavāf* [circumambulation]. That is, I start from one corner [*rokn*] of the House of God. I need to draw this for you [see Figures 2.1 and 2.2].
>
> In my mind, I have divided each side of the House of God into two and I have also divided the [lunar] month into two. I begin here [*pointing to the corner*] and each day I am standing facing that part, for 15 days. I move from this rokn and I pray inside here.

During the first fifteen days, she has in her mind's eye one half of the wall. She stands in front of it and while praying she evokes the presence of the Prophet, Hazrat-e Mohammad. "I tell myself he prayed here and I am now praying here too" (see Figure 2.2). For the following fifteen days she is with Hazrat-e Ali (the Prophet's son-in-law); then she goes on to Hazrat-e Fatemeh (the Prophet's daughter and wife of Hazrateh Ali), Imam Hasan, Imam Hussein (the grandchildren), and so on, until she reaches Imam Musa Kazem (the seventh Imam):

> Then again [for another fifteen days], I start here, with Imam Musa Kazem who is my mother's ancestor.[47] I feel close to him [*bāhash kheili ma'nūsam*]. I tell him, "Look, your granddaughter is praying,

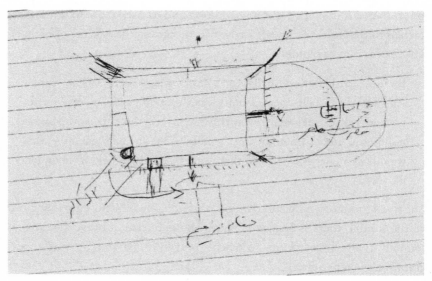

FIGURE 2.1. Maryam's drawing of the Kaaba for explaining her technique for concentration.

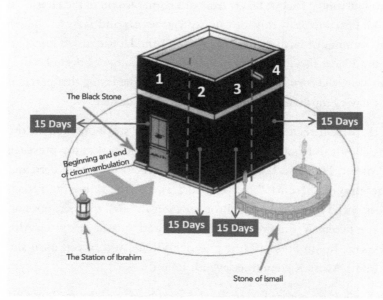

FIGURE 2.2. Maryam's imaginary circumambulation when she performs her namaz.

do remember to help her children. . . . My parents [they are deceased] are there, my siblings, and my children. I pray with all these people present.

Maryam spoke of this technique as quite effective. She connected her movement around the House of God to the timing of a religious gathering, a *rowzeh*, that her parents used to hold once in the middle of every lunar month.[48] At that point in the month, her location coincided with the gathering.[49]

When I presented this technique at a workshop in London a few years ago, scholars of Catholicism who were present were struck at what they saw as similarities with the Stations of the Cross, where at each station, believers imagine the moment in Christ's passion that the station represents.[50] As in Maryam's mind's eye, there is a progression from one place, one moment, to another. Doing the Stations of the Cross, as depicted in many paintings, is a spiritual pilgrimage. Maryam also spoke of what she imagined she was doing in terms that are used for the hajj pilgrimage—circumambulation, praying where Hagar is buried, and so on. A comparative study of religious imagination could lead to new understandings of religion and of forms of religiosity .

When Maryam stands in front of the House of God and imagines the Imams and her parents, siblings, and children with her, one might ask what kind of namaz she is performing. Is it congregational or individual? It is both and neither. Between what Maryam has been taught or has heard about namaz over a lifetime and what actually transpires in her performance of it, her imagination, along with various kinds of experiences, intervenes. And many people and holy figures who are invisible to us are fully present in her namaz. This imaginary circumambulation is buoyed by the presence of her deceased parents and her children and siblings in her prayer.

Conclusion

In this chapter, I have taken up the question of what can make a namaz go well or badly. I argue that ritual is a site of simultaneous and at times contradictory desires and commitments. It is the site of love, devotion, fear, commitment, doubt, discovery, practice, routine, and "repetition." As our ethnographic exploration of namaz shows, a ritual like namaz is not a once-and-for-all matter but an occasion for the play of imagination and a great deal of reflection.

Each time one stands to pray, one cannot know at the beginning how that particular session will unfold. I argue that the implications of this phenomenon should lead us to a rethinking of ritual. It is not that "repeated" acts never become rote or mindless; it is that they do not inexorably become so. The stipulated poetics of the namaz do not prevent variability and unusual choices of nonstandard suras or the communication of questions and anxieties to God. In fact, it is often these very possibilities that give moral and emotional force to the act of ritual prayer. Reciters strive to create a presence in the words of the namaz and to achieve a certain companionship with the divine. That one can tell God what one wants while using His words shows that the form-content relationship is not fixed and can change daily. This is perhaps a result of the fact that one utters the Qur'anic verses every day in many different contexts. Hence, the form-content relationship does not remain static, nor does the reciter's imagination.

When the salam is uttered as the last part of the namaz, the reciter may go on to do other things and step out of the prayer rug. Often though, she sits on the sajjadeh, relaxes her body, and follows the namaz with different kinds of do'a. The next two chapters are devoted to prayers that are conversations with God and prayers that have been composed by Imams.

What Are We Up To When We Pray?

Spontaneous Conversations with God

When the shepherd we met in the Introduction was talking to God, without a script, he was doing a kind of prayer called *do'ā*. Do'a is an Arabic word, from a root meaning "calling out," "reaching out," or "summoning." It means asking the one we address to turn toward us. Do'a allows one not to search for rules and etiquette and to say what one's "longing heart desires," as God revealed to Moses in Rumi's poem. It is, furthermore, a form of worship (*'ebādat*) that is widely practiced but is not compulsory. Unlike *namāz*, do'a is not required, and yet I never met a believer who did not engage in it for that reason. Doing do'a is *mostahabb*—those who perform it become favored (*mahbūb*) in the eyes of God. Do'a is spoken of by some religious scholars as a "natural need" and a "necessity," not just for Muslims but for human beings in general.[1] I heard from many people that do'a makes a reverse journey as compared to the Qur'an. *Do'a* are sent upward to the heavens by God's creatures, whereas the Qur'an was sent down to them. This kind of exchange is seen as opening up a space for an intimate relationship between believers and the divine.

One of the most interesting aspects of examining different forms of worship within the same religion is that our generalizations about that religion ("Islam is *x*"; "in Islam *y*") and about how believers conceive of God are challenged. In fact, one difficult question is how we can make sure to have at least an empirically accurate understanding of the ways in which God is thought about and addressed in any given religion. When we hear some of the women discussed in the following pages relate what they say to God during their do'a sessions, God appears to be closer than He does in namaz. The characterization of God as "the Beloved" in mystic discourse encourages conversations with Him that fall in and out of recognized categories of "prayer." Experientially, do'a allows for a less well-defined practice and exhibits a more capacious conception of God—a God who can be addressed in Persian (rather than the Arabic of the namaz) and who wants to hear from His creatures even at their most mundane and personal. There is something paradoxical about do'a: it is neither required nor a ritual in the usual sense of the term, but doing it shows perhaps a stronger commitment to the existence and presence of God than ritual prayer does because one is addressing an invisible being voluntarily and at a time of one's choosing.

What are the implications of conceptions of God seemingly shifting or being multiple depending on what religious act we examine? In addition to the surprising ways in which an ethnographic study of do'a changes our perceptions of how God is thought about, do'a, by the same token, helps us better understand the complexity of Muslim subjectivity—it can hardly be characterized by examining one ritual, no matter how central that ritual is to the religion. The relationship to God is not unchanging and monolithic, and therefore God does not remain one thing. In a gathering of Muslims and Christians in 2011, convened by Rowan Williams, the former Archbishop of Canterbury, and organized by the interfaith group Building Bridges, participants discussed prayer in both religions. Rowan Williams makes a point in the preface to the resulting volume that is helpful here:

> To speak about prayer is to speak about where and who we are, not simply to speak about an activity that begins and ends; it is certainly not simply to speak about a way in which human beings attempt to get in touch with a remote and distant God. *Prayer is about the way in which a relationship is realized and sustained.*[2]

The ways in which prayers are used to construct a relationship with God are a central part of my initial interest in this present project. The examples of actual do'a included in this chapter will make this point clearer.

Unlike namaz, which is taught from an early age, do'a is among the religious activities that are not explicitly taught, perhaps because it is not required. In doing do'a, one is largely on one's own. Some women told me that in childhood, they were encouraged to talk to God to tell Him what they wanted and what was on their minds. At times when a relative was sick, their parents would tell them to do do'a so that the relative would get better, because "God favors children's prayers," but they were not instructed on how to talk to God.[3] A frequently heard saying attributed to the Prophet is that do'a is *mokh al-'ebada* (the essence of worship).[4] The Qur'an speaks of it favorably. One of the most famous verses, widely quoted by many people, is the encouragement to do do'a: "Call on me and I will answer" (40:60). This verse appears on signs adorning the walls of various shops. People encourage each other to turn to God and ask for help while quoting this verse. Do'a is believed to have a protective quality, shielding those who engage in it from catastrophe and misfortune. Some people recite prayers taken from the Qur'an over sick children (and adults) and immediately blow air towards them to spread the words of the prayer on their bodies.[5]

There are various other terms that differentiate to one degree or another kinds of prayer—some of these terms are Arabo-Islamic, and some have survived from pre-Islamic times. Among the former are *zikr* (remembrance), most closely associated with Sufis but not exclusive to them, and *monājāt* (whispered prayers).[6] There are many kinds of zikr—a well-known one involves enunciating the names of God.[7] Practicing zikr is meant to put one in the thought of God. Among Persian terms for prayer, the most prominent are *niyāyesh* and *rāz-o-niyāz*. Niyayesh dates back to the Pahlavi language and is a term used by Zoroastrians and Muslims. It is often interchangeable with do'a, but it is supposed to be a prayer without request and largely a prayer of praise and gratitude. The term do'a is used for two rather distinct acts; it is therefore important to understand how they are distinguished. *Doing do'a (do'a kardan)* means talking spontaneously to God—whether to show gratitude, share anxieties, make requests, ask questions, or just to address Him, without one particular purpose. One can do do'a anywhere and at any time—on the bus, while walking, before falling asleep, and so on. However, when the term *do'a* is used with the verb *khāndan* (to read or recite), it refers to reciting prayers composed by Imams that are available in prayer books—hence not spontaneous praying. We will examine some of the differences between the two kinds of do'a later in this chapter; and the next chapter is entirely devoted to Imams' composed prayers, in Arabic.

In the following pages, I write about spontaneous prayer that is done in Persian. In the do'a book market, collections of praise poems are also called niyayesh. Raz-o-niyaz (secrets and needs) is another term for an intimate, confessional, conversation; it is also the name for a *goosheh* (melody) in Iranian classical music in the mode of Homayoon.[8] There is little sense in drawing hard and fast boundaries around acts of prayer. They are all ways of addressing God, they overlap, and they are about learning to spend time in divine company.

Do'a shares similarities with prayer in Christianity. Leaving aside the use of prayer books in church services for now, Muslims and Christians talk to God using their own words for a variety of purposes. I have taught several classes on prayer and poetry to undergraduates in the last few years at my university in the United States. In most of these classes, a major-ity of the students were Christians of various denominations, and I was surprised to find out that many go to church rather regularly. In talking about spontaneous prayers, it turned out that sometimes they feel they can-not just launch into talking to God—they first need a way of starting the conversation. One of the popular ways of "breaking the ice," as they said, was to recite the Lord's Prayer. After that, they felt more comfortable us-ing their own words to start a conversation. Similarly, among the women in our group, some adopt and adapt certain phrases from sources such as well-known prayers, poems, and perhaps even artworks with spiritual writ-ings that capture their attention, and use them to frame their own prayers. Beginning with such phrases, almost as greeting formulas, eases them into finding their own footing in the conversation. Often these phrases are vocatives, each beginning with *khodaya* (Oh God), *ey khodayeh mehra-ban* (Oh kind God), or *khodaya beh haqq-e in rooz-e mobarak* (Oh God, in honor of this blessed day). *Beh haqqeh* is a formula, and after it, many different things can be requested: for example, "in honor of this blessed day please heal all those who are sick." A friend suggested that we can call these framings "threshold" phrases, because they allow the worship-per to enter the space of prayer.[9] Of course, if one simply wants to address a short request—"please help my friend regain her health"—one may not need to be eased into do'a. On some days and for some people, it is easier to engage in such conversations, and on other days, it is harder.

Before moving on to listen to examples of spontaneous do'a, let us note briefly that there are do'a that are expressed collectively in gatherings that are also in Persian and spontaneous. These are not personal conversations, and they often reflect what is happening in the broader world. For example, climate change matters have become almost a constant part of Iranian prayers. People are quite worried about the long-standing drought and the subsequent loss of major rivers and lakes. When they see fresh snow on top of the majestic Mount Damavand, which can be observed on days where there is not too much pollution, they thank God and show gratitude for the snow. In fact, a widely practiced routine that defines the everyday life of Tehran residents is to look toward the north as soon as they wake up to see if Mount Damavand is visible. That is one of the best barometers for the level of pollution. In recent years, their prayers include pleading with God for an end to the wars in Syria and Yemen, and for keeping war away from Iran. Acts committed at home and around the world in the name of Islam are a cause of great distress for them—they feel helpless while they keep repeating, "but this is not Islam." Not once, though, did any of these women or anyone I came into contact with while in Iran attribute, for example, what ISIS does to Sunnism as a whole. While Saudi Arabia's ruling families and Wahhabism do receive criticism in Iran—one could hardly imagine a form of Islam further from 'erfān mysticism—conversations with my interlocutors rarely included the expression of sectarian views. If anything, I was surprised at how often I heard that the way Sunnis pray or do other acts is preferable to what Shi'as do. I emphasize this point because while outside Iran one frequently hears about the Sunni-Shi'a divide, inside Iran the picture is far more complex, and the discourse is less sectarian.

Let us now listen to a few examples of spontaneous prayers. What can they teach us about being a Muslim? What are people up to when they pray?

A Long Chat with God

At times, do'a turns into a long conversation whose unfolding content is unpredictable, even for the reciter as she allows her mind to wander. Prayer can wind and roam and become an occasion for posing some of the most difficult questions that we all face. Maryam, who was almost seventy at the time of this conversation, described some of her long prayer sessions:

> In do'a, sometimes you get this feeling of joy—you realize that your whole being has just been taken over by love and you can give this love too. This is a great feeling. You think of the whole universe, the whole world, and that there is only God. This moment is very important. This is not a moment where you want anything from God. This love actually comes into existence in silence and not in speaking.
>
> Now at this time you feel that love, that kindness, that rain of mercy, that rain of love, and your heart swells up and you think there is no one else [but God], and in reality there isn't.

This "feeling of joy" and the connection to the universe and to God is the experience of *hāl* that we discussed in the Introduction—that change of state in one's emotions that is sudden and unpredictable but crucial from the point of view of 'erfan mysticism in understanding the presence of the divine.

But then, Maryam explained, her thoughts became darker. And she thought to herself: "We are all here for a short time. It is really one moment—just like those shadows that Plato talked about. We think that what we see is reality but we only see shadows, we do not see the real." Anthropologist Tanya Luhrmann, who studies American evangelicals, also uses the allegory of Plato's cave to illustrate the "dilemma of human knowledge." The idea is that the world is far more complex than our ability to understand it, and we become aware therefore that "what we take to be true may be an illusion, a wispy misperception."[10] Maryam seemed to have a similar thought when she said that we do not see the real—that our knowledge is imperfect.

She then explained the kinds of questions she asks God in her do'a, and how she unexpectedly reached a "difficult" moment:

> I asked God, those who have left us, where did they go? Where are my parents now? And here it becomes difficult. And so one says to God immediately, I leave everything in your hands. It is also said in the Qur'an when it talks about the soul [*rūh*], God says this is a matter

that you should leave in my hands [Sura al-Isra': 85]. It is not that these are bad thoughts; it is that they do not have an answer. . . . I try to distance myself from these emotions but it is difficult.

She finished by saying that although "it happens rarely," it is possible to do niyayesh and "reach a state that is beautiful."

As I mentioned in the Introduction, the 'erfan concept of hal is part of the everyday vocabulary of lay Iranians whether educated or not. There is an attentiveness to how one's hal changes in the course of any kind of worship (or other moments). Maryam began by talking about that moment of feeling great joy and love that she said "comes in silence" and does not last very long but is overwhelming. She then went on to give another example:

I was doing namaz recently and suddenly this hālat [state] came about which was great. I was standing there facing the House of God [in her mind's eye], and then it was as though space became light blue around me. It was so pleasant and I felt drenched in kindness, in the soft cloud of kindness. Of course, these visions were just in my imagination. They didn't have a reality to them, there was nothing, and yet that feeling transpired, that good feeling came about.

When Maryam is enveloped in love and feels the kindness of God, she has the impression of being surrounded with light blue space and a soft cloud of kindness, but at the same time she pauses to say that these are just her imaginings. She is reflexive about what is happening to her feelings in the course of praying and what she is conjuring versus what is "reality." But the fact that the soft cloud of tenderness is not reality does not lead her to abandon praying altogether or to make it a more restrained exercise, and possibly more real. As she put it, "there was nothing, and yet that feeling transpired."[11]

Significantly, toward the end of the description of her prayer, Maryam questioned whether what she has just described is in fact do'a:

These thoughts come with doing do'a. Are they do'a? In reality probably not, but they come hand in hand. They lead me to tell myself: Don't complain; it is what it is. This is the moment you live in; don't ruin this moment, this day. To accept my state of needlessness, that is what I should be able to do. I must be thankful, and that is the best thing I can do.

She answered her own question by saying that certain thoughts *come hand in hand* with doing do'a. In effect, she was saying that do'a does not have hard and fast boundaries. The doctrinal categories go only so far and what people do probably often exceeds them. What worshippers end up sharing emerges in the course of talking to God and may not have any particular theologically agreed-upon name—supplicatory, petitionary, praise, gratitude—none of which would quite capture the conversation Maryam described. Her do'a also shows that she is adept at doing it and has a well-established relationship with God. According to her, there are states one reaches in do'a that take time to arrive at—the talking must go on for a while for one to reach a point where things stream out and it becomes much more of a conversation rather than accomplishing a particular religious act with a beginning and an end. In other words, once a conversation with God starts, it is not always possible to give it a name and characterize it as one kind of activity.

In her prayer, there are, in addition to joy and love, what she calls "difficult thoughts" about the point of life, about what she is doing on this earth, and about where we go after we die. She particularly thought about this question after her parents died, wondering where they were. When she travels, she struggles with the idea that she is leaving them behind. Does it make a difference to them when she is out of town? She told me that these questions never end, but she often tells herself that they are nonsensical because her parents are no longer alive.

Is there a different kind of reality to the feelings, ideas, and imaginings that transpire in the course of prayer—one in which the speaker is well aware of the absence of a blue cloud of tenderness out there, but one that nonetheless transforms her emotional state? Indeed, Maryam seemed to be doing a back-and-forth between what appeared to her, what she understood, what might or might not be real, and her questions. Those who characterize religious people as irrational, lacking critical faculties and self-reflection, would not raise an eyebrow about someone walking in a park on a nice sunny day and suddenly feeling light and full of cheer, brimming with an inexplicable joy. In both of these cases, nothing outside the one who holds a conversation with God, and the other who walks in the park has changed. The world out there remains what it has been. Yet, one person is considered irrational and the other as perfectly understandable. Toward the end of her prayer, Maryam told herself she must not complain. Clearly, the addressee of her words is not just God but herself as well.[12]

When she speaks of a state of joy or ecstasy (*halat-e vajd*) and says that there is nothing except God, one hears echoes of the mystic concept of unity of being (*vahdat-e vujūd*) that considers human beings manifestations of one God—like an ocean and its waves.[13] There is only the ocean; the waves do not have a separate existence. What matters is that feeling of connection—the joy (or longing or sorrow) that one feels when that connection with the divine is made. These are all present in her description. She does not call herself, and neither do any of these women, a follower of 'erfan—because according to them, considering oneself an *'ārif* (mystic) without years of study and practice would be too presumptuous and a true 'arif would never actually say that she is one—but she has read and discussed 'erfan ideas in poetry and in classes and, as the others do also, holds them in high regard. This has clearly offered her a way of seeing and articulating such matters. The soft cloud of kindness and the light blue space around her is a description of the hal that overcame her in that moment.

Call on Me and I Will Reply

We have heard some of Mina's stories in the previous chapters. She is the retired high school teacher who taught social studies at the same high school where Maryam taught and who is a few years younger. I visited her at her house, and she also took part in several group discussions that I organized over lunches and dinners.[14] In one of these gatherings, Mina told us about a special exchange with God that she will never forget. It was at a time when her father was in a hospital in Tehran:

About thirty years ago, my children both had the flu. My mother had broken her leg and was staying home; and I was at school when she called and said, "Your father is not well; we have to call an ambulance and take him to the hospital." I went to the school principal and asked permission to leave for the day. She said you can't go. By the time I got to the hospital, my father had gone into a coma. Days passed, maybe twenty days or so, and my father continued to be in a coma. One night I went to the hospital to stay with him as usual, and I had taken five sets of exam papers with me to correct. But there were so many and my mind was not working. I tried to get an extension, but the principal said I absolutely had to hand in the papers the next morning. I fell asleep while correcting them. Next thing I knew, I was woken up by the sound of the dawn azan. As soon as I heard the azan, I broke down and started to cry. I said, God, if you are testing me, I just can't. Why are you doing all of this? Everything is going wrong, I will not talk to you anymore, I will just not have anything to do with you. I just kept sobbing. Then suddenly I heard my father say, "Can someone give me some food, I am hungry." I couldn't believe it. The nurses were so surprised. Then they said we have to first ask the doctors if it is okay to give him food. I said forget it. I went and got him bread and cheese and tea, and he ate with gusto too.

She added: "And then I asked God to forgive me, to forgive that I doubted his mercy."

It was clear to those of us listening that Mina was convinced God had heard her. He heard her anger and despair and so had something to do with her father waking up. She apologized to God and asked for forgiveness because she had doubted His mercy—doubted that He was paying attention to her. The moment she expressed her acknowledgment that God had not in fact forsaken her, everyone around the table began to cry. Over and over, I was told by many of my interlocutors that the most important thing for them was to feel that God had not forgotten them—that He was watching over them.

At times when people become angry with God, it can lead to a complete rupture and a stopping of all prayers for at least some time. I heard from many of the women that at one point or another in their lives, they did *qahr* with God—meaning they stopped talking to Him (*ba khoda qahr kardam* [literally, "with God I did qahr"]). Qahr happens in close relationships—it is a moment of rupture and deep disappointment, so deep that the person no longer wishes to talk to the source of this disappointment. Even the most pious woman I interviewed told me that in her twenties, she temporarily stopped talking to God. She did not explain the reason, but she was the only woman among the group I interviewed who did not have children, and she hinted at this as a defining aspect of her life. Although she appeared to have regretted this decision when she was younger, she also expressed her relief that at this later moment in her life she did not have children.

Maryam told me that while she has never done qahr with God, her relationship has experienced many "vulnerable" (*hassās*) moments.[15] One that she remembers particularly well was when her mother had had a difficult operation. In addition to that, she said:

My husband was at the hospital after a stroke. And I had lost my teaching post. I had left one of my daughters in the US [due to the Iran-Iraq war] so she could finish high school and go to college.[16] And my other daughter was with me but I could not afford to pay for her school and had no idea where to get the money. It was a really vulnerable moment in my relationship with God. I was feeling so terrible on that day.

I was walking down the street and I suddenly saw a mosque. I decided to go inside but it was locked. So I started banging on the door. Eventually the caretaker came out and said, "*khānūm* [Madam], what is going on, what do you want?" I said, "Open the door of the mosque, I want to go in. A mosque is the house of God, you have no right to close its doors." So he opened the door and I went into the *shabestān* [prayer hall]. He let me be alone. I started shouting and crying: "God, what is going on? What are you making me go through? Please help me, I need help, I am pleading with you."

I think in that moment, I really had lost my mind; I was not in control and was ranting. I did a namaz, I prostrated, I was acting like a madwoman. Eventually, I calmed down and started to feel better. I took a deep breath and went to the caretaker. I gave him some money and I apologized to him. He had been so nice and gentle with me. I could not have done what I did at home or anywhere else.

Maryam ended by saying that "not much really changed" after her beseeching God, but her mother's health did gradually improve, and she learned how to cope with the conditions better.

At times, there is a complete rupture in the relationship with God. Aziz jan is about ninety years old and among the few in the generation of these women's mothers whom I was able to talk to over a period of several years. She is Pari's great aunt. She said that at some point she completely stopped praying for years because she was so angry with God. When she was fifteen, her parents forced her to marry a man who was "perfectly nice," but she did not like him. She was "totally in love" with her school and her classes and all she could think about was the schoolyard where she played with her classmates. The last thing she wanted to do was to get married, and although she locked herself in her room on the wedding night, it was to no avail. She felt betrayed both by the women in her family and by the men:

> A few years after getting married, I became pregnant. I still had not left prayer [tark-e namaz] but life became so hard for me that I did qahr with God and stopped praying. I wanted to move back to Tehran with my family because my father's assignment [in the city where we lived with my husband] was over and they were moving back. So I tried to convince my husband to move with us, with our little son and my family. He refused, because I heard his father tell him, "If you go with them, they will always say that the groom is eating off the hands of his father-in-law because you don't have a job there and you don't know anyone." So he refused to go with us. My own father said, "Well, you take your son and come with us," and I said, "I am not going to have my child live fatherless." My husband's father had told him this thing, and so when he told me he was not coming with us to Tehran at the last minute, after I had sold everything we had, I was extremely upset. After that, I did qahr with God. I just said, this life is too difficult, I can't. Then for years I did not pray.

Years passed. She had three more children and she still was not praying. Her sister had decided to do the hajj, and on the day she was leaving, as she was getting on the bus to go to the airport, she said to Aziz jan: "When I'm in Mecca, I am going to ask God to help you take up namaz again." Aziz jan replied to her, "No need for you to ask God. *You* ask me and I will do it." Aziz jan did begin to pray after that but "not like the old days. . . . I never went back to praying like before the qahr."

Note that she says, still with evident hurt and anger, "No need to ask God. *You* ask me and I will do it." Aziz jan and her sister were extremely close throughout their lives and eventually they lived together after their children were grown and her sister's husband died. They spent night and day together. Their hair grew white at the same time, and they kept it with a similar length and cut. They dressed like each other and, given their familial resemblance, seemed like inseparable twins. People commented on their closeness. Aziz jan's sister became far more religious and organized monthly group do'a sessions and other religious gatherings for about forty women that still continue several years after her death. It is this sister and their closeness that are at the center of Aziz jan's stopping her qahr with God. She makes it clear that she will do namaz because her sister is asking her—no need for God to do that.

I asked Aziz jan if she does do'a. She said, "Yes, I talk to God but I only talk to Him, not to Ali, Naghi, Taghi, only God. And I don't *read* do'a [from prayer books], maybe a couple that I have learned from my niece, but otherwise I just talk to God." She says with humor that she does not pray to Ali, Naghi, and Taghi—rhyming names of Imams. This kind of joking about the number of Shi'a Imams has become far more pronounced since the revolution, as the government has undertaken a vigorous campaign of publishing a seemingly endless number of books and producing documentaries on the lives of the Imams as exemplary beings who should be emulated.[17]

As If She Is Standing in Front of Him

People often say with admiration that so and so talks to God *as if she or he is standing right in front of Him.* Maryam, Mina, and Aziz jan all clearly talk to God in that way. Mina described what she called a niyayesh that she will "never forget."

Once a serious problem came up for my daughter. I was very upset about it. It was night and after I finished my namaz, I went to my room and turned off the light and began to do do'a. I was crying, and I wanted to know what I had done that my daughter would suffer like this. I just thought she is so young; she does not deserve such a terrible thing to happen to her. Well, apparently, my daughter was passing by and she heard me. So she entered the room and turned on the light and said with great distress: "*Maman*, if you say these things to God, then your namaz is invalid." I asked why, and she replied, "Do you not say *allaho akbar* [God is great]? What does that mean? That means God is generous and will take care of you. Either you believe in that or not."

What Mina did in that room in relation to God sounds similar to what we do when we want to have a serious word with someone—a relative or a friend. We go to a room with them, close the door, and ask them to explain themselves. In namaz, one of the main suras that is recited emphasizes how God has not been born nor has He given birth—He is therefore across an ontological divide from us, an entirely different Being, all knowing, all wise. In contrast, the God who is addressed in do'a does not seem to be across such a great divide. He is close by and reachable. And he is being asked to account for Himself—He is not being treated as perfect. Whereas in namaz there is more of the idea of God as all powerful, perfect, and omniscient, in do'a, once in a while, God has to hear one's anger and account for His decisions. Note also that the kind of Persian used to talk to God is not a special language that people must invent to talk to God. It is on the whole an everyday, vernacular style of Persian.

Let us look at one more example of a conversation with God that illustrates the rather ordinary language that is used and the fact that God is addressed in a way that can hardly be categorized as a religious act with its own name. Parvin described one of her recurrent conversations with God:

I wake up at five in the morning and begin to do do'a after namaz. Often, I see the same bird that comes close to the window, and I ask God, "Khodaya, it is still very dark, where has this bird come from and what is it doing here?" The bird comes every day and begins to sing; it is so beautiful. I ask God, "What is it saying?" I can't under-stand it but it is so early [that] I think it must not be looking for food because it is dark; it cannot find anything.

Here is an example of a conversation with God that mainly consists of asking a question one might ask anyone else—what is this bird doing in the dark and what does it want? Parvin described a back-and-forth about the bird in which she engages routinely. She added: "I then look at the trees and it is as if they are all doing a *tasbīh* [praise prayer] to God—this is also in the Qur'an, we just need to harmonize ourselves with these."[18] She takes the sight of the morning breeze gently swaying the trees as a lesson for herself—she must learn to harmonize with nature, with the world, as the trees do. After telling me about this early morning conver-sation and how well she feels at dawn, she is reminded of a universally beloved half line from Hafez that mentions the breeze:

Sahar bā bād migoftam hadis-e ārezūmandī

At dawn I was telling the breeze the story of my longings

She then said: "I like this do'a, and I recite it often." Somewhat surprised, I asked her: "This Hafez verse is a do'a? She replied: "Well . . . Hafez knew the whole Qur'an and all of his *ayāt* are in some ways like the Qur'an." Her use of the word *ayat*, usually reserved to mean Qur'anic verses, rather than the word for poetic verses (*beyt*), is an example of how thoroughly the worlds of prayer and poetry can intermingle—the Qur'an mingling with Hafez, Rumi, Saadi, and others—exactly what Hojjat al-Islam Qara'ati objected to, as we saw in the Introduction.

Many of these women told stories about talking to God at dawn. As they put it humorously, "Dawn is a time when God is less busy." Hence, one has the feeling that He has more time for a private conversation. The difficulty of waking up at dawn is a major topic in religious writings on namaz, especially among those who have just started to pray.[19] But for these women who have been waking up at dawn for a long time, it has become not just easy but a time of day that they find *extra*-ordinary. They look forward to it because somehow dawn prayers tend to be more memorable. Maryam said:

Dawn is a very good time—your thoughts are not here and there. It is as if you can be alone with God and you find yourself in front of that House [in Mecca]. At that early morning hour, you still have hope for the rest of the day.

Franklin Lewis, a scholar of Persian literature, has written on the importance of dawn in Persian poetry. He notes many mentions of dawn and the "easterly early morning breeze," "the fragrant breeze of morning," in Hafez's divan. His translation of the poem Parvin recites reads:

At dawn I was telling my tale of yearning and desire
A call came, saying "be assured of the divine blessings."

As Lewis notes, dawn is also recognized in the Qur'an as the time of do'a and of the recitation of the Qur'an.[20]

I have already illustrated the ways in which the believer's relationship with God seems to shift depending on the kind of worship. There is also a certain amount of ambivalence about how close one ought to get to God. One might think that experiencing a sign that God is present is always positive. But it can be a frightening event. Parvin told me that several years ago her sister was diagnosed with a debilitating illness. Parvin became extremely despondent. At the time of her namaz, she began to beseech God from the bottom of her heart and express her distress and disbelief about her sister when she suddenly heard a loud and frightening voice asking, "What do you want?" It did not have a kindly tone, and she felt so scared she had to sit down. She looked around to see if someone had just entered her house. She listened carefully but there was no one. She was not sure how to reply: "Here I was deep in pleading with God, and suddenly I was not sure how to answer the question about what I wanted." She characterized this experience (which she told me about several times in various conversations over the years) as frightening. She can still hear that voice. While there is a great deal of discourse on ways to get closer and closer to God, there is also the fear of *getting too close*, lest one enter, as Parvin explained, "another world" from which that voice had come.

One can see in these stories and do'a sessions certain kinds of ambivalence toward God, as I just mentioned. Yes, one ought to love Him, revere Him, believe in Him, and recognize His utter perfection. One must see His absolute kindness everywhere. But almost inevitably, this long-term relationship has many ups and downs. What focusing on do'a teaches us is that conceptions of God, even for the same individual, are varied rather than monolithic. The intimacy of the language used, the kinds of things shared, the demand for God to account for His actions, and the occasional presence of anger seem to blur the absoluteness of the divide between Him and His creatures. I think using Persian as opposed to Qur'anic Arabic in these do'a sessions also plays an important role. While these women can read and understand Qur'anic Arabic, they cannot converse in it. The mostly ordinary Persian that is used in do'a does much to personify God, all doctrinal characterizations of Him as an entirely distinct Being notwithstanding. Hence, the very act of spontaneous prayer transforms the ontological divide, at least momentarily. The all powerful, all knowing God who "has not given birth nor is He born" becomes an addressee to whom many kinds of emotions may be directed.

When God Is "the Beloved"

In 'erfan philosophy, as expressed in prose, poetry, stories, and songs, God is the Beloved. What are the implications of this conception? Rumi and those who came after him articulate the idea in unforgettable words and images. I have chosen a poem by Rumi that describes the worshipper's prayer to the Beloved:

At the time of evening prayer
everyone spreads cloth and candles,
But I dream of my beloved,
see, lamenting, grieved, his phantom.
My ablution is with weeping,
thus my prayer will be fiery,
And I burn the mosque's doorway
when my call to prayer strikes it.
Is the prayer of the drunken,
tell me, is this prayer valid?
For he does not know the timing

and is not aware of places.
Did I pray for two full cycles?
Or is this perhaps the eighth one?
And which Sura did I utter?
For I have no tongue to speak it.
At God's door—how could I know now,
For I have no hand or heart now?
You have carried heart and hand, God!
Grant me safety, God, forgive me. . . . [21]

Theorizing the worshipper as the lover and God as the Beloved has profound consequences for shaping that relationship and the ways in which worship may be carried out. Even if, as I suspect to be the case, God is only sometimes "the Beloved," one can end up in all kinds of conversations with Him—conversations that fall in and out of the strictly religiously named categories we have, such as do'a, zikr, and niyayesh (or in English, praise, gratitude, and supplication). There is nothing new in speaking of God as the Beloved, as He has been referred to in this way for centuries. Rumi wrote the poem just quoted in the thirteenth century. And speaking to God unscripted and in Persian has always been a possibility and practiced by some. But just as religion was mainly a subject of explicit discussion and debate among clerics and secular intellectuals before the revolution, so were understandings of the implications of 'erfan for religious practice and for the relationship to the divine. There has emerged a discourse on practical 'erfan that has found its way into the everyday exchanges of laypeople from a variety of social backgrounds. At the moment it is an explicit and frequent subject of conversation among many who do not necessarily consider themselves experts on 'erfan. As we can see from the various do'a just narrated, the content and form would be difficult to imagine if the dominant feeling toward the divine was one of awe. In these cases, the ideal of addressing God as if standing in front of Him and the intimacy of showing disappointment and asking Him to explain himself demonstrate the absence of awe, fear, or distance.

Many of these women believe that their mothers and fathers rarely talked to God in the ways that they do. Perhaps their parents felt more fear toward God than women in our group. The kind of prayer where one sits and just talks to God at length, without any particular agenda, seems to have become more widely practiced after the revolution. I was told that the women's parents recited Arabic prayers—their mothers reciting from the Qur'an and from prayer books, and their fathers preferring the Qur'an alone. They characterized their parents' approach and that of the generation before them as *mowrūsi* (inherited) and *ābā va ajdādī* (fathers and ancestors). These terms are meant to capture the fact that, as it was explained to me, those generations relied far more on what they were taught by their elders than on seeking to understand the reasons behind ideas and acts. They did not do "their own research." Although many of the women's parents were familiar with 'erfan poetry and could recite its verses from memory, there was no force imposed by the state to worship or understand Islam in particular ways—though the preference was for Islam not to play a major role in public life and politics. Hence, while the relationship between the 'erfan approach to religion and divinity and the more legalistic approach has been historically uneasy and often contentious, most laypeople did not find it to be that relevant to their daily lives. After the revolution, on the one hand, 'erfan-inflected thinking grew through many channels, and at the same time, following the death of Ayatollah Khomeini, *organized* mystic groups were pressured to go into hiding and disband or be punished with jail time and worse. This again shows the ambivalence of the state toward mysticism.

One might think, as some secular Iranians tend to do, that 'erfan is restricted to the middle classes, who as one person put it "do not really want to pray and do other religious acts," and so they cling to mysticism. While one cannot deny that class plays an important role in approaches to religion and that mysticism is interpreted in different ways, the spread of 'erfan-related ideas and 'erfan-minded individuals and groups is hard to overestimate. The appeal of 'erfan cuts across class and gender lines—it appeals both to those for whom Islam is a major guide in their lives and those who find in 'erfan a highly promising cosmology that can help them escape the secular/religious binary. Let us return to the Qom Seminary's description of do'a that was mentioned in the Introduction:

Do'a is the spiritual relationship between the creator and the created, and the thread of connection between the lover and the Beloved. Do'a is to recall the Friend in one's heart and to utter His name on one's tongue, and the key to being granted [generosity]. It is the way to get close to God, the essence of worship and the life of the spirit [ḥayāt-e rūḥ]. Do'a is the turning of the humble servant full of need to the doorway of the eager God without needs. God is so eager for His servants that He said, "If you do not come to me and do not ask me for anything, I will not pay attention to you." Hence, now that the High God has opened the door of do'a and monajat for His servant and has given him/her permission to be present in His company, the servant must guard the mutual courtesy and ethics and behave in such a way that is suitable for the high God.[22]

The website then cites several verses of various poems by Rumi to reinforce these points about do'a. This is a measure of the high regard for Rumi, and by extension for 'erfan ideas, held by an institution that has historically been at best ambivalent about and more often hostile to mysticism.

Persian and Arabic: The Concept of *Fazīlat*

In the realm of *written* do'a, there are certain kinds of prayers—such as some verses of the Qur'an that have come to be considered independent do'a and others that have been written by the Imams, all of which are in Arabic—whose recitation accrues *fazīlat* (virtue). Recitations of these do'a are also mostahabb acts.[23] According to the *Masnavi* class teacher, Arabic words used in religious contexts are felt to be *rāz-alūd* (imbued with holiness and mystery), that is, appropriate to worship. Persian is certainly used in the establishment and maintenance of one's relationship to the divine, as we just saw, but it is not perceived to have the kind of mysterious efficacy that Arabic does. One might draw a parallel with a time when the Lord's Prayer was recited exclusively in Latin. In that case, the difference between its Latin recitation and simply beseeching God in vernacular English or French was likely similar to this kind of distinction that some Iranian Muslims make. Similarly, those who used to say the Hail Mary in Latin were probably skeptical about its efficacy in any vernacular language. But eventually, because church services turned to the use of the vernacular for all purposes, prayer in vernacular languages became common, though not necessarily beloved and accepted by all. In mosques in Iran, the *khotbeh* (sermon) is in Persian, though it is often interspersed with Arabic expressions and with verses from the Qur'an. There is a difference between the recitation of a sura when the intention is to perform a religious act and the mere reading of that sura in Persian. But because the relative places of Persian and Arabic as languages of religion are in flux, there are disagreements over why a recitation in Arabic is a religious act but a reading of the same sura in Persian is not. On television, prayers are recited in both languages, though Arabic dominates. Persian subtitles appear when the prayer is in Arabic. Increasingly, Persian has come to play a larger role as a language of worship.

The women in our group have diverse positions in relation to the notion of fazilat. Interestingly, those who object most strongly to privileging Arabic over Persian in do'a (not in namaz) are the ones who take issue with the whole idea. Elaheh, Parvin, and Pari are in this group. They do not believe Arabic prayers have a particular kind of fazilat. Nor do they agree with the use of zikr and prayers in set numbers.

But Mina thinks that "zikr saves us from stray thoughts" and is useful for "seeking refuge from thoughts that trouble us." She said, "I think this helps prevent emotional illnesses [*bimāriy-e ruhi*]." She continued:

> I myself, whenever I have troubling thoughts [*āzār dahandeh*], I seek refuge in God [*beh khoda panāh mibaram*]. I treat myself to nineteen *bi-ism allah al-rahman al-rahim* [In the name of God, the Beneficent, the Merciful]. If it [a troubling thought] comes at namaz, I do one round of *bi-ism allah* with tasbih [prayer beads].

Note that she uses the very first verse of the Qur'an (and of every sura)—"In the name of God, the Beneficent, the Merciful"—to ward off bad thoughts. This is one of the most popular zikrs. Usually, the reciter holds prayer beads in one hand and counts with the beads. Another example is doing *tasbih-e hazrat-e Fatemeh* (the Prayer of Hazrat Fatima). It consists of thirty-four *allaho akbar*, thirty *sobhan allah*, and thirty *al-hamdo li-allah*, at times with minor variations in this order. Maryam, Mina, and

Parvin said that their mothers and grandmothers taught them to do this. They explained: "First, one says that God is great; next, one reminds oneself that God is pure of all that is bad [*monazzah az hamey-e badihā*] and hence He can keep you away from what is bad; and then one expresses gratitude [*shokr*] for being kept far from what is bad in this world."

Commenting on whether choosing Arabic or Persian makes a difference, Maryam said: "If you had asked me ten years ago, I would have said yes, but now I don't think it makes any difference to God in what language you pray." She gave me the example of a zikr that Aziz jan's sister taught her, using different names of God. It was *yā fattāh* ninety times, at any time of day, and several times in the same day when she faced a "knot" (*gereh*) in her life and she wished it to be opened (*goshāyesh*). *Ya* is a vocative in Arabic. *Fattah* comes from the root f-t-h, meaning "to open." If one has financial problems, one might say *ya rāziq* from the root r-z-q, meaning "what God gives creatures for their daily sustenance." Maryam used to put her hand on her mother's leg where she had tumors and say *ya shāfī* (oh healer) many times. "Zikr gives you strength in your heart when you are worried—it offers some calm as you go about your day and you say these names," Aziz jan's sister had explained. But now when Maryam wants something from God, she is likely to make the request in Persian just as often as doing the zikr in Arabic.

None of these women made mention of a concept that religious leaders call *ehtiyāt* (caution) in relation to choosing a language for prayer. When asked whether one should do do'a in Persian, most clerics assume they are being asked about written Arabic do'a, and they reply that one should at least recite in both Persian and Arabic, for reasons of "caution" (recall the previous discussion of namaz and *qonūt* in Persian). In order to make sure that one is fulfilling a religious duty, one must use caution and pray in Arabic.[24] There are ayatollahs who believe that fazilat refers only to the ideal of spiritual transformation, and that would be the reward itself. For example, as Ayatollah Mohsen Kadivar explained to me:

> The idea of fazilat is to obtain spiritual *savāb* [reward]. It is clear that if do'a can be the source of spiritual transformation and personal cultivation then fazilat and savab cannot mean anything else. But sectarian kinds of interpretation imply that reciting do'a even

without spiritual transformation has merit and reward. In this case then, reading an Arabic text is thought to be the source of the reward and hence the translation of the do'a is regarded as lacking that particular feature. It is clear that this interpretation is indefensible, and I know of no credible source [mostanad-e mo'tabar] for it.[25]

Thus, the related idea of ehtiyat is not one that he would employ to justify the use of Arabic. Among the ranks of those called religious intellectuals in Iran, this position is typical. Such ambivalence toward the importance of Arabic is not new to the postrevolutionary period. However, previously it was not commented on so widely across different groups.

There are many suras or parts of suras in the Qur'an that are used as do'a. They are a pleasure to recite because of their sounds, their rhyme schemes, and their rhythm. People like to recite them aloud to themselves and especially to others in order to share this pleasure. I transliterate two here and urge the reader to try to read them out loud a number of times. I have transliterated the words so as to indicate the way they should be pronounced and have purposely left out the translations so that the reader can focus on the sounds of the language alone.

Sura 113 (The Dawn)
1. Qul a'uuzo bi rabbil-falaq
2. Min sharri maa khalaq
3. Wa min sharri ghasiqin iza waqab
4. Wa min sharrin-naffaa-saati fil 'uqad
5. Wa min sharri haasidin iza hasad

Sura 114 (The People)
1. Qul a'uuzo birabbin naas
2. Malikin naas
3. Ilaahin naas
4. Min sharril waswaasil khannaas
5. Allazee yuwaswisu fee suduurin naas
6. Minal jinnati wan naas

Other examples of such suras appear in Chapter 4.

Conclusion

Muslim subjectivity is often portrayed by exclusively examining that which is obligatory. I think that offers a misleading and an incomplete picture. There are many acts that Muslims engage in that are mostahabb, and do'a is one of them. One can learn a great deal through a close look at do'a. Do'a shows how individuals engage in highly personal and serious dialogue with God. In doing so, they depart from a monolithic view of God and enter a changing relationship with Him. Among other things, the actual act of addressing God in everyday Persian seems to transform His place so that He is no longer across an ontological divide. Furthermore, although we routinely say that Islam is a monotheistic religion, we should note as well, as the example of Aziz jan's experience and practice demonstrates, how these women were socialized into becoming Muslims, that this is a monotheism produced and shaped with the presence of many others—siblings, mothers, fathers, ancestors, and special holy figures with whom a worshipper has found a particular affinity. Robert Orsi observes, "Humans are always accompanied, and any account of a single human life must include these others that accompany that life, for better and for worse."[26]

It is clear that few people start praying on their own without having grown up in a family where others pray. After the revolution, those who seemed to have "discovered" religion rather suddenly in their adulthood were commented on negatively. They appeared to believe anything they were told about Islam, or they came across as claiming far more religiosity than those who had grown up with religion. It was common to hear observations like "so and so was a Muslim *before* the revolution," as contrasted to individuals who had grown up in families where the parents did not pray and religion was neither a set of acts nor a topic of conversation at home. The distinction between those new to religion and those whose families were religious became highly meaningful after the revolution. Perhaps at the heart of this distinction is the question of who accompanies members of each of these two groups in their religious journey.

At the time the women I met with went to school, when the shah was in power, religious teaching at school was not extensive, particularly not in elementary school. That has changed now at all levels of the public education system. After the revolution, the inclusion of prayer halls in schools (and public offices) became obligatory, and now all Muslim students and teachers have to go to the prayer hall at the time of the azan.[27] Hence, school has become a far more significant source of religious education. Moreover, this rather doctrinal religious education is perceived as being fundamentally different from the learning about religion that goes on at home.

People "follow" a religion in all kinds of ways, including by performing acts that are compulsory and others that are not, or to state this another way, acts that are well-defined and those that are far less so. Do'a is not an act that has a specific pedagogy. Worshippers make it up as they go along, using their imagination, their experience, and whatever related sources they may have been exposed to, such as poetry, prayer books, the media, and discussions with others. I argue that an ethnography of these varied acts, such as the one presented in this chapter, shows that God is neither conceptualized nor worshipped in just one way. The relationship with God is capacious and experiences vulnerabilities and ruptures. Maryam resorts to Plato's shadows—the idea that we do not see the real and so we cannot judge the logic of God's decisions. But even resorting to shadows and being unable to see the real was not enough to prevent her from going to the mosque and shouting at God.

Finally, what we can note about inward speech, inasmuch as we can hear it in these women's stories, is that it is a back-and-forth between assertions and questions.[28] This speech does not seem to be locked in a secretive, inner recess of those who pray, inaccessible and incomprehensible to others. It is very much like speech directed at others. It is probably not possible to know everything that people say in conversations with God, and some of it might be so private it will never be shared with others. Nevertheless, we should challenge our implicit assumption that only publicly performed rituals, semiotically available and audible, can be studied.

The following chapter is about do'a that are written by Imams and appear in prayer books. What is the role of women in the uses of what we might call Shi'i liturgy? What is the print culture of prayer books, and how have they become diversified after the revolution? How do Persian and Arabic fare in this market?

CHAPTER FOUR

Movable Mosques

Prayer Books, Women, and Youth

And when worshippers ask you about me,
they should know that I am near
and I answer their call if they call on me.
So they must also answer mine
and have faith in me to find guidance.

Qur'an, Sura al-Baqara, 186

In these verses, God tells the Prophet to remind believers that He is near and will answer if they call on Him. Spontaneous prayer (*do'ā*), Qur'anic prayer, and *namāz* are ways of calling on God. There is also a large body of prayers composed by the Imams, or believed to have been composed by them. Various scholars have put together collections of them in prayer books. These prayers are referred to as do'a as well. The reading and recitation of such prayers is *mostahabb* (favored) and not mandatory. But as we will see, many people like to read them on various occasions.

Historically, such prayers have met with some degree of skepticism over their authenticity. The chain of transmission or narration is so long that there are inevitably doubts about how an original composition by an Imam could have survived so many generations. Did Imam Jafar Sadeq really compose such and such a prayer? Has it arrived to us intact, or have people with their own agendas about Islam "planted" ideas in it? Some of the most popular prayer books make claims that only increase readers' doubts: often an Imam is reported to have said that a certain prayer will solve one's problems, absolve the reciter of sins, or guarantee her entry into paradise. Would any Imam actually say such things? The postrevolutionary reflexive turn has expanded the debate about such prayers and, by extension, about the status of the prayer books that contain them, with skeptics taking the position that this is the kind of Islam that tells follow-ers one doesn't have to work hard to be a true Muslim—simply reciting some prayers will send one to heaven. Interestingly, the preference for Persian comes out most strongly in relation to these Arabic do'a, claimed to have been written by Imams. If one is to talk to God from the heart and say what one desires, why use other people's words (even if they are Imams), and why in Arabic?

The propagation of such prayers has been carried out in numerous ways. These are not prayers that people are taught in childhood—that kind of pedagogy is usually reserved for prayers from the Qur'an. I found that Imams' prayers are the last kind of prayer that people learn—some learning just a few and others many more. They are recited in gatherings and individually and are broadcast on radio and television. Older prayers books offer instructions on various rites for every day of the week and often for the resolution of problems (*moshkelāt*). These can include health and financial difficulties as well as anxieties about one's children, mar-riage decisions, and so on. The prayer books offer advice about what to do and which prayer to recite, how many times, and when.

In the following pages, I will first provide a brief history of prayer books, from the beginning of the twentieth century to the present, includ-ing their print culture and the changes that can be observed in the prayer book market. What kinds of new prayers are being offered to readers, and to which kinds of readers? We will then move to the ideas and practices of the women in our group with regard to prayer books.[1] I explore the role of women as consumers of such books, and as authors of some of the newer ones in this genre that have become available in the last decade or so. I will interweave the views of the women with those of religious authorities. As reflected in the more recent prayer books, ideas about what constitutes a do'a have multiplied and changed since the revolution. Women's specific uses of prayer books and their authorship of prayers in Persian, which are sometimes called "simple *'erfān*," play a major role in such changes. More recent prayer books aim to attract a younger and more educated public—they make attempts to address the historical prob-lem of the authenticity of such prayers and the promises about resolving life's problems through the simple recitation of do'a.

The Qur'an as a Prayer Book: "I Only Recite the Rabbinas"

Broadly speaking, prayer books have, historically, been viewed negatively because their existence has seemed likely to detract attention from the Qur'an. Equally importantly, those who hold this view believe that the Qur'an itself contains prayers of all kinds and so fulfills all the needs of those who want to pray. Nevertheless, as we will see, there are a fair number of prayer books in circulation in Iran, even if no political power or institution has ever lent support to standardizing them or making them an official part of worship—at least not explicitly. Indeed, it may come as a surprise to those for whom prayer books play a central role in religious services to learn that for Iranian Shi'i Muslims, prayer books are not part of any official or regular service offered by mosques. There are no *standard* and officially sanctioned prayer books equivalent to, for example, the Book of Common Prayer for Anglican and some other Protestant denominations or the Roman Missal for Catholics. On Fridays, when people go to mosques, perform the noon prayer, and listen to a sermon, the imam at the mosque may recite suras of various lengths from the Qur'an, but no verses from prayer books. The preacher often translates and interprets what the Qur'anic verses mean. And there may be call and response interactions between the preacher and the congregation: for example, when the prayer leader voices a request, such as "God, please heal all those who are sick," and the congregation responds by saying *amen* or *elahi amen* (roughly, "may God help it happen"). There have been attempts to centralize mosque activities and to offer prepared sermons on a variety of topics and historically significant events. These prepared sermons, called *fish-e manbar* (memo for the pulpit; from the French word *fiche*) are available on several websites, most notably the central masjid.ir. On some evenings, certain do'a from prayer books are recited and interpreted in gatherings and classes.[2]

The Qur'an is routinely used as a prayer book. The high reverence for this sacred book—and among Iranians in particular, the historical preoccupation with whether an adequate translation into Persian is possible—has limited the attention given to this particular function of the Qur'an. It is not hard to understand why most people would be reticent to refer to the Qur'an as a prayer book—the designation would make it one among many others, whereas the Qur'an is considered to be unique.

On a daily basis, one of the main ways in which worshippers develop a relationship with the Qur'an is to read and recite do'a—at times individually, at other times in gatherings, and at still other times, by paying a professional reciter (*rowzeh-khan*) to recite a do'a. Such prayers are broadcast on television and radio as well. They may be complete suras or parts of suras that are liturgical and have a hymnal quality.[3] This use of the Qur'an and the emotional bonds that emerge as a result are at least as important, if not more so, than reading it from beginning to end for its "meaning," as one would do with any other book.[4] The importance of meaning comes in and out of focus, but the aesthetic and emotional dimensions, as I argued in Chapter 3, are crucial.

One frequently hears, "There is this do'a in the Qur'an that says . . . " Such do'a have their own names, separate from the name of the sura. For example, the prayer Ayat al-Kursi, a popular Qur'anic prayer across the Muslim world (and the one mentioned in Chapter 2 that Maryam's father encouraged her to memorize), is part of the Sura al-Baqara.

> God—there is no deity except Him, the Ever-Living, the Sustainer of [all] existence. Neither light nor deep sleep can overtake Him. To Him belongs what is in the heavens and whatever is on the earth. Who is it that can intercede with Him except by His permission? He knows what is before them and what will be after them, and they encompass not a thing of His knowledge except for what He wills. His *kursi* [throne] extends over the heavens and the earth, and their preservation tires Him not. And He is the Most High, the Most Great.[5]

The Prophet Muhammad, Hazrat-e Ali, Imam Reza (the eighth Imam), and Musa Ibn Jafar (the seventh Imam, also referred to as Imam Musa Kazem) are reported to have expressed their high regard for this prayer. It is believed to have special virtues and benefits.

There are many parts of the Qur'an in which God is directly addressed in a supplicatory manner. These addresses are generally of two kinds. Throughout the chapters of the Qur'an are verses of various lengths that begin with *rabbina* (Our Lord) followed by a variety of supplications. It happens routinely that these verses are recited without reading the entire sura of which they are a part.[6] Some of these do'a have come to be considered appropriate for particular times of the year, such as Rama-zan ("Ramadan" in Arabic), the month of fasting. Here are a few more examples from other suras:

> Our Lord! Bestow on us endurance, make our foothold sure, and give us help against the disbelieving folk" [2:250]

> Our Lord! Forgive us, and our brethren who came before us into the Faith, and leave not, in our hearts, rancor against those who have believed [59:10]

> Our Lord! Perfect our Light for us, and grant us Forgiveness: for You hast power over all things [66:8][7]

Two of the ayatollahs whom I interviewed, Qom Seminary graduates with doctorates from European universities, told me that they recite do'a only from the Qur'an, especially "the beautiful rabbinas," because they are sure of their source—there is no doubt about their authenticity. In order to accrue religious merit or deepen one's knowledge, many people do strive to read the Qur'an from cover to cover. But what circulates, gets quoted, is recited as a stand-alone do'a, and figures into the arts of recita-tion played on radio and television does not include all 114 suras. While the use and memorization of Qur'anic do'a is likely an old practice, it is also the case that certain practices encouraged the recognition and use of certain suras as individual do'a. For example, prayer scribes (do'ā nevīs) wrote certain prayers on pieces of paper to offer to those seeking help for a variety of reasons.[8] With the advent of publishing and the increase in lit-eracy in the early decades of the twentieth century, it is reasonable to sug-gest that printing sets of individual suras as small booklets helped spread knowledge about some of them more than others and further buttressed the prayer book aspect of the Qur'an. Such practices make do'a object-like, and people speak of being "given" a do'a. For example, Maryam, Mina said, "gave me *āman rasūl*" (2:285–86; "the Messenger has believed [in what was revealed to him]"), and Mina now recites this do'a in times of need. Some ask a relative, a cleric, a mystic, or a friend for a do'a (or a *zikr*) that is relevant to their particular needs. This publishing practice is not limited to Iran; it is widespread in many other Muslim countries.

Some short suras are perceived to be particularly poetic in form, and their content can easily be related by the worshipper to her daily and changing concerns. These were often referred to by my interlocutors as the suras "toward the end of the Qur'an," and they are also published as single do'a or combined with a few other similarly short ones. As mentioned in Chapter 3, examples specifically cited by my interlocutors are al-Sharh (The Relief, sura 94), al-'Asr (Time, or Declining Day, sura 103), al-Nasr (Victory, sura 110), al-Ikhlas (Sincerity, sura 112), al-Falaq (Daybreak, sura 113), and al-Nās (Humankind, or The People, sura 114). There is therefore a long-standing practice of publishing and using certain parts of the Qur'an more than others.

The Book of Sajjad and Keys to Paradise

When we enter the realm of non-Qur'anic do'a, we are almost immediately in the company of the Prophet and members of his family (*ahl-e beyt* [literally, "members of the house"/home/family]).[9] Those who belong to this household include Hazrat-e Ali, Hazrat-e Fatima (wife of Imam Ali and daughter of the Prophet), and their eleven descendants beginning with Imam Hassan. Some members of the beyt are believed to have authored prayers. In discussing prayers written by descendants of the Prophet, the Qom Seminary website first characterizes the Prophet's family in relation to the Qur'an:

> The Qur'an is written Islam, and *ahl-e beyt* are its enunciators.
> The Qur'an is the way, and *ahl-e beyt* are the guides.
> The Qur'an is the law, and *ahl-e beyt* know the law and execute the law.
> The Qur'an is the torch, and the Imam holds the torch.
> The Qur'an is wisdom [*hekmat*], and *ahl-e beyt* are the models of this wisdom.[10]

The implication seems to be that what they say and do is directly inspired by the holy book and hence they are trustworthy. The son of Imam Hussein is believed to be the author of one of the two best-known prayer books in contemporary Iran. The older one is *Sahifeh Sajjadieh* (Prayers [or Scripture] of Sajjad, or Psalms of Sajjad; its full name is *Sahifeh-ye*

Kamele-ye Sajjādieh). The more recent one is *Mafatih al-Jinan* (Keys to paradise), first published in 1925. *Sahifeh* is the oldest prayer book used by Shi'a[11] and, as just mentioned, is attributed to the fourth Imam, the great-grandson of the Prophet, Ali ibn Hussein, known as Zein al-Abedin, who later acquired the title "Sajjad," meaning a person who prostrates in prayer (referencing the fact that he prayed a great deal).

His prayers emerged out of the context of the single most important event in the history of Shi'ism. In 680 CE, Imam Hussein, Imam Sajjad's father, challenged the passing of the caliphate to Mu'awiyah's son Yazid. Heading a small army, he went toward Kufa to fight, but he and his supporters were met by Yazid's army in Karbala (Iraq). They were deprived of water and, greatly outnumbered, killed along with their families. Imam Sajjad survived because he was too ill to fight, but he witnessed the killing of many of his family members.[12] People say that for this reason his prayers are particularly poignant and heartfelt. Hence, the historical context bestows an incomparable pedigree on *Sahifeh Sajjadieh*.[13] Imam Sajjad composed fifty-four "psalms."[14] Although the chain of transmission (*sanadiyyāt*) of these prayers is lengthy, those in the chain were his children, who helped to disseminate the prayers. His children can be traced back, and so the prayers are found to be trustworthy. The prayers in this book are considered to be lofty, eloquent, heartfelt, beautiful, and profound. Those who see the prayers' chain of transmission as a reason for doubting their authenticity have been in the minority.[15]

Any prayer book containing prayers from the Imams is necessarily in Arabic, as all were Arabic speakers. These prayers are published in Iran mostly in bilingual editions. Publishers of prayer books seem to have become keen on enlisting well-known religious figures to translate and correct errors in the text. As a result, prayer books are advertised not only on the basis of the credentials of the original author(s) but also on the basis of the credentials of the translator and compiler who is ideally a well-known contemporary religious scholar. According to the website of the Qom Seminary, which has twenty-five separate entries for this prayer book, *Sahifeh* has been translated by eighteen different translators. In translating the work into Persian, many have tried to preserve the poetic quality of the original Arabic.[16]

The second most popular prayer book, after *Sahifeh*, is *Mafatih al-Jinan* (Keys to paradise). Edited by a scholar-cleric named Sheikh Abbas Qomi (1877–1940), it was compiled as a collection of previously published prayers. Qomi explained: "Some pious brothers requested that I study the popular *Miftah al-Jinan*[17] and keep those prayers that have *sanad* [proof, documentation], and what I cannot find sanad for, exclude, and add some prayers that are credible [*mo'tabar*] but not mentioned in that book; therefore this humble [self] fulfilled their request and arranged the book in that way and gave it the name *Mafatih al-Jinan*."[18] *Mafatih al-Jinan* is the first true popularization of non-Qur'anic prayers,[19] and it overtook *Sahifeh* in terms of readership.[20]

In order to add to the credibility of prayer books and to encourage their purchase, they almost always contain a number of suras from the Qur'an at the beginning. Whether the inclusion of suras was controversial, how the practice was sanctioned, and by whom remains to be explored. *Mafatih al-Jinan* is a hefty book, and most editions run more than one thousand pages. The table of contents itself runs to several pages. The edition that I own, for example, belonged to my mother. It was published in 2003.[21] It begins with eighteen suras from the Qur'an and goes on to do'a to be recited after namaz and on each day of the week. It has various kinds of nonobligatory namaz, such as that of Hazrat-e Fatima; it has rites for Fridays, rites for fasting and other months, and prayers (*ziyarāt*) for pilgrimages to various saints' tombs. Almost all do'a books are divided into do'a, zikr, and ziyarat.

Mafatih al-Jinan became ubiquitous in the decades after the revolution. Copies can be found on the bookshelves of mosques and shrines alongside the Qur'an. Many homes have a copy (perhaps received as a gift), even if it is not read by family members. At times, it is distributed for free at funerals, commemorations, and anniversaries of deaths. In hotel rooms, there is often a copy of the Qur'an and a copy of *Mafatih al-Jinan*. This practice continues to be objected to because of the implication that one can read *either* one *or* the other. The most famous critic of *Mafatih al-Jinan* is Ali Shari'ati (1933–1977), a seminal and prolific figure in the intellectual and political life of Iran.[22] His views on this prayer book are well-known and circulate widely by being frequently quoted.

Shari'ati seems to have spoken on behalf of many who were bothered by this book's widespread availability, lamenting that ever since its appearance on the market, people were reading the Qur'an less.[23] In his book *Niyayesh*, Shari'ati returns again and again to the gulf between *Mafatih al-Jinan* and *Sahifeh*:

> Those small souls whose heart is as big as a thimble and whose flight of thoughts reaches the tip of their nose, they are comfortable and content and assured that with . . . one pilgrimage to Shah Abdul Azim and one offering of food and a bit of alms and a few pages reading of the *Mafatih al-Jinan* . . . they finally have all the keys to the gates of paradise; what more could one want?[24]

As we will see, similar views were echoed by some of the women in our group. When Shari'ati turns to *Sahifeh*, he sees in it the most important sociohistorical context for the formation of Shi'i prayers. He enumerates features of Islamic prayer such as eloquence and literary beauty—the musicality of the "speech, word, sentence and the entire text." He sees in Islamic prayer,

> the element of thought, meaning that the entire text of Islamic prayer from beginning to end (*Sahifeh* is the perfect example) is about *khodā-shenāsi* [theology] and *ensān shenasi* [human-ology, anthropology], ethical principles, social principles and the rights of individuals and classes [toward each other], and there is also the expression of fear and escape from the ups and downs of individual and collective ethical issues.[25]

To these he adds a fourth feature:

> because of the historical context of the composition of *Sahifeh*, a social and political element [exists] . . . in Shi'i prayers.

> Under conditions when Imam Sajjad had absolutely no recourse to political or military protest, he had no hope for continuing the struggle and given the social and political conditions, there was the danger of annihilation and the forgetting of [Imam Hussein's] thought and the movement for justice, rights, and humanism [*ensan dūsti*]. . . .

Only one person was left and that person was not free of responsibili-
ties, the responsibility to his own soul, the soul of someone who must
keep alive within himself, with this thought, this emotion, memory,
and commitment, keep himself alive with prayer. And [also] as an individual who has the responsibility of keeping, defending, spreading
this message and keeping the thought, emotion and giving it to the
future generation, [he] must make use of do'a as armament for social
and intellectual struggle.[26]

Shari'ati holds up *Sahifeh* as *the* model for Shi'i prayers. It is clear
that for him, *Mafatih al-Jinan*, having been compiled by a cleric-scholar
who was not widely regarded as learned and erudite, and who gathered
prayers for daily concerns such as headaches, lack of funds, and so on,
could not possibly compete with *Sahifeh*. It is also clear that when he
says "Shi'i prayers" he means the body of *written* prayers that Shi'a recite
and not prayers that are spontaneous conversations addressed by Shi'a to
God in Persian. While he says nothing against spontaneous do'a, he does
not dwell on it or elaborate on any aspect of it. Nor does he comment
on choice of language between Arabic and Persian. Given the immediate
political context of the time when he was writing—the repressive rule of
Mohammad Reza Pahlavi—and Shari'ati's open opposition to what he
believed to be an unjust system—he saw *Sahifeh* as having great political
and social relevance.

Who Wrote That Prayer? The Problem of Authenticity

By far the biggest and most sustained objection to prayer books is that they
are thought to contain prayers whose authenticity cannot be satisfactorily
substantiated. They lack a sufficient level of sanadiyyat.[27] Sanadiyyat belongs
to '*elm-e hadis*, or science of hadis, a discipline that is part of the curriculum
at seminaries—where substantiation of what the Imams have said, done,
and recommended is of paramount concern. The degree to which various
individuals and groups show skepticism with regard to any given hadis (or
even most hadis) is a major fault line that divides practicing Shi'i Muslims
in Iran. Among Sunnis, that science is devoted to the Prophet's acts and sayings, but among Shi'a it includes the Prophet and the Imams.

The *Mafatih* states, for example, "It is narrated from Musa ibn Jafar that whoever recites Ayat al-Kursi after any namaz, will be protected from harm." Several *fazilat* (virtues, efficacy) are mentioned based on what the Prophet "and others" have said about this prayer. It is also added that one could enter heaven by reciting it. Of particular interest is that as the list of reliable narrators goes on, we move from the Prophet and his descendants to Shi'i ulema who are known to have undertaken the gathering of hadis and prayers from older manuscripts (for example, the tenth-century Kulayni and Ibn Babawayh). Hence, the chain of transmission reads:

> Kulayni and Ibn Babawayh *and others* according to trustworthy documents [*sanad*] narrated from Imam Muhammad Baqer, Peace be Upon Him, that Gabriel went to the Prophet Joseph (Peace be Upon Him) in jail and said, say after each namaz: "Oh God! In this problem of mine offer an opening and a way for me to exit it and give me sustenance from where I can know and from where I cannot."[28]

Kulayni and Ibn Babawayh are well-known among religious scholars but neither is an Imam—they are not one of the *ma'sūm* (innocents, saints, Imams). Imam Muhammad Baqer died in the early eighth century so neither of the scholars could have known him firsthand. And who are "the others"? Is it possible that an Imam would say that by reciting some prayer one enters heaven, or is that some kind of advertisement by the publisher to increase the sale of the prayer book, or perhaps some cleric who wanted to encourage lay believers? This is one of the main sites of contention both among clerics and between them and lay believers. Religious websites are filled with questions such as the one just posed. Responding to what some see as outrageous claims and promises, mention of such specific rewards is generally avoided in more recent prayer books that are clearly aimed at a more educated and middle-class readership.

The scholar of Islam and translator of *Sahifeh* William Chittick argues that ultimately, the content of prayers illuminates their worth, regardless of their authenticity. He adds, "for most Muslims" this content is the basis for their engagement with certain prayers, rather than a preoccupation with the identity of the author. He is right in his assessment of the historical reactions to *Sahifeh*—the book he is writing about. However, with regard to prayer books such as *Mafatih al-Jinan*, there has been far more contention, both among clerics and among educated laypeople in particular after the revolution. Ayatollah Mohsen Kadivar, while expressing a desire to produce a prayer book based on a revamping of *Mafatih al-Jinan*, points out that the recitation of such do'a is only mostahabb and not obligatory. Therefore, he argues, one must not exaggerate the importance of authenticity. He goes on to say that one should always adopt a cautious attitude in reading do'a books, but because one does not *have to* recite such prayers, their sanadiyyat should not play too big a role.[29]

A problem exacerbated in relation to authenticity is that Persian speakers are not able to judge the language of such prayers because they are *always* in Arabic. Readers' access to bilingual editions makes it possible for them to know what a do'a is about. Stories and jokes circulate about the wrong choice of Arabic prayers whose themes are not understood. Two experiences, one conveyed by Maryam and another by the teacher of the *Masnavi* class I attended in my summers in Tehran, convey the point:

> Recently, the husband of an acquaintance died. I went to his funeral and found that this guy who normally works in some unclear capacity at a mosque that I know had been tasked with reciting appropriate do'a from the Qur'an. But he recited a do'a that is not only entirely inappropriate for the occasion of the death of someone because it has nothing to do with death but also very contentious because it has no sanadiyyat—[it is] not clear who wrote it. Its text [in Arabic] is full of curses, curse this, curse that. It was a cold afternoon, he was going on and on, and people were losing their patience. I was getting very upset about the choice of this prayer. Later, I talked to the uncle of the woman who had organized the funeral and asked him: "Do you know what do'a he was reciting? Do you understand what it was saying?" He said, "No, not at all." When I explained the content to him, he was quite taken aback and promised to go and tell the man off. I said, "No, don't do that, because those who have hired him in the mosque might not like what you have to say and then they will turn against you. Why don't you just advise him to recite a popular sura from the Qur'an, such as the Yasin and others like it, on such occasions?"

Maryam happened to know that do'a precisely because it is one of those highly contentious ones: that is, few believe that an Imam could have actually composed it. Her friend's uncle, although he works in a mosque, did not seem to have much knowledge of the world of do'a; but neither apparently did the man who had been hired for this purpose by the mosque.

The *Masnavi* teacher told me a similar story:

> Recently I went to someone's burial and heard some man recite prayers into the ears of the deceased, as is customary. He kept saying in Arabic these sentences that each start with the imperative, *"If-ham!"* [Understand!]. I went to him later and asked whether he knew what he was saying. He said, "No." I said, "Well, why don't you say it in Persian so that you know what you are saying and maybe there is a chance that the deceased will understand too?"

To continue for a moment with the subject of choice of language, none of my interlocutors mentioned the concept religious leaders call *ehtiyāt* (caution) in relation to the language of prayers. As briefly discussed in Chapter 3, when asked whether one should do do'a in Persian, most clerics say that for reasons of "caution," one should at least recite first in Arabic and then if desired also in Persian—meaning that in order to ensure one is fulfilling a religious duty, one must pray in Arabic. But there are ayatollahs who believe that fazilat refers only to the ideal of spiritual transformation and that would be the reward itself, as Ayatollah Kadivar explained. According to him, there is nothing intrinsic in the Arabic that would provide more reward or more merit. Thus, the concomitant idea of ehtiyat is not one that he would employ to justify the use of Arabic. The ambivalence toward the importance of Arabic is not new to the postrevolutionary period. However, previously it was not widespread among lay believers and was largely articulated by secular intellectuals. I asked Ayatollah Kadivar: What should one's position be with regard to the number of repetitions attached to certain Arabic do'a or phrases, with the implication that the number itself matters? He replied that if one truly believes in the efficacy of a do'a, it is just possible that what one wants out of that recitation will actually happen. One must not dismiss such practices out of hand and assume that there is generally a lack of response to do'a.

"Dear Young Reader": Updating Prayer Books

The market for prayer books in Iran is vast—there are many bookstores stocking different categories of prayer books in most major cities and especially in shrine cities such as Qom and Mashhad. There is great competition among publishers and among some clerics—not only does the market seem relatively lucrative but there are few copyright constraints on older (especially prerevolutionary) prayer books. Publishers can publish well-known or obscure prayer books with many kinds of modifications in quality, length, format, shape, and price, and even use similar titles for diverse content, without fear of legal repercussions.

Before the revolution, perhaps excepting some editions of *Sahifeh* and *Mafatih al-Jinan*, most prayer books were produced on cheap paper and aimed at the less educated readers and lower classes. Since the revolution, the prayer book market strives to capture a more middle-class and educated readership. It is a long way from what Constance Padwick wrote of in the 1950s when searching "bookshops of the Muslim world" and finding only "a pile of humble little prayer-books."[30] One sees a great change in the appearance of prayer books, their content, and their price. The line between formulaic prayers and spontaneous, conversational prayers (in Persian) is being blurred. There is an emphasis on speaking from the heart, and this is reflected in the emergence of new kinds of prayer books, as we will see shortly.

Although *Mafatih al-Jinan* is not respected in the same way as *Sahifeh*, its ubiquity has made it a lucrative brand. Publishers seem to have distributed and/or sold it to mosques, shrines, and hotels—this is likely how copies of this book began to appear everywhere alongside the Qur'an. Therefore, different forces have contributed to its reach. The general shortage of paper that lasted through the 1990s led publishers to choose books that were safe investments, including prayer and poetry collections. These collections were well-known and likely to be bought by libraries, mosques, shrines, religious foundations, charities, and bazaar merchants. They are also favorites for offering as gifts. *Mafatih al-Jinan* fit these various constraints and desires well.

In a wide-ranging interview with a researcher-librarian at a Qom-based religious research center in the summer of 2014, I was told that

Mafatih al-Jinan has acquired the status of a *sar qofli*, roughly meaning "key money." He explained that the reason it became popular is that it has an *'ammi* (popular, vernacular) character: "for every kind of pain, everything, it matches those pains. The whole book is organized in this way." He went on to explain that "publishers are profit seeking," and so there are countless editions of this book issued by innumerable publishers.[31] Moreover, publishers consider the publication of prayer books as a way of acquiring religious reward (*savāb*) while simultaneously hoping to make a profit. This overlap is another source of suspicion for those who are skeptical about prayer books.

In the last few years, a number of well-known grand ayatollahs have published their own prayer books, and some connect their books in one way or another to *Mafatih al-Jinan* while simultaneously critiquing it. Two prayer books that have become relatively well-known are *Kolliyat Mafatih Novin* (Keys to the new), published in 2011 by Ayatollah Makarem Shirazi (b. 1924), and *Mafatih al-Hayat* (Keys to life), a 2012 work by Ayatollah Javadi Amoli (b. 1933).[32] The latter is advertised as "the second volume" of *Mafatih al-Jinan*, because its aim is to help teach readers how to live in *this* world—a backhanded reference to the claim of *Mafatih al-Jinan* to be the keys to paradise. Yet, *Mafatih al-Jinan* is not included in the lengthy bibliography of *Mafatih al-Hayat*, and the author, unlike the publisher, makes almost no mention of it. The book has two introductions, one written by the publisher and the other by the author. The publisher states:

> With all encompassing command of the revealed sources and with complete reaping of the book [Qur'an] and *sunnāt* [hadis] and also of reason [*'aql*][33] . . . the great hadis scholar of our times his Honor [*jinab*] Hajj Sheikh Abbas Qomi, May God Have Mercy on Him, made the road [*sulūk*] of believers and the connection between human beings and God [*ertebāt ba khoda*] smooth through three kinds of worship, namaz, do'a, and ziyarat, and helped them reap savab [religious merit] and reward [*pādāsh*]. [Aytatollah Javadi Amoli saw that] another book was necessary that would be considered it second and complementary volume . . . and therefore this book received the name "Keys to life."[34]

From the introductions to *Kolliyat Mafatih Novin* and *Mafatih al-Hayat,* it is clear that the main challenge is to attract a young, educated, middle-class readership, people who would not read *Mafatih al-Jinan*—a prayer book that neither addresses such an audience nor has been updated, according to the two authors of these more recent prayer books. *Kolliyat Mafatih Novin,* by Ayatollah Makarem Shirazi, is much closer to the contents of the old *Mafatih al-Jinan* in that it provides both popular Qur'anic suras and do'a for particular problems and occasions. However, in its extensive introduction, the author mentions that he has excluded non-credible or poorly documented prayers, and claims about entering paradise and so on are largely absent. The point is repeatedly made that while the old *Mafatih al-Jinan* was fine for its time, *Kolliyat Mafatih Novin* combines contemporary language and content that is aware of the needs of the younger generation, who are frequently directly addressed. Also unlike *Mafatih al-Jinan,* which has no explicit addressee, both of these books directly address the reader with phrases such as "dear readers" and "dear young readers." They are each more than one thousand pages in length and are priced for the salaried middle class. *Kolliyat Mafatih Novin* was first priced at 12,000 *toman* and has reached 35,000 by now. That price is way beyond the means of the urban and rural lower classes for whom this amount of money would feed their families for a few weeks. Similarly, depending on the edition, *Mafatih al-Hayat* is priced around 20,000 toman. By 2017, the book had gone through 179 printings, nine of which had a circulation of twenty thousand. It should be kept in mind that there are many religious libraries, research centers, and foundations, and such high numbers do not necessarily mean that this many laypeople are reading such books.

Mafatih al-Hayat is not a typical prayer book in that it has lengthy prose sections about "how to live in this world," as is stated in its introduction. Section headings include "Dealing with Oneself," "Dealing with Those Like Oneself," "Dealings between People and the Islamic System," "Human Beings' Dealings with Animals," and "Human Beings' Dealings with the Environment." It seems inspired by self-help books, many of which have been translated from English and are widely available in bookstores. Each of these major sections has chapters devoted to the topic, and brief stories and prayers are included from Imam Jafar Sadeq, the Prophet, and Imam Ali. The book does not include most of the popular prayers. The range of topics addressed in *Mafatih al-Hayat* is vast. It moves from mundane matters of daily life such as what to eat, how to keep one's health (based on sayings from the Prophet and the Imams), and what to wear, to how to deal with others such as "neighbors," "our Sunni brothers," and "people of the book," and also discusses justice, ethics, dealings with the Islamic government, distribution of wealth, animal rights, and treatment of the environment. This book clearly aims for a different public than that addressed by *Mafatih al-Jinan*. Except for a small section at the end,[35] it includes no recommendation for doing a rite on a particular day or reciting a certain prayer a set number of times.

Let us now turn to *Kolliyat Mafatih Novin*. Like *Mafatih al-Hayat*, this book was compiled by a team of two researchers and two translators, and although their names appear on the copyright page after the name of Nasser Makarem Shirazi (without his title), the book is known as his. *Kolliyat Mafatih Novin* and *Mafatih al-Hayat* both carry copyright notices, unlike the old *Mafatih al-Jinan*, so no other publisher can issue them without permission. At the time of my writing, *Kolliyat Mafatih Novin* was in its twenty-ninth printing. I came across it first in the shrine of Shah Abd al-Azim located in Ray, southeast of Tehran. Many copies could be found on the portable bookshelves located in the large prayer hall. This was a rather surprising sight, as the *Kolliyat Mafatih Novin* was stacked alone, with no other prayer book nearby, such as the more usual *Mafatih al-Jinan* that used to occupy such spaces at mosques. This seemed to be a deliberate edging out of *Mafatih al-Jinan* by the shrine management.

The recent prayer books show a set of influences from multiple sources—trying to cover all bases to entice readers. On the one hand, they use the language of numbers, just like self-help books. For example, *Kolliyat Mafatih Novin* lists "nine advantages" of the book, "ten suggestions for achieving sincerity,"[36] "ten special features," and so on. I summarize what appears in the introductory pages of the book as its "nine advantages" here:

This book has been prepared using today's language and literature and is usable by all classes [*hame-ye qeshr-hā*]; the translations are fluent and eloquent; all prayers and *zikrāt* and pilgrimage prayers are reported [*naql*] from credible [*mo'tabar*] sources and every one of their sources is indicated in footnotes on the same page; . . . weakly supported and questionable narrations have been avoided; it has a special organization that makes it easy to use; necessary material that did not exist in the old *Mafatih al-Jinan* has been added; conditions and factors for the answering of prayers and the rites, mores [*adab*], and preparations for pilgrimages are explained in detail; and on the whole it has become a book that for the wayfarer [*sālek*] on the path to God (in particular the young) is beneficial and constructive in this spiritual and moral journey.

Emphasis on fluent and contemporary language throughout is an allusion to the overly Arabized and heavy language of religious books in Iran, including some prayer books, such as *Mafatih al-Jinan*, which has a curious and inconsistent style with many Arabic terms and stilted Persian. Although the two ayatollahs who are the authors of these books would not self-identify as followers of 'erfan, they use the language of 'erfan. In *Kolliyat Mafatih Novin*, the believer is referred to as *sālek*, which refers to one who seeks the path to God as a wayfarer. And each section introduction is said to "help [the reader] arrive at the spiritual and mystic states of prayer [*halat-e 'erfani*], of do'a."[37] The justification given for compiling yet another prayer book is that times and readership have changed:

But because this book was written for its particular time and place and had a particular addressee [*mokhātab*], it was necessary to [subject it to] an extensive revision; to eliminate its shortcomings, and to eliminate certain topics that had been criticized by those who do not mean well [*bad khāhān*]; then give it a new [*novin*] organization and on the whole to produce a prayer book that from *all viewpoints is comprehensive and appropriate for our age and time—in particular for the young generation who seek God* [*khoda jū*; literally, "God seeking"].[38]

The difference from *Mafatih al-Jinan* can be seen especially in the advice given to "our young generation":

> Our . . . advice to our dear readers, especially to the young genera-
> tion who have faith and are pure of heart, is that *more than paying
> attention to the number of do'a, they should care for the quality
> and spiritual hāl o havā* [state of feeling], and they should know that
> reciting one Kumail or Nudbeh or Abu Hamzeh or [the prayer of]
> Arafeh of Imam Hussein with presence of the heart can produce such
> transformation and revolution in human beings [*ensan*] that a new
> chapter might start for [him or her].[39]

Thus, reciting the words of an Imam with presence of the heart can lead to spiritual transformation, regardless of how many times each prayer is recited. It is the *hāl* that transpires (one hopes) and the possible "new chapter" in one's spiritual life that matter. The fazilat is in the transformation that these prayers bring about in the reciter, and so the prayers accrue higher merit for the reciter.

Some prayer books do not display the name of any well-known cleric but count on their contemporary appearance and practical function. For example, a two-book set published by Qom-based Omm Abihaa is called *Ertebat ba Khoda* (Connection with God).[40] This title capitalizes on an old and popular 'erfan-inspired expression that, according to some, captures the heart of any act of worship. There is also a television talk show with that name. *Ertebat ba Khoda* contains prayers for travel, leaving the house, the first night of the lunar month, and pilgrimages to Mecca and the shrines of various Imams, including "pilgrimages from afar" (*ziyarāt az rāh-e dūr*).[41] The series has a colorful laminated cover showing the tiled dome of a mosque in an orange hue on the top half and a dusk sky with birds flying on the bottom half. On the back of the cover is a verse from the Qur'an: "Ask Me and I will answer you" (40:60). The edition I bought was the twenty-third, published in 2014 (Iranian year 1392), in 5,000 copies. This book in the series is clearly made for a middle-class market, judging by its price[42] and by the fact that its second page has a dedication form to fill out: "This book is offered by _____ to _____." Such prayer books look substantially different from older ones in terms of cover design, font, number of colors used, and paper quality.[43]

In addition to publishers, charity organizations and wealthy individuals, in particular bazaar merchants, print and distribute free prayer pamphlets, at times just one small heavy paper page that is laminated and has a do'a in Arabic on one side and Persian on the other. This kind of small laminated page with colorful Islamic design borders is meant to be distributed as a gift, and comes with titles such as "Do'a for Shunning All Evil and Difficulties," "Do'a for Relieving Fright and Stress," or "Do'a for Protecting Faith, Life, and Property."[44] Individuals also reprint books such as *Mafatih al-Jinan* on the occasion of a parent's passing and place the deceased parent's name and at times photograph inside the covers.

In sum, there is a category of recently published prayer books authored especially by clerics and their teams (though some appear without a named author) that walk several fine lines. They try to conform to certain ideas historically associated with what prayer books ought to offer, and at the same time, they strive to appeal to the younger generation by the use of some of the most popular 'erfan concepts, such as hal, the journey, the wayfarer, and so on. They emphasize presence of the heart, understanding, and spiritual transformation—moving unevenly further from or closer to some of the main features that *Mafatih al-Jinan* was so successful in establishing.

Tea with a Taste of God: Non-Clerical Authors, Persian, and "Simple 'Erfan"

These days, religious bookstores in Iran are filled with shelves upon shelves of colorful and attractively produced prayer books. Although no explicit signage separates them, some of the more recent prayer books are quite distinct from the kinds we just discussed. What directions have recent prayer books taken? What is new? What has changed? First, compilers and editors of prayer books are no longer exclusively clerics of various ranks. Young laypeople, both men and women, are authoring books that are categorized by publishers and booksellers as prayer books. As we will see, the most successful of these young authors are women. Second, these books are entirely in Persian. No longer is it the case that a written do'a must be in Arabic. The Persian is poetic and vernacular and the themes are viewed as directly inspired by 'erfan. The style is often called 'erfan-e sādeh (simple 'erfan). In such books, the Persian is not there just as a translation but as a language of religious devotion in its own right.

One series, called *Niyayeshhā* (Prayers) is entirely in Persian, and includes titles that, for example, translate to *Me and My Preoccupations* and *Me and What I Do Not Like*.[45] As mentioned in the previous chapter, *niyāyesh* is a term for prayer that is at least as old as Zoroastrianism in Iran and is in current use by both Zoroastrians and Muslims. For this reason, native speakers of Persian do not necessarily link it to a particular religion, and it has perhaps more of a ring of "modern" spirituality. Each volume in the series carries the same introduction stating that "organizing a good life that is oriented to *ta'ālā* (God) and the building of constructive and ethical relations with other people (*mardom*) depends on many conditions, chief among them the golden rule that 'what you like for yourself, like for others,' and 'what you don't desire for yourself, don't desire for others.'" The text goes on in this vein, until we come upon this section heading: "The Following Points Are Worthy of Your Attention." Numbering each point, the authors state:

> 1. In this [note]book [*daftar*], we have tried to choose those niyayesh that are simple and fluent [*sadeh va ravān*], avoiding concepts that are difficult and hard to understand, [niyayesh that] *would be useful for today's young generation* and those whose understanding does not require interpretive and hermeneutic [*tafsir va ta'vil*] efforts. 2. Long sentences have been shortened, and in some cases when the vocatives (*khodaya!*) and (*elahi!*) [O God and O Lord] have been hidden, we have brought them out.[46]

But, one wonders, which "long sentences," and who has "left out" the vocatives? It turns out that deep inside the introduction, the claim is made that each niyayesh is based on something said by the Imams that has been culled from various books.[47] Again, this is an example of wishing to cover all bases.

The desire to attract young readers is even clearer from the statement on the back cover of books in this series, where the use of the words *do'a* and *niyayesh* alternates:

Although do'a is speaking to the creator of existence, it is at the same time speaking to oneself and to society. Hence, [we] should pause at the depth of its concepts and the breadth of its meanings to find and use the code and the secret of individual [*fardī*] and collective [*jam'ī*] education [*tarbiyat*].[48]

To assert that a do'a is talking to oneself (as well as to one's creator) is a rather contemporary idea. The same can be said of the themes that are covered, which probably would have been found rather odd by earlier generations: "What I don't like about my relationship to myself"; "What I don't like about my relationship to others"; "What I don't like about my relationship to God"; and finally, "What I don't like about my relationship to nature." In one last chapter, there are sections on famine, lack of rain, scorched meadows, and overconsumption.

But the most successful new genre of prayer books is made up of those written by young women such as Erfan Nazar-Ahari—a poet and, at the time of the publication of her first book in 2006, a doctoral student in philosophy. *Chay ba Ta'm-e Khoda (Tea with a Taste of God)* is attractively produced and priced at several thousand toman.[49] This book became a phenomenon and has spawned a whole genre of books that are said to present simple mysticism appropriate for people of all ages. In 2016, the book won an award at the twelfth annual Festival of Children and Youth and was given another prize by the Center for Children's Intellectual Development. By this time, it had gone through eighteen printings, and the cost rose from 2,500 to 9,000 toman. The author has now written similar books for the Tehran publisher Ofoq, with titles such as "Where Have You Left Your Wings" and "Every Dandelion Is a Messenger."[50] The books are designed to be offered as presents, and I was given a few by two of the younger women I talked to—then in their mid-forties. Simple mysticism books, often written by female authors, using plain and contemporary prose and poetry inspired by the voluminous heritage of 'erfan literature are in great demand and popular across generations. Websites reviewing such books are fairly numerous and contain large numbers of comments by readers.

We are now ready to delve into how the women in our group, and women more generally, use and shape the body of (written) prayers that circulates in a variety of ways among individuals, groups, classes, and gatherings.

Women and Shi'i Liturgy

Several of the women in our group have taken a general position against *Mafatih al-Jinan* at this point in their lives, though the strength with which they hold this position varies. I asked Maryam how *Mafatih al-Jinan* entered her life in the first place. She explained that in 1990, she came back to Iran from the United States, having left Iran with her two small daughters in 1985 when Tehran began to be bombed by Saddam Hussein. When she returned, she had little money and found out that she had lost her teaching post in a public high school. She was reinstated after months of effort. After she began teaching again, her husband had a massive stroke (as related in the previous chapter). One of her colleagues at work brought a collection of small booklets to distribute. Some had one sura from the Qur'an and others contained non-Qur'anic do'a. Maryam said that her colleague distributed these on the occasion of her own father's passing. They had titles such as "For Getting Rid of Life's Difficulties." Up until that point, she had never bought prayer books or paid much attention to them. But she began reading the ones that her colleague passed around and eventually bought more books like them. One of the booklets her colleague gave her contained a verse from the Qur'an and explained that "if you recite it eleven times, your day brightens." Maryam continued:

> You know when you begin to do something like this, you don't really believe in it, you just do it. Then one day at my mother's house I met a relative of hers who had come from Karbala [Iraq]. She was so nice-looking and I liked her a lot. I don't know what happened but suddenly she recited this same verse. I was so taken by that. I said with surprise, "You read this too?" She said, "I read this every day and I have taught it to my children as well." Once I heard that, I befriended the do'a much more. It had so much more of an effect on me.
>
> It also gave me the feeling that I could make matters better for myself by *doing something*. I would recite these on the way to work (having to take three buses each way), or while walking, and I felt a

positive energy from the universe [kā'enāt]. Whatever you do, if you do it from the bottom of your heart [samīm-e del], it becomes somehow effective [kār sāz misheh].

At times the path to prayer can be unusual. Parvin gave Maryam a copy of a book translated into Persian by a woman of their mothers' generation, Guity Khoshdel (b. 1926), that led Maryam to like saying do'a more than she had in the past. The book had been written by the American author-illustrator Florence Scovel Shinn (1871–1940).[51] Shinn spoke of "how one ought to work on one's mind and keep it positive." Maryam told me, "This book became the Qur'an for me for a while." "Imagine," she said, "I began reading do'a because the father of a colleague passed away, and then because of a relative in Karbala, and my love of the book of an American author who did similar things as me, such as hold regular gatherings." Little by little, she sought out prayer books and came across the *Mafatih al-Jinan*. She participated in women's gatherings where the book was used, and she and her mother established a routine of reciting certain prayers together on Friday evenings. But years later, her mother (her coreciter) passed away, her living conditions changed, she met others whose ways she liked, and she stopped reading this book:

I don't really use the *Mafatih* anymore. First, because I used to read it with my mother, and since she passed away, I don't like it as much. Second, I was always quite surprised that when my father was alive he never opened the *Mafatih*. Then in the last few years I began taking courses with Mr. Malayeri [a Rumi teacher] and although he has attended the seminary [howzeh] himself, he does not seem to really believe in the *Mafatih* from the way he talks. Also Dr. Shari'ati said that from the time *Mafatih* appeared everywhere, no one reads the Qur'an anymore.

But still, there are prayers I like, such as the prayer of Kumail, and although it is included in the *Mafatih*, that is a separate matter from the *Mafatih* itself. Kumail's meanings [ma'ānish] are very beautiful. There are a few other prayers I like: for example, the do'a of Abu Hamza Somali, about Imam Hussein going to Kufa and Arafat.

It is really from his heart [*az qalbesheh*]. I like *Sahifeh Sajjadieh* a lot more than the *Mafatih*.

The Kumail prayer mentioned by Maryam, and always included in prayer books, is one of the most-loved prayers among these women. It is said that Gabriel taught it to the Prophet Khidr, and Imam Ali taught it to his friend Kumail, hence the name. The authenticity of Kumail is not, for the most part, in doubt, and this prayer is included in *Mafatih al-Jinan*, though it can also be found in other sources.[52]

While one cannot be sure of the readership of *Mafatih al-Jinan* during the decades immediately after its publication, it is clear that at the moment, it is read mostly by women. Many women told me that their fathers, brothers, or husbands did not like or in any case did not use the book. This is similar to the historical pattern of the gendered use of prayer books among Christians.[53] Because prayer books are not used in mosques as part of regular services and because women do not play major roles in organizing mosque activities, prayer books such as the *Mafatih*, which give specific instructions about what to do on every day of the year, act as movable mosques for women who take turns in organizing activities in their own homes. They do not follow every instruction and in fact often come up with a variety of their own creative ideas in these gatherings that are not in the prayer book.

I was told by my interlocutors that *Mafatih al-Jinan* is popular because it gives explicit instructions about what to do, when, and how many times; and it explains exactly what kind of reward each prayer offers. For example, readers are advised to recite a certain prayer eleven times and then visit the grave of some holy figure; or "reach with hands to the sky and say this phrase and whoever does that God will forgive all his sins."[54] It also often promises the reciter *ejābat* (God's fulfillment of her request). Simin said, "*Mafatih* is viewed as being expressly for *bar avordan-e hājāt* [the realization of one's needs]." But *Sahifeh* is "these beautiful conversations with God" and for spiritual needs alone. It is characterized as "true niyayesh" because the reciter does not ask God for anything—she recites the lines without an eye to any reward or any exchange.

Elaheh, who was in her early-sixties at the beginning of my fieldwork, is from a well-known religious family. Her father, who is now deceased, was a highly respected translator of the Qur'an. She is a frequently invited speaker to many classes, in particular those on the Qur'an. Elaheh said, sarcastically, that these days, publishers "come up with the prayer book of Omm Davood,[55] Baba Aameleh . . . they just keep producing these books and pamphlets. . . . Who says you can learn anything from reading these?" She continued:

> Mafatih is too facile, it makes one's job too easy. It effectively says, "read this and you will be connected to God." It is being a true Muslim that is very difficult. And they have even planted some stuff in it like "tie such and such do'a to yourself if you want such and such." Recall the words of Ali Shari'ati on the Mafatih.

We return here again to the anxiety about what is in prayer books such as Mafatih al-Jinan. Elaheh uses the expression "planted" (kāshtan) to underline the problem of sanadiyyat and authenticity. According to her and many others, this planting is crucial because it can shape answers to the question of who is a true Muslim. Is it the compiler of Mafatih al-Jinan or is it one of the Imams who promises that if you recite such and such prayer thirty-four times, you will get your wishes? Could this not be planted in the text because the compiler wants to sell his book?

Such tejārat (doing business) with God is what many of these women are strongly against. Elaheh said:

> Once a man who was my father's student came to him for reading Hajj Mulla Hadi Sabzevari's Manzūmeh [Treatise] together. He told my father, who was on his way to Mashhad [where the shrine of Imam Reza is located], "Please take this ring and drop it into the inner shrine." My father said, "Can I give it to someone who needs it?" He then sold the ring and gave the money to a grocer in a neighborhood where he knew two university students whose fathers were farmers [that is, poor], as credit for their groceries.

Elaheh finished this story by saying, "You see, people just choose to do what is simpler. The man wants to use his ring as an offering to the eighth Imam so that he [the Imam] recommends him to God." Of course, those who cannot spare a ring are in the majority, and so in their case doing business with God would be an act such as reciting a prayer or a verse a certain number of times. Elaheh believes, "They tell you to read the *Mafatih* so that you won't go and read Saadi because it is Saadi [as opposed to *Mafatih al-Jinan*] who keeps you away from *khurāfāt* [superstition]."

Parvin told me, "I don't read the *Mafatih*, I think I need to first read the Qur'an. I don't even own a copy." She said that *Sahifeh* is superior to *Mafatih al-Jinan* in several ways:

> There are prayers from *Sahifeh Sajjadieh* that we listened to [on the radio] at dawn during the month of Ramazan when we were children. There was a dawn prayer that belonged to Imam Zein al-Ab-din. I think those kinds of do'a are maybe at the highest levels of 'erfan. . . . I read once through all of the prayers in *Sahifeh*; they are about morality and ethics and behavior and when you read these you ask yourself: higher than this [*bālātar az in*], what do you want? Within the confines of words, what is it you would like to express [more than this]?
>
> In my opinion the Imams are also *'aref* [mystics] . . . one cannot know them unless one reads everything they have written. We are not used to doing research. We must read and research and not accept everything. I now think this way: whatever is from our ancestors, from our past, I need to research it and explore it. I don't want to prejudge it but I also need to find out for myself.

One can see the success of attempts, recounted in the Introduction, to assimilate the Imams and their exemplary lives to the tradition of 'erfan. Many people routinely refer to Imams as 'aref, or mystics. Without knowledge of how this merging could have transpired, one is at first struck by this attribution. The edition of *Sahifeh Sajjadieh* that Parvin read and distributed is bilingual, and she has read the Persian translations more than the Arabic originals. As with other prayers written in Arabic, those who translate them into Persian make an effort to keep the poetic quality of the original. Parvin still reads some of the prayers because they are beautiful and because she likes their themes.

The rejection of *Mafatih al-Jinan* does not mean that the women refuse to go to female-only gatherings that use prayers from it. Very few of the women in our group and in fact very few of the women I know in general, even the ones who do not pray, avoid religious gatherings organized by family and friends due to their dislike of the prayer books used at such gatherings. If the text of the prayers they like happens to be included in *Mafatih al-Jinan* and they own a copy, then they will use it for those occasions. Here lie the multiple and simultaneous roles that women play in both the critique and the propagation of Shi'i liturgy.

Conclusion

In her analysis of medieval books of hours, Virginia Reinburg characterizes them as offering worship that was "individual and collective, private and public." They provided a "domestic link to the liturgy," allowing women a participatory role in Christian worship.[56] This latter point is crucial. Based on my fieldwork and that of Azam Torab carried out decades earlier on lower-middle-class women in Tehran,[57] prayer books are used by women across class lines, and even most ideological lines, to organize, plan, and perform various collective rites at home as primary actors. Mosques have historically been male-dominated spaces, and women rarely get a chance to play major roles in their functioning. As I mentioned, *Mafatih al-Jinan* and similar prayer books serve as movable mosques. They offer ideas about how to undertake religious acts that do not have to be performed inside a mosque. Several women said that although they do not like *Mafatih al-Jinan*, they like many things about the gatherings. They like getting together, cooking special kinds of food and sweets, setting the tablecloth on the floor, deciding who will recite what, and the like. There is a tremendous amount of creativity generated in these gatherings. For example, many ideas come into existence in the course of planning the gatherings, and there is much improvisation during the ceremonies. Deciding what one ought to cook, determining what kind of poetry should be recited or sung, inviting singer/reciters and (Sufi) musicians, and standing up at the end of the evening and holding hands while praying out loud are not practices that are written down anywhere. These were mentioned by the women as aspects of such gatherings that they particularly enjoyed. They find them exhilarating. Some of the ideas offered by prayer books get adapted for major gatherings, such as celebrations of the birth of the Prophet (*mowludi*) and also the births of other Imams, *nazr* gatherings called *sofreh* (literally, tablecloth) or *sofreh-ye nazr* (cloth of vows), and collective readings of the Qur'an and of certain prayers in regular monthly gatherings. Were it not for these gatherings—and let us remember that they have greatly proliferated in kind and frequency since the revolution, *Mafatih al-Jinan* might not have received as much attention.

Women have several effects on the kind of liturgy that is central to religious gatherings and celebrations and that is epitomized by *Mafatih al-Jinan*. While that book soared in popularity for a while after the revolution, it has now gone through multiple critiques from intellectuals, lay believers, and clerical scholars who have published their own prayer books. The role of women in shaping and diversifying Shi'i liturgy extends to the composition of devotional prose and poetry in Persian. As we saw previously, the most successful author of simple mysticism is the woman who wrote *Tea with a Taste of God*. She succeeded in publishing sixteen books in this genre between 1996 and 2013. But much of what is composed by women and recited in gatherings remains unpublished, though some works are published online. There are women who have founded 'erfan groups that have weekly classes, CDs, books, and videos of their founders reciting prayers and poetry available on their websites. A prime example of this trend among women is the well-known Haideh Khadem.[58]

What is the role of do'a in articulating the characteristics of a true Muslim? Eschewing all ideas of fazilat and religious merit, Elaheh believes that

> do'a is a spark [*jaraqqeh*]. We light a matchstick so that we can light a lamp with it. A do'a is a spark for good deeds. My father used to say, when you get in a car, say this prayer: "God protects you for He is the most merciful." But then he would add, saying this means that afterward, you do not honk, you don't go down a one-way street the wrong way.

As we saw, there are fundamental disagreements among the women in our group and among scholars and clerics such as Shari'ati, Sheikh Qomi, Ayatollah Makarem Shirazi, Ayatollah Javadi Amoli, and Ayatollah Kadivar. Moreover, a choice between Arabic and Persian is profoundly implicated in such debates. As ideas about prayers have changed and have come to be challenged in the decades since the revolution, the status of Persian as a language in which one can address God has been strengthened, as evidenced by recent prayer books that are exclusively in Persian; so have the multiple roles that women play in the realm of do'a. The idea that Arabic has a mysterious sacred quality fit for divinity and religion persists, but it is now being openly challenged.

A study of prayer books illuminates the ways in which the Qur'an is used as the prime book of do'a. The body of hadis that, since the reign of the Safavids in particular, has been researched, tended to, and grown,[59] continues to offer grounds for both inspiration and skepticism. What did such and such Imam say after all: to pray in order to obtain keys to heaven or to cultivate the inner self or to oppose oppressive regimes, as Shari'ati advocated? Or do we pray to find a path to God and tend to the construction of a relationship with Him and walk toward true Islam? The dominant position forged over the past few decades is that the path to follow is articulated by the Qur'an and the Imams and also by 'erfan whose eternal poets are the interpreters of scripture par excellence.

Conclusion

What comes to be defined as belonging to the realm of religion is treated by the believer as material to work with, to think about, and to imagine with. In that process, acts, rites, rituals, ideas, and beliefs do not remain untouched, unchanged, and unchallenged. Reading scripture, doing rituals, engaging in recommended ethical acts (*mostahabbāt*), conceptions of God and the quality of believers' relationship to Him, the obligatory and daily recitation of fixed forms such as *namāz* prayers, all these change in the hands and minds of the believer. They become transformed as one enters different stages of life into different communities and relationships and as the world changes. Such material becomes a source for ongoing internal dialogues as well as exchanges with others. Namaz in nineteenth-century Iran was likely thought of quite differently and performed differently from namaz at the present moment. Similarly, namaz at age twenty is unlike the experience at age seventy. As one's experience with namaz grows, one learns to practice it rather than repeat it.

The Qur'an is read, reflected upon, and puzzled through not by everyone but by many. Not every part of this text has received equal attention or gained equal popularity. At times, some parts are deliberately ignored and left unread because they are not found to be entirely comprehensible or maybe relevant. Several of the women told me that they skip some parts because they disagree with the content. In one of our last group discussions in the summer of 2015, Pari told us that she does her morning namaz whenever she wakes up:

> I do not think that I am obliged to pray [*muqayyad nistam*] in the morning, noon, and night five times, and to be frank, it has been years that I no longer have this belief [*bāvar*] because in general I

feel that it is me who has the need to pray; it is not the great God [*khoday-e bozorg*] that has any need for my praying. I like very much to begin my day, whenever I wake up, eight or five in the morning, to say *bi-ism allah al-rahman al-rahim* and do my namaz. When I sit in the bus, I have no need for doing the *vūzū* [ablutions]—"*hīch ādābi o tartibī majū, harcheh mikhāhad del-e tangat begū*" [Don't search for manners and rules, say whatever your longing heart desires].

We might remember this line of Rumi's from the Introduction. To explain why she does not follow the usual *adab* for doing namaz, Pari cites Rumi's verse spoken by Moses to the shepherd based on God's revelation to him. After the namaz, she recites from memory some of the *rabbina* prayers in the Qur'an. There are ten of them that she particularly likes. For example:

Lord, do not take us to task if we forget or make mistakes. Lord, do not burden us as You burdened those before us. Lord, do not burden us with more than we have strength to bear. Pardon us, forgive us, and have mercy on us. You are our Protector, so help us against the unbelievers [2:286].

When she began reciting this verse, the other women present joined in. This was a usual occurrence—once someone began reciting a prayer or a poem, others would quietly accompany the reciter and they would say it together. Pari, like many others, said that she loves this prayer in the Qur'an. However, she also explained:

Now look here, I have done a bit of *fūzūli* [playful intervention, nosiness, meddling] here in the *āya* of the Qur'an [*the others chuckle*]. Instead of saying, "so help us against the disbelievers," when I recite, I ask God to "help me *against my own malice*" [mixing Persian syntax with the original Arabic, she says], *Fa ansurna 'ala khubs-e tīnatī*. I put this phrase in because I say let's leave the poor *kāfar* [disbeliever] alone, what is it to me? I mean my own meanness is really here [*pointing to her heart*] and that is worse than unbelief.

I had never before come across this kind of fuzuli. In the ensuing discussion, most agreed that one's own meanness is a more substantial matter than someone else's unbelief. Here is a good example, one among many, of how religion has come to be reflected upon and debated among different groups of Muslim Iranians after the revolution. Some of the women were not sure about whether one should change the word of God and what the implications of that would be. Pari argued that she needs to tell God what *she* wants. She suggested that if we read the Qur'an in order to talk to God, understand Him, and construct a relationship with Him, then we should ask ourselves: "Who is speaking to whom? It is *me* who is asking God for what I want." She pointed out that she was reciting a prayer *addressed to God*, so she changed it according to what was in her heart. In this case, it matters little that the words are changed, though they are God's words. She is being sincere. And at the same time, the reciter herself is also an addressee so that a back-and-forth routinely develops in working with religious material and it becomes an internal (and in this case external) dialogue.

Most of these women own several different translations of the Qur'an, as was mentioned in previous chapters. The increasing number of people who spend time reading the Qur'an systematically, carefully, and regularly while comparing different translations has resulted in laypeople having favorite translators. They are able to argue about why one is better than the other. There are at times vast differences in style and choices of terminology. The women bring these together with recent interpretations broadcast on radio and television and evaluate them.

It is instructive to look at a page of a Qur'an owned by Elaheh (see Figure C.1). On the pages of another Qur'an, she had used a highlighter as well. Many of these women's Qur'ans have markings and comments written in the margins, sometimes just a note to explain a word to themselves. But the fact that the Qur'an comes to be treated in this way by a non-cleric and nonexpert shows the degree to which religion has become an object of reflection for many people since the revolution.

It would not be reasonable to suggest that the ideas and practices of these women are shared by a majority of Iranian Muslims. But their cases illustrate some of the specific ways in which Iranian society currently grapples with questions of religion. A crucial example of this grappling is the daily performance of ritual prayers, namaz. From the outside, this ritual appears to constitute the quintessence of a rote and mindless act.

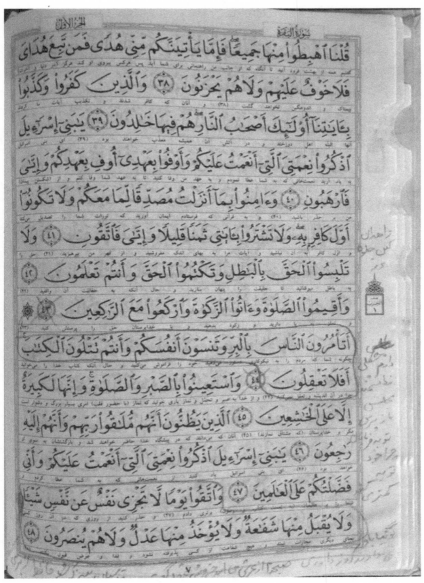

FIGURE C.1. A page of Elaheh's Qur'an. Photo by the author.

Iranian Muslims largely recite the same verses from the Qur'an in Arabic—a language that a majority do not know well—and they "repeat" these verses five times a day, day after day after day over decades. How could these verses—even if those reciting them did somehow understand Qur'anic Arabic, and even if they were choosing nonroutine verses—not lose their meaning and become rote after a while?

In Chapter 2, I showed in detail how false this appearance is. First, these Qur'anic verses are being recited not read, and hence the relationship that is built with this oral text over time is not predicated exclusively or even primarily on what the form "says." The forms are fixed but not the imaginations and the daily contexts of the reciters, whose ideas, queries, needs, and moods are in flux. In ritual recitations, there is no necessary or constant relationship between form and content, as just discussed. Furthermore, my interlocutors view namaz as communication with God. They use the words that are the verses of the Qur'an—hence God's language—to tell Him what *they* want to say. The fixity of the forms and the fact that the women are not the authors of the words do not limit the content of this communication. When they succeed in telling God what they want to say, they create what they call a presence in the space of this worship; they achieve co-presence with the divine. This is considered to be a "good namaz." Contrary to the prevalent (secularist) view that religious rituals are repeated—that they are copies of copies—and that one performance is like any other, the fact that these women tell God many different things while using the words of the Qur'anic suras shows clearly that this ritual is practiced, though of course it might at times end up as a "bad" or mindless session. Performers come to see rituals as sites for all kinds of queries, puzzles, and articulations of goals and desires. These might change daily. Crucially, when someone begins the recitation of namaz, or any other ritual for that matter, she does not and cannot know in advance how that particular practice session will go and where it will end in terms of her emotions and her experience. One cannot know whether one's concentration will hold, whether one will create a presence, or whether one will feel *hāl*. What Pari said about changing a word in a Qur'anic verse to be able to express what she wants is in some ways similar to what happens in the course of the recitation of namaz.

There is an interaction with a fixed text, and the reciter reflects on what she actually wants to say to God.

Language and ritual both precede the subject, but at some point, in ways that are not entirely clear, individuals make their own connection to these structures. Speakers of the same language all end up finding their own presence in the signifier with various degrees of success. No two speakers of the same language sound exactly alike. Similarly, with rituals, believers understand, articulate, and practice them and find connections to them that change over time and are rarely exact copies of what they have been taught. And practices and reflections do not remain the same throughout an individual's life. Ethnographies of rituals such as namaz contribute to an understanding of how an imponderable variety of individuals at different stages of their lives make a ritual their own.

Religious ideas and practices are almost always subjects of complex exchanges between the self and various communities of believers who as individuals might disagree on any number of matters relating to such practices. Hence, even those who do not frequent mosques and who perform most of their prayers at home are fully aware of other discourses and are in dialogue and at times sharp disagreement with them. Not only has the home become a quasi-public space after the revolution, due to restrictions on various kinds of gatherings, there are many communities to which these women belong—in particular, the various classes they regularly attend. Using the rather vague concepts of the public and the private to speak of different kinds of Islam and of religious appropriation does not shed light on the complexity of the simultaneous agentic deliberations that are going on. This is in particular the case in the context of Iran, where religion has become an object of scrutiny in the public sphere.

A good namaz requires concentration (*tamarkoz*), sincerity (*kholūs*), and presence of the heart (*hozūr-e qalb*). In the case where the reciter's mind wanders, there is disagreement between some clerics and among lay believers about the value of such a namaz—whether it will have its intended transformative effect in honing one's ethical approach to the world (though the legal validity of namaz does not depend on such factors). The discipline of namaz is first and foremost meant to make a better person out of the believer, one who does not lie, cheat, or take what is not hers.

The postrevolutionary revisiting of religion and the sharp debates that have ensued have greatly lessened the distinction between the elite (*kha-was*) and the laity. This has also led to questioning the need for clerics in mediating believers' relationships to the creator.

What intervenes in the thinking that a certain kind of religious practice is good enough for the majority, and that the mere performance of a ritual obligation can make for a true Muslim (among other things), is the centuries-old presence of *'erfān* theorization in the form of classical poetry about experiences of the divine. In Chapter 1, I offered an ethnography of how this poetry is encountered from childhood, both at home and school. It is through this poetry that one learns the value of avoiding turning religious acts into mere duties. And it is also this poetry that teaches about the dreadfulness of pretended piety, religious hypocrisy, and the supreme value of hal. It encourages reflection on the value of religious acts, or any act in fact, that is done in and with the thought of God. Hal teaches one that the value of doing religious acts is in an unmediated relationship and connection to the divine that is spontaneous and unaffected by searching for "manners and rules."

The work of prayers and poems that come to be much loved over decade after decade of one's life and that evoke strong emotions on being heard or recited cannot be explained with analyses that focus on their meaning or a "full understanding" alone. Semiotic analyses depend on the material availability of some linguistic form to be analyzed. But linguistic forms evoke particular voices and memories. Their sounds are embodied. These "presences" are not easily available for ethnographic observation. It would be like saying that the relationship individuals make with an old architectural structure in their town is entirely understandable based on an art history approach to studying its formal features. I argued in Chapter 1 that while semiotic analyses are necessary, they are far from sufficient for grasping the reason why certain texts have such sway, and remain vital and beloved for centuries.

I began this book with the larger question of what we mean when we say someone is religious. I hope to have shown that understanding religiosity requires detailed empirical research. An Islamic government with a desire to Islamize all aspects of private and public life has served as the major spur toward the production of debates about religion and divinity. 'Erfan poetry, with its challenges to visible piety and dry religion, has offered lay believers the concepts and vocabulary to challenge legalistic approaches to prayer and to religion more generally. The increasing presence of 'erfan has created a fundamentally paradoxical situation for the Islamic republic: for centuries, the visibility of public acts in the service of religion has been articulated as a sign of *riyā* (insincerity) in this poetry. Visible signs are not to be trusted, yet for women wearing a headscarf is obligatory, even if they are not believers. The republic, founded by a cleric who wrote 'erfan poetry, has become increasingly caught in the contradictions of its wishes. Insincerity is institutionalized through such laws.

I end this book with the words of Parvin. She described how, when she was thirteen, she began having her "first why questions" (*avvalin cherā-hā*). She was particularly concerned about the existence of so much inequality around her. She said that the first couplet she learned was from the eleventh-century poet Baba Taher Oryan:

> If I could reach the celestial wheel
> I'd ask why is this like that
> You have given some one hundred blessings
> And others, bread drowned in blood[1]

Parvin continued:

> I heard later that God got angry at Oryan for this poem, but I don't believe it. I don't think God gets angry at questions. Baba Taher was an *'ārif* [mystic] and this is what he thought. Is it not the case that we come into this world to gain *ma'refat* [gnosis] and wisdom [*shu'ūr*]? By asking this question, he was walking toward knowledge. We say that Islam, and Muslim, mean that one must have a head bowed in submission [*sar-e taslīm*]. But if we want to submit, then how can we ask questions and how can we learn? Are we to just say yes, right, to whatever they tell us is our true religion? No, I don't think so.

Inside and outside Iran, there is tremendous cynicism and pessimism about the direction of the revolution and about the ruling elites in the various organs of state. Reasons for this pessimism are not lacking.

Repression, coercion, and corruption continue, with ebbs and flows, four decades after the uprisings that led to the downfall of the Pahlavi regime. But simultaneously, the revolution has led to a rethinking of and deeper reflection on fundamental questions about religion. The challenges of the dilemmas that individuals face under a regime that attempts to coerce everyone to be a believer have had and continue to have profound implications for the present and future of the country. It has been a religious education on a mass scale. In this respect, the revolution has not been a failure. There are groups that follow what some state authorities tell them, and they foster ideas and practices that represent what is called, as we have seen, a Shari'a-minded, legalistic Islam. But alongside these there are many others, such as the group of women we have heard from in this book, who continue to hang on to religion while simultaneously striving to question and debate Islam beyond questions of obligation and regulation. Analyses of Iranian society that ignore this maturing of reflections on religion miss a great deal. They tend to see only the regime and the opposition to it, both painted in monochromatic terms. Iranian society is said to be made of up of those who are hopelessly fanatical about religion and those who oppose the fanatical regime. But as I have tried to show, there is a great deal of questioning and discussion that is nourished and sustained spiritually, intellectually, and aesthetically by the vitality of public debates. What true Islam is continues to be debated. It seems unlikely that this debate will suddenly come to an end from some kind of resolution. What has been learned by laypeople as a result of the theological education of the last few decades will not vanish even if the moment of debate might pass owing to the imposition of limitations on the public sphere in Iran.

Glossary

ā = aa

ū = uu

ī = ii

adab	Inner and outer refinement and conduct; a highly valued cultural elaboration of cultivating one's character in ethics and aesthetics.
ādāb	Ways, manners, etiquette.
akhlāq	Ethics, temperament, behavior.
'ārif	Mystic.
āya	Qur'anic verse (*āyeh*, in Persian pronunciation).
azān	Call to prayer.
do'ā	Prayer.
dolla rāst	Going through the motions of prayer, without sincerity.
'ebādat (pl. *ebādāt*)	Worship, ritual.
ehtiyāt	Caution.
'erfān	Mysticism, Sufism.
esqāt-e taklīf	Getting a (religious) obligation done.
fazīlat	Virtue, merit.
hāl	A complex mystical concept that is meant to capture the presence of the divine. It may occur to the wayfarer as a sudden feeling of ecstasy or profound sadness.

harām	Religiously forbidden.
jā-namāz	Prayer cloth.
kholūs	Sincerity.
khotbeh	Sermon.
Masnavi-e Ma'avī	A six-volume work by Rumi that contains hundreds of stories, often told in dialogue form, that are meant to teach the principles of love and devotion to God, of the mystic ways. It has been referred to as the Qu'ran in Persian. The title is frequently translated as "Couplets of True Meaning," though it could also be translated as "Spiritual Stories."
monājāt	Whispered or intimate prayers.
moshā'ereh	Poetry contest.
mostahabb (pl. *mostahabbāt*)	A religiously recommended act that makes the individual favored in God's eyes.
namāz	Obligatory prayer made up of Qur'anic verses.
niyāyesh	Prayer; a term used by Zoroastrians and Muslims. Usually a prayer of praise.
niyyāt	Intention.
qahr karden	To initiate a rupture in one's relationship with a friend or family member or with God.
qāl	What is said (from Arabic *q-ā-l-a*, "to say").
qasideh	An ancient form of poetry—an ode, usually a praise poem.
qonūt	Extra and voluntary prayer added to namaz.
rak'at	A prayer cycle in namaz.
rokūu'	Bending and placing one's hands on one's knees, in prayer.

sajjādeh   Prayer rug.

salāt   The Arabic name for ritual prayer (namaz).

sojūd   Prostration in prayer.

sūra   A chapter of the Qur'an (sūreh in Persian
                    pronunciation).

tavāf   Circumambulation, for example, around the
                    House of God (Kaaba) in Mecca.

vājeb   Religiously required act, an obligation.

zikr   Remembrance, a form of prayer to put one in the
                    thought of God.

Notes

1. See, for example, Adelkhah, *Being Modern in Iran.*

2. Behrooz Ghamari-Tabrizi explains this quite well in his book *Islam and Dissent in Postrevolutionary Iran.*

3. Ibid., 83; emphasis added.

4. See Ilahi-Ghomshei, "Principles of the Religion of Love in Persian Poetry," 77.

5. Khorramshahi, *Divan-e Hafez,* 118–19. I have slightly changed the original Persian; using fewer synonyms to make the English more readable.

6. Although his actions as the Supreme Leader of Iran stood in contradiction to these facts, Ayatollah Khomeini spoke about presence of the heart and about there being as many ways to reach God as the number of our breaths, and he wrote poems intended to be mystical and using the symbolic vocabulary of wine and the lover.

7. Given the relative absence of theological debates in the public sphere in Europe and the United States over the last few decades, one might ask whether it takes a revolution for such debates to occur. I would argue that in the United States, for example, many Christian denominations have been formed due to the availability of a legal infrastructure for such groups and their acceptability. But the state in Iran, before and after the revolution, has not allowed and does not now allow splinter groups who disagree with one another on theological grounds to form separate denominations. The legalization and ease of forming denominations is a double-edged sword. On the one hand, the freedom to form one's own sect allows for fresh inquiries that may otherwise be stifled by the larger group. But, on the other hand, actual theological debates often then move out of the public sphere. Whereas the political stakes of disagreements between established religions on the one hand and cults and new religions on the other may attract media attention, the theological stakes are not high because neither the state nor the church is imposing religion coercively. The debates in Iran have become existential because the state claims both religious and political power. Among the Muslim population, everyone is a "Shi'a" with a small, equally undifferentiated minority of "Sunnis." Certainly, there are many different kinds of Shi'as and Sunnis, but they are formally and legally uniform. There are also Sufi groups with their own leaders, histories, and practices, though after the death of Ayatollah Khomeini they have been increasingly harassed and silenced. But the fact that one cannot simply split off and go one's own way means, among other things, that debates over theological differences are kept alive in the public sphere.

8. From Arabic *'awām.*

9. Bilingual Qur'ans have been around for centuries, but the desire to participate in debates has pushed many Iranians to spend time actually reading at least parts of the

Qu'an so that they can have their input into conversations about Qur'anic interpretation.

10. See Shahab Ahmed's trenchant critique of scholars who represent Islam in this way for all times and places, in *What Is Islam?* 117–29. On the importance of ambiguity and ambivalence in "human and historical Islam," see 36–46.

11. Ibid., 120.

12. On the history of translations of the Qur'an into Persian, see Zadeh, *Vernacular Qur'an*; on Arabic language ideology, see Haeri, *Sacred Language, Ordinary People*.

13. Asad, "The Idea of an Anthropology of Islam."

14. See, for example, Amanat, *Iran: A Modern History*; Katouzian, *The Persians*; and Atabaki, *Iran in the 20th Century*.

15. See Anzali, *"Mysticism" in Iran*, for an explanation of how the term *'erfan* came to be preferred to *Sufi*. I follow his usage.

16. Doostdar, *Iranian Metaphysicals*.

17. For general information about Rumi, see "Rumi, Jalāl-al-Din," *Encyclopædia Iranica,* http://www.iranicaonline.org/articles/rumi-jalal-al-din-parent.

18. For the history of cultural centers (*farhang-sara*), see the website of the Cultural and Artistic Organization of the Municipality of Tehran, www.farhangsara.ir (in Persian).

19. See Mojaddedi, "Rumi, Jalāl-al-Din viii," *Encyclopædia Iranica*, http://www.iranicaonline.org/articles/rumi-jalal-al-din-teachings. Abdolkarim Soroush, a prominent religious intellectual and a prolific author, with his own website in English and Persian, has presented lectures on the *Masnavi* at many American universities, including Harvard University; some of these lectures are accessible on YouTube. He has also published an edition of the *Masnavi*.

20. Attributed to Nur al-Din Abdel Rahman Jami (1414–1492). See Ahmed, *What Is Islam?*, 307.

21. For this summary, I use various translations, including my own, as indicated in the following notes.

22. Arasteh, *Rumi the Persian, the Sufi*, 144.

23. Rumi, *This Longing*, 19–22.

24. Ibid.

25. Rumi, *Rumi: Swallowing the Sun*, 16–18.

26. My translation.

27. Coleman Barks has translated these lines as: "Say whatever and however your loving tells you to / Your sweet blasphemy / Is the truest devotion" (Rumi, *Essential Rumi*, 167).

28. For a brief excerpt from the opera, composed and performed by the Mastan and Homay group, see "Moses and the Shepherd," YouTube, July 10, 2010, https://www.youtube.com/watch?v=w6JNXHOTi20.

29. Avery, "Foreword: Hafiz of Shiraz," xiii. *Hafiz and the Religion of Love*, xv.

30. Perry, "New Persian," 90.

31. *Rumi: Swallowing the Sun*, 16–18. One could say that these verses' acceptance of many languages is inspired by the Qur'an itself, in whose pages there is no injunction to read it exclusively in Arabic, contrary to much writing that characterizes the holy book with such orthodoxy.

32. See Farrell, "Latinate Tradition as a Point of Reference"; and also Yarshater, "Ventures and Adventures of the Persian Language."

33. The book was translated into English in 2017. See Zarrinkoub, *Two Centuries of Silence*.

34. al-Qushayri, *Epistle on Sufism*; al-Hujweri, *Kashful Mahjub*. For more recent

writing, see Zarrinkoub, *Jostejoo dar Tasavoff-e Iran*. For writings in English, see, among many other works, Sells, *Early Islamic Mysticism*; and Nasr, *Islamic Philosophy from Its Origin to the Present*. For a brief source in English, see *Encylopædia Iranica*; for a source in Persian, see Wikifeqh.

35. Although the concept of hal and the concept of "real presence" in Catholicism are not the same, there are some intriguing overlaps. Hal is viewed as an indication of the presence of the divine, similar to the real presence of God in the Host. In both cases, the clergy dislike the fact that they are unable to control it. As historian of religion Robert Orsi states, "This is the Church's problem with the real presence: controlling access to it. Such control is one of the surest grounds of ecclesiastical and political power, not only over the laity but over the rulers of nations, too. Yet presence continually exceeds the Church's efforts to contain it." Orsi, *History and Presence*, 2.

36. Setad-e Iqam-e Namaz-e Keshvar [National organization of namaz], accessed January 8, 2020, http://namaz.ir.

37. In modern Arabic vernaculars, the sound "th," as in English *nothing*, no longer exists. *Hadith* in classical Arabic has that sound, but in modern vernaculars and in Persian, the word is *hadis*, with an *s*.

38. Losensky, "Sa'di," *Encyclopædia Iranica*, http://www.iranicaonline.org/articles/sadi-sirazi. It should also be noted that Saadi, Rumi, and Hafez are not viewed as representing uniform understandings of what it means to be an ethical and true Muslim. However, insofar as Qara'ati is concerned, that is less important than the idea that they could be guides to Muslims.

39. "Hafez," in *Encyclopædia Iranica*, http://www.iranicaonline.org/articles/hafez.

40. See Asriran news item 282342, accessed October 6, 2015, www.asriran.com; also see Javann, accessed October 6, 2015, https://www.Javann.ir/002hYt.

41. "Naqd-e Shi'r-e Mowlavi Tavasott-e Hojjat al-Islam Qara'ati," https://www.aparat.com/v/io8Zw/; and also "Moosa va Shaban beh Qara'at-e Mohsen Qara'ati," http://www.bbc.com/persian/blogs/2014/05/140507 _ l44_nazeran_gheraati_masnavi.

42. "Younesi va tada'i ma'ani sokhanan-e masha'i," https://www.tasnimnews.com/fa/news/1393/02/14/358505/.

43. For a comparative study of sincerity in denominations of Christianity, Judaism, and Islam, see Haeri, "Sincere Subject." The discussion is inspired by the work of Webb Keane in his book *Christian Moderns*.

44. It was recently reported that some of the most popular 20th-century poets and authors, such as Nima Yushij, Medhdi Akahavan-Sales, and Houshang Ebtehaj, and even the classical poet Khayyam, are being eliminated from textbooks. Although so far it does not seem to be the case that most classical poets are being removed, much was written in the media about the possibility of doing so in the near future. See "Intiqad az Hazf-e Nam-e Bozorgan-e Adabiyat-e Iran," https://www.bbc.com/persian/iran-50311057.

45. For recent work on mysticism in Iran, in addition to Anzali's *"Mysticism" in Iran* cited earlier, see Ahoo Najafian's "Poetic Nation" (2018), which focuses on Hafez and argues that Iranians' self-understandings are "uniquely associated with poetic and mystical" traditions "epitomized" by Hafez. Seema Golestaneh's "The Social Life of Gnosis" (2014) examines mysticism beyond literature and poetry and how it is "reconfigured" in everyday life.

46. "Rābete-ye Ma'navi beyn-e 'āshiq va Ma'shūq" [The spiritual relationship between the lover and the beloved], Wikifeqh, May 22, 2017, http://www.wikifeqh.ir/%D8%A2%D8%AF%D8%A7%D8%A8_%D8%AF%D8%B9%D8%A7.

47. Relative to studies of ritual acts in Islam, there is far less writing on do'a in Western social scientific literature. Muslim subjectivity is routinely defined in terms of ritual, obligatory duties as articulated in legal writings. In Iran, however, there is a fairly large body of theological writing on do'a that continues to the present. To cite only two of the more recent writings: see Khomeini, *Sirr al-Salat*; and Shabestari, *Naqd Bunyadha-yi Fiqh va Kalam*.

48. The distinction dates back to the time of Reza Shah, who in 1928 established Uniformity of Clothes laws and forbade men, with some exceptions, to wear turbans and robes (what most wore at the time). They had to appear in public in hats and European suits.

49. Dinani is an expert on the renowned Shahab al-Din Suhrawardi, the founder of the School of Illuminationism (in the 12th century). See Dinani's personal website: Gholamhossein Ebrahimi Dinani: Filsoof va Andishmand-e Irani [Iranian philosopher and thinker], accessed August 28, 2019, https://ebrahimi-dinani.com.

50. On how this program came to be, see "Ravayat-e Mansoori Larijani Darbare-ye Dinani," https://philosophyar.net/interview-withmansoori-larijani. For reports that he had spoken favorably of this dance, see "Ezharat-e Dinani darbare-ye Raqs-e Arefaneh va Fatva-ye Maraji' Taqlid dar Radd va Takhta'e-ye ān" [What Dinani said about mystic dance and the fatwas of sources of emulation in their rejection], https://www.mashreghnews.ir/news/119654/%D8%A7%D8%A8%D9%87%D8%.

51. The verse continues: "[It is] the work of Allah, who perfected all things. Indeed, He is Acquainted with that which you do" (Qur'an 27:88), https://quran.com/27/88.

52. Setrag Manoukian makes this point as well in *City of Knowledge in Twentieth Century Iran*.

53. Mujtahed Shabestari was unable to publish his last major work in print, so he published it on his website. It comes to just under 700 pages, spans a wide variety of topics, and includes two essays on Rumi (pp. 59 and 65), where he refers to the *Masnavi* as Rumi's "reading of the world," meaning Rumi's interpretation of the world. Shabestrari, *Naqd Bunyadha-eh Fiqh va Kalam*, http://mohammadmojtahedshabestari.com/1282-2.

54. Youssefzadeh, "Situation of Music in Iran since the Revolution." Music continues to be controversial and hotly contested. For example, a sole female voice is banned from the media unless the performer sings in a private venue for a female-only audience. For this reason, a number of popular singers have had to leave Iran.

55. See Haeri, "Sincere Subject."

56. See for example, Nasr, *Three Muslim Sages*.

57. Moore, "Friendship and the Cultivation of Religious Sensibilities." See also Furey, "Body, Society, and Subjectivity in Religious Studies"; and Orsi, *History and Presence*, where he speaks about the religious subject who does not face God and religion alone but who is "accompanied."

CHAPTER ONE

1. *Masnavi*, Book 1, in Rumi, *Rumi: Swallowing the Sun*, 34.

2. In Persian, *bar jānam neshast*.

3. For a recitation of this poem, accompanied by a ney, see "Persian Poem (Molavi/Beshno as ney)," YouTube, April 12, 2015, https://www.youtube.com/watch?v=X68AGcXgPt4.

4. For historical views, see Spooner and Hanaway, *Literacy in the Persianate World*; and Ahmed, *What Is Islam?*

5. Smith, "Religion, Religions, Religious." Also see the introductory chapter of Shahab

Ahmed's *What Is Islam?* which offers a welcome exploration of the boundaries of Islam versus any local cultures; Asad, *Genealogies of Religion*; and Orsi, *History and Presence*.

6. Anthropologist Michael Jackson's essays on how religiosity is not necessarily dependent on religious institutions, texts, or doctrines and his use of poetry in sketching this argument ethnographically around the world is inspiring. Jackson, "The Palm at the End of the Mind."

7. Similar to *beyt bāzi* among Urdu speakers.

8. Eliot, "The Love Song of J. Alfred Prufrock," https://www.poetryfoundation.org/poetrymagazine/poems/44212/the-love-song-of-j-alfred-prufrock.

9. Simms and Koushkani, *Art of Avaz and Mohammad Reza Shajarian*, 144.

10. In the summer of 2012, I watched a television series called *Mosha'ereh Tabestani* [Summer poetry contest]. See *Mosha'ereh*, Channel 7, accessed June 18, 2019, http://tv7.ir/portal/iribprogramsinfo/%D9%85%D8%B4%D8%A7%D8%B9%D8%B1%D9%87.

11. Hanaway, "Amīr Arsalān," *Encyclopædia Iranica*, http://www.iranicaonline.org/articles/amir-arsalan-a-prose-romance-of-the-genre-dastanha-ye-ammiana-popular-tales.

12. See Metcalf, *Moral Conduct and Authority*; and Hamid Dabashi, *World of Persian Literary Humanism*.

13. See Fischer and Abedi. *Debating Muslims*; and Ahmed, *What Is Islam?*

14. She divorced her husband shortly after she married, and never had children. She wrote a number of poems about the emotional lives of mothers and their children.

15. Parvin E'tesami, *Nightingale's Lament*, 114.

16. It was hard to locate a translation of this poem; I found these few lines on the web page *Prophet Moses* (AS)—Part 1, http://eram.shirazu.ac.ir/www2/CD1/www.iua-net.org/Books/Stories_of_Prophets/moses1.htm.

17. Kadkani, *Ba Cheraq va Ayne* [With light and mirror], 459–65. The author also notes the writings of those who doubted her talents and denigrated her work.

18. See also Moayyed, *Once a Dew Drop*.

19. Far more has been written on her than on Etesami. See, e.g., Farrokhzad, *Literary Biography with Unpublished Letters*. Also see Farrokhzad, *Sin*; and Hillman, *A Lonely Woman*. Her influence on the women in our group came much later in their lives but, surprisingly, her name did not come up in our discussions.

20. Mirhadi, *Ta'sir Madares Dokhtaraneh dar Towse'eh Ijtima'i Zanan dar Iran*; Farsani, *Asnadi az Madares Dukhtaran az Mashruteh ta Pahlavi*. See also Rostam-Kolayi, "Origins of Iran's Modern Girls' Schools"; and Rostam-Kolayi, "From Evangelizing to Modernizing Iranians." I thank Jasamin Rostam-Kolayi for lending me two of these studies.

21. The first group of women who received their degrees from Harvard University graduated in 1963. Women became full members at Oxford University in the 1920s.

22. Birašk, "Education," *Encyclopædia Iranica*, http://www.iranicaonline.org/articles/education-x-middle-and-secondary-schools.

23. Only men who could convince the authorities of their religious education and get permission could continue to wear turbans and robes. Many men gave up. They were obliged to wear European suits, leather belts, leather shoes, and a hat that the Shah himself designed, called the Pahlavi hat, later replaced by felt hats imported from Europe. See, for example, Atabaki and Zurcher, *Men of Order*; Lindisfarne-Tapper and Ingham, *Languages of Dress in the Middle East*; Chehabi, "Staging the Emperor's New Clothes"; and Chehabi, "The Imam as Dandy."

24. Jewish and Zoroastrian friends from Yazd pointed this out to me. Upper-class women who had spent time in Europe, or for whom European clothes had been brought

to Iran, did appear in public with hats and long coats even before the ban, so this behavior was not entirely unheard of.

25. See the wonderful collection of photographs gathered by the Harvard University project Women's Worlds in Qajar Iran. Accessed May 17, 2020, http://search.qajarwomen.org/search?lang=en&filter=genres_en:photographs.

26. Amin, *Making of the Modern Iranian Woman*. I searched for studies and data on women in public life during the 1950s and 1960s and was unable to find any. In an email exchange with Camron Amin, he confirmed that most historical studies of Iran, including those that focus on women, stop around the late 1940s.

27. Amin, *Making of the Modern Iranian Woman*, 3.

28. The excitement about the possibilities for public life and the many kinds of social activities they could engage in was still clear in their voices when they discussed those decades of their lives. Speaking about her high school days, Mina said proudly: "At that time, my high school had many societies [*anjuman*], we had the Literature Society, the Journalism Society, and so on. I was a member of the Literature Society. . . . In any case, this wonderful teacher we had, God rest his soul, really established the foundations of our training in literature. This was in the seventh, eighth, and ninth grades." Mina also said that her school took theater seriously, and the students put on major plays, including those of Shakespeare. Looking back, the women seemed incredulous at "how good" their public schools were when they were growing up. Mina went on to say, "Unlike now, almost all our teachers were men and they were pretty good. . . . Our physics teacher was the famous Mr. Mirforoushan. Imagine that at that time he taught us the theory of light [*mabhaseh nur*], and then once I got to high school I knew it so well I did not need to be taught again."

29. Schayegh, *Who Is Knowledgeable Is Strong*.

30. See Breyley and Fatemi, *Iranian Music and Popular Entertainment*. To listen to Marzieh go to "Marzieh," YouTube video, July 17, 2010, https://www.youtube.com/watch?v=JUI_993Vlmw&list=RDJUI_993Vlmw&t=5; Bauer, "Marzieh," https://www.britannica.com/biography/Marzieh.

31. Delkash: A Dream of Sound, http://delkashmusic.tripod.com. See also Naficy, *A Social History of Iran*, vol. 2, 211. To listen to Delkash, go to "Vigen & Delkash-Bordi A Yadam," YouTube video, October 2, 2008, https://www.youtube.com/watch?v=nOEpJWF8LMo.

32. Thanks to the efforts of Jane Lewisohn, all programs are archived online. See the Golha website, accessed January 8, 2020, http://www.golha.co.uk.

33. Simms and Koushkani, *Art of Avaz and Mohammad Reza Shajarian*, 145.

34. Pirnia, with Nakjavani, "Golhā, Barnāma-ye," *Encyclopædia Iranica*, http://www.iranicaonline.org/articles/golha-barnama-ye.

35. In his study of poetry in a Yemeni tribe, Steven Caton writes at length about the "soft power" and the "verbal persuasion" that poetry achieves among the tribes in settling disputes. Caton, *"Peaks of Yemen I Summon."*

36. Abu-Lughod, *Veiled Sentiments*, 241.

37. The *Encyclopædia Iranica* defines *ghazal* as follows: "Persian love poetry is mostly embodied in a verse form called *ḡazal*, a short lyric poem of some seven to fourteen lines. The unit of gazal, as in most other forms of Persian poetry, is a line (*beyt*), which consists of two hemistiches (*mesrāʾs*) with a distinct caesura between the two. As a rule, each line contains a complete statement; sometimes the entire poetic statement is contained in one hemistich, and the second hemistich is then used to either emphasize the idea expressed in the first hemistich, or reiterate it in a different way, or illustrate it, or to introduce a new

idea, or else as mere padding to complete the meter." Yarshater, "*Ḡazal* ii. Characteristics and Conventions," http://www.iranicaonline.org/articles/gazal-2.

38. Davis, "Sufism and Poetry." Ghazals usually have between seven to fourteen lines. Each line can have a separate theme and does not have to be related to the one after it. The hemistiches are short, and hence syntax does not get a chance to play a big role.

39. Lewisohn, "Religion of Love and the Puritans of Islam," 176–77.

40. Puett and Gross-Loh, *The Path*, 132–33.

41. Ahmed, *What Is Islam?*, 340–42. He makes the point, as have others, that the centrality of classical poetry stands also for the whole of the "Balkans to Bengal complex" (see p. 18). By using this term, Ahmed calls attention to geographies that are often ignored in the popular imagination and often even in academic works that link Islam only to Arabic-speaking countries or to the Middle East. He calls lands that show the great influence of Islamic mysticism and the Persian language in the form of their poetry (and songs) "the Balkans to Bengal complex," which includes Bosnia-Herzegovina, Turkey, Iran, Central Asia, Afghanistan, North India, and the Bay of Bengal.

42. From Arabic *wasf al-hal*.

43. This is taken from one of the better translations of Saadi. See Saadi, *Selections from Saadi's Gulistan*, 21.

44. All men and women are to each other
the limbs of a single body, each of us drawn
from life's shimmering essence, God's perfect pearl;
and when this life we share wounds one of us,
all share the hurt as if it were our own.
You, who will not feel another's pain,
no longer deserve to be called human.
Translated by Richard Jeffrey Newman (unpublished).

45. I accompanied her to her poetry and Qur'an classes. Both classes met in private homes, and all attendees were adult women, but the teacher of the Qur'an class was a man in his mid-fifties.

46. Kermani, *God Is Beautiful*, vii.

47. Kermani also describes the importance of the aesthetic reception of the Qur'an: "Turning to Islam, however, we encounter an odd paradox: Islam's aesthetic dimension is of central importance to the Muslim self-image, if only because the Muslim Prophet's greatest—and, according to many theologians, his only—confirmatory miracle is the beauty and perfection of the Quranic language; yet, at the same time, the aesthetic dimension has hardly figured at all in the Western view of Islam, art historians' research aside. Hardly any academic writer would deny that Muslims experience the Quran aesthetically—as a poetically structured text and as a musical recitation—and that the reception of the scripture as an aesthetic phenomenon is one of the essential components of Islamic religious practice, at least in the Arabic speaking world. Nonetheless, although the aesthetic reception of the Quran is so important and obvious, it has never been proportionately reflected in Oriental studies. . . . The limited resonance of such efforts is evident not least in the fact that general descriptions of Islam as a rule still completely ignore the importance of aesthetic considerations within the Muslim religious world." Kermani, *God Is Beautiful*, vii.

48. Nafisi, "Introduction"; emphasis added.

49. Meskoob, *Iranian National Identity and the Persian Language*, 50.

50. Ibid., 171.

51. In the table of contents, the last page is stated to be page 207, but the actual last page is numbered 205.

52. Translated by Franklin Lewis in Rumi, *Rumi: Swallowing the Sun*, 34–36 (emphasis in the original).

53. "Zabaneh Farsi" [The Persian language], http://www.wikifeqh.ir/%D8%B2%D8%A8%D8%A7%D9%86_%D9%81%D8%A7%D8%B1%D8%B3%DB%8C.

54. Andrew Bush makes a similar point in his study of Sufi poetry in Kurdistan. See Bush "Offer of Pleasure," 517.

55. Ferdinand de Saussure's conception of language as *langue*, the abstract system, and *parole*, the actual speech of individual speakers, does not make mention of the fact that we hear *parole* in actual voices; it cannot exist without being attached, as it were, to particular voices. The question then becomes, what are the implications of this for analyzing the complex interactions between linguistic and cultural practices?

56. Other important scholars have articulated the idea of presence in distinct terms: for example, Mikhail Bakhtin in many of his works, including the essay "Discourse in the Novel." Walter Benjamin, in his essay "The Storyteller," speaks of presence in this way: "The storyteller's traces cling to a story the way traces of the potter's hand cling to a clay bowl" (56).

57. de Certeau, *Practice of Everyday Life*, 137. I see a connection between this idea and Emile Benveniste's elaboration of Saussure's idea of the sign. Benveniste asks us not to forget that between the signifier and the concept, there is also the "thing itself" out there in the world. See Benveniste, *Problems in General Linguistics*.

58. Barthes, *Mourning Diary*, 14. Writing about his mother's passing, Barthes says: "How strange, her voice which I knew so well, and which is said to be the very texture of memory . . . I no longer hear."

59. Gumbrecht, *Production of Presence*.

60. Gumbrecht, *Production of Presence*, 18.

61. Robert Orsi, *History and Presence*, 2. Orsi explains how "in an intellectual culture premised on absence, the experience of presence is the phenomenon that is the most disorienting, most inexplicable" (64).

62. Ibid., 62; emphasis added.

63. Shayegan, *Panj Eqlim-e Huzur*, 14.

CHAPTER TWO

Parts of this chapter appeared in my article "The Private Performance of Salat Prayers: Time, Repetition, and Meaning, " *Anthropological Quarterly* 86, no. 1 (Winter 2013), 5–34. I thank *AQ* for permission to reproduce sections of that article here.

1. Asef Bayat rightly argues against characterizing engagements with Islam "from within" always "in terms of religious revivalism, or as an expression of primordial loyalties." Bayat, *Life as Politics*, 3–4.

2. Orsi, *History and Presence*, 3.

3. For one of the earliest anthropological studies of prayer, see Marcel Mauss's *On Prayer* (published in French in 1909). Mauss expresses surprise that anthropologists and historians have treated prayer in generalities and have not paid sufficient detailed attention to it. That observation remains largely true with a few exceptions. For studies of *namaz/salat* by anthropologists, see Bowen, *Muslims through Discourse*; Henkel, "Between Belief and Unbelief"; Mahmood, "Rehearsed Spontaneity and the Conventionality of Ritual";

Mahmood, *Politics of Piety*; Simon, "The Soul Freed of Cares?"; Haeri, "The Private Performance"; Lambek, "Localising Islamic Performance"; and Parkin and Headley, *Islamic Prayer across the Indian Ocean*. Also see note 30 for this chapter, which discusses Khomeini's writings on namaz; Katz, *Prayer in Islamic Thought and Practice*; and Padwick, *Muslim Devotions*.

4. In conversational Persian, the long vowel [aa] becomes [oo] (as in "food") when it occurs before nasals. Hence *namaz-khoon, tehroon, iroon*, etc.

5. In a piece titled "A Christian Perspective on Muslim Prayer," Daniel Madigan observes: "It is a great pity—indeed, a gross injustice—that almost the only images of the Muslim ritual prayer seen by people in the West are the accompaniment to television news reports of violence and radicalism. Those who lived through the violent decades of the Irish 'Troubles' can imagine what the corrosive effect would have been if every report of an IRA attack had been illustrated by images of Catholics at Mass" (65).

6. This is a rather long way from times when Christians admired the devotion displayed by Muslims performing namaz. See, for example, Christian and Mittermaier, "Muslim Prayer on Picture Postcards."

7. Elaheh, for example, told a story about how mosques have changed. She said that a few decades earlier, when she and her sister "were still young and beautiful," they were window shopping in Isfahan when they noticed a few young men following them. After a while, they realized they could not shake them off, and so they decided the best thing to do was to walk into a mosque. It was summertime and the weather was hot. Elaheh and her sister entered the mosque and immediately felt the cool air, the feel of tile floors under their bare feet, and the safe surroundings. She commented: "This is what mosques were also meant to do—to provide shelter from heat and cold, and safety from unwanted attention or danger."

8. See Fischer and Abedi on differences between Sunnis and Shi'as with regard to Friday prayers. Fischer and Abedi, *Debating Muslims*, 120–21.

9. *Dehkohda Dictionary*, s.v. "namaz."

10. Khan, "The Acoustics of Muslim Striving."

11. One of the most beloved azans in Iran was recorded by the late Mu'azzinzadeh Ardebili. He recited this azan in the Persian classical mode, *bayat turk*, hence the azan has an "prelude" (*pish-daramad*) that most azans do not. He also recited it without this prelude. To listen, access https://www.youtube.com/watch?v=NotoOHfKFaE.

12. Manuals are available that describe the minutest details of the ablutions. My aim is to present the main idea briefly.

13. One widely known and shared joke is the substitution of "because I fear my father" for "to get close to God."

14. Every cycle ends after one stands up following sojud, except the very last one, where, after sojud, one sits up and recites the tashahhod and then salam when the prayer ends.

15. Angelika Neuwirth explains that it is likely the *bism allah* was not a part of al-Fatiha, in which case the sura starts with al-Hamd. She believes that this is the likely reason why Shi'as refer to the sura with this name. See her *Scripture, Poetry, and the Making of a Community*, 164–66.

16. Sells, *Approaching the Qur'an*, 43; see also Neuwirth, *Scripture, Poetry, and the Making of a Community*, chap. 6.

17. Neuwirth, *Scripture, Poetry, and the Making of a Community*, 164.

18. Sells, *Approaching the Qur'an*, 42.

19. Ibid., 136.

20. Mahmood, *Rehearsed Spontaneity*, 827–53; also see Mahmood, *Politics of Piety*.

21. According to Constance Padwick, "There are several variants of the much-used 'Prayer of Ya Latif,' some said to have been taught to travelers in the desert by Khidr, another said to have been the prayer of Jacob when Judah brought him Joseph's coat as a sign that the latter was alive (Qur'an, 12:93)." She observes that "it is noteworthy that in prayer, the Name of God constantly associated with His activity is al-Latif, the Kindly." Padwick, *Muslim Devotions*, 254.

22. To give an idea of the content of some of these suras, here are a few examples:

Al-Sharh (The Relief)
Did We not expand for you, [O Muhammad], your breast?
And We removed from you your burden
Which had weighed upon your back
And raised high for you your repute.
For indeed, with hardship [will be] ease.
Indeed, with hardship [will be] ease.
So when you have finished [your duties], then stand up [for worship].
And to your Lord direct [your] longing.

Al-Falaq (The Daybreak)
Say, "I seek refuge in the Lord of daybreak
From the evil of that which He created
And from the evil of darkness when it settles
And from the evil of the blowers in knots
And from the evil of an envier when he envies."

Al-Nas (Mankind)
Say, "I seek refuge in the Lord of mankind,
The Sovereign of mankind.
The God of mankind,
From the evil of the retreating whisperer—
Who whispers [evil] into the breasts of mankind—
From among the jinn and mankind."

23. They say, for example, three *allaho akbar* or this verse from the Qur'an (2:201): *"rabbina aatina fil dunya hasana va fil akherateh hasana . . . "* (Our Lord! Give unto us in the world that which is good and in the Hereafter that which is good, and guard us from the punishment of Fire).

24. See the websites of Ayatollahs Araki, Behjat, Tabrizi, Khoei, Fazel-Lankarani, Golpaygani, Sistani, and Makarem Shirazi, among others.

25. In the social sciences, most studies of this ritual prayer have examined its congregational performance, and this focus has both skewed the study of namaz toward men and reproduced the notion that for all Muslims everywhere not praying at the mosque is somehow religiously disfavored. See Parkin and Headly, *Islamic Prayer Across the Indian Ocean*. Major exceptions are Mahmood, *Rehearsed Spontaneity*; Mahmood, *Politics of Piety*; Henkel, *Between Belief and Unbelief* ; and Haeri, "Private Performance of *Salat* Prayers. See also Katz, *Prayer in Islamic Thought and Practice*, which offers debates

similar to those that take place among Iranian Shi'as on the question of an ideal prayer from a Sunni point of view.

26. "*Namaz-eh Jamaa'at*," Wikifeqh, accessed August 21, 2019, http://www.wikifeqh. ir/%D9%86%D9%85%D8%A7%D8%B2_%D8%AC%D9%85%D8%B9%D9%87.

27. For example, see Fanella Cannell's discussion of the "mistrust of the experiential in ritual" on the part of some anthropologists in her "How Does Ritual Matter?" Extending beyond anthropologists, this phenomenon can be seen also among scholars of religion.

28. Many Muslim women, in particular those outside Muslim-majority countries, have taken steps toward attending prayers led by women. The American scholar of Islam Amina Wudud became well-known in part due to her leading prayers in 2005 in New York. See also Pnina, "Seeking Recognition."

29. I find a similarity here between the idea of practice and that of iteration as explored by Jacques Derrida. Arguing against John Searle that a citation or use must be "serious" rather than in jest, Derrida claimed that on the one hand, the serious could be a special case of that which is acted rather than the opposite. And that on the other hand, each iteration is open to new meanings because, each time, the citation is (re)contextualized. Derrida does not deny that a convention must be recognized for it to be a convention (or a performative), but he calls attention to the fact that the recognizability does not render the meanings of the convention closed to further possibilities. The insight captured by the openness of iteration seems to me to be similar to the conceptualization of the namaz as practice rather than repetition. See Derrida, *The Ear of the Other*.

30. There is a great deal of writing on the idea of stations that one may reach in practicing the namaz/salat in the course of a lifetime. Many theologians have written about stations in their *asrār il-salat*, or "mysteries or secrets of the salat," including Ayatollah Ruhollah Khomeini. The latter's *Mysteries of the Salat* was perceived to be too difficult, and he was encouraged to write another version that would be more suitable for the general public. This version has been translated into English and published by Brill as *The Mystery of Prayer: The Ascension of the Wayfarers and the Prayer of the Gnostics*, 2015. Ayatollah Khomeini then wrote *Adab As-Sala* in which he discusses various subjects including stations of the salat, covering topics that have to do with ritual purity and the clothes one must wear, and moving on to the spiritual stations and the particular understandings that the one who prays should hope to arrive at. In the second Chapter of *Adab Salat*, titled "The Stages of the Stations of the People of Suluk," he begins with this passage: "Know that there are for the people of *suluk* [journey], in this station (i.e., paying attention to the humility of servitude and the Glory of His Lordship) and other stations, countless stages and degrees, only to a few of which we can generally refer, since comprehensively knowing all their aspects and counting all the stages are beyond the capacity of this humble creature: '*The ways to Allah are as numerous as the breaths of the creatures*.'" Ruhollah Khomenei, *Adab As-Salat*. The last statement, in bold in the original, is a reference to a *hadis*.

31. Parvin described al-Hamd in this way: "In the namaz, in the seven ayas [of al-Hamd], we talk to God, we tell him that He is kind and merciful, we ask that we be guided to the right path. . . . Then when we say, 'It is you we worship and you we ask for help,' this is not just us, that 'we' encompasses all existence. Like David when he did namaz, he was harmonious with all of existence; the same with Suleiman, it is as if all of existence is praying and remembering God." The stories of David and of Suleiman in the Qur'an are about how, when they pray and show gratitude, all of nature prays with them.

32. The terms can be found in the work of Abu Hamed al-Ghazali (d. 1111) and have been in use by many others at least since that time.

33. This is similar to what Webb Keane describes about Protestants. See Keane, *Christian Moderns*; and Haeri, "Sincere Subject."

34. She is a retired high school teacher in the same generation. I did not have a chance to speak with her outside of this group gathering.

35. In her study of a group of pious, lower-middle-class women in Tehran, Azam Torab finds: "A basic feature of ritual activity is that meanings are not fixed but implied. ... Because [ritual activities] are open-ended, new interpretations are possible. ... [They] give rise to new understandings, enabling actors to negotiate the self, the social and the cultural." Torab, *Performing Islam*, 24.

36. Culler, *On Deconstruction*.

37. Talal Asad argues against scholars who see in the "doctrine of untranslatability" applied to the Qur'an, the "fixed literalness" of language that defines "the Moslem religion." Asad, *Secular Translations*, 58.

38. The absence of any strict form-content relationship is apparent in John Bowen's study of salat in Indonesia: "The *salat* is not structured around an intrinsic propositional or semantic core. It cannot be decoded semantically because it is not designed according to a single symbolic or iconic code. In particular times and places Muslims have construed the *salat* as conveying iconic or semantic meanings, but as part of particular spiritual, social, and political discourses." Bowen, "*Salat* in Indonesia," 615.

39. Orsi, *History and Presence*, 2.

40. See, for example, Bashir, *Sufi Bodies*, 68–74.

41. See the English translation by Richard Jeffrey Newman in Saadi, *Selections from Saadi's Gulistan*, 57–58.

42. The starchy ascetic puffed up with prayers and me
With meagre means, drunken ways and poverty—
Betwixt and between, let's see who God will favour.
Lewisohn, "Religion of Love and the Puritans of Islam," 180.

43. Hafez, Malek, and Zakani, *Faces of Love*, 78–79.

44. "*Namaz*," Wikifeqh, accessed December 12, 2015, http://www.wikifeqh .ir/%D9%86%D9%85%D8%A7%D8%B2.

45. He went to college, was recruited to join the army during the war with Iraq, and spent a few years at the front. When he came back, he began a thorough and methodic study of major Islamic texts, and he decided to become a teacher of the Qur'an.

46. A good namaz is often described with the help of adjectives such as *jānāneh* (vital; an adjective derived from *jān*, which means both body and soul), and the verb *keyf dashtan* (have exhilaration). This latter expression is used to describe many experiences that "hit the spot." At times, the verb *chasbidan*, meaning "welding," "bonding," or "sticking," is used, in the slangy expression *michasbeh*.

47. Her mother was a *seyyed*, a "descendant of the Prophet." She was born and raised in Tehran, but her mother's father was from Iraq. He had traveled to Iran, married her grandmother, and then stayed there. The kinship to Imam Musa Kazem, a seyyed (d. in Baghdad in 799 AD), is through her Iraqi grandfather.

48. A *rowzeh* is a religious gathering where a paid professional reciter comes and recites various pieces from the Qur'an and from the repertoire of Persian and Arabic religious songs and poems. It is also often held to commemorate the passing of a family member or

an imam, or the birthday of an imam. Organizing a rowzeh has savab, or religious merit.

49. I am reminded of Tanya Luhrmann's discussion about "those who loved to pray." They became "so absorbed in their prayer that the ordinary world could fade for them, and their sense of time and place and self would alter. They talked about how vivid their internal world became." Luhrmann, *When God Talks Back*, 133.

50. The workshop, Comparative Ethnographies of Prayer, was organized by Fenella Cannell at the London School of Economics. The scholars of Catholicism who spoke of the similarities were William "Bill" Christian and Robert Orsi. Later, Bill Christian, in a November 8, 2017, email to the author, wrote: "The cultivation of intense remembering like that, whether of the stations of the cross or other moments in the life of Christ or Mary, are part of spiritual exercises like those of Ludolphus of Saxony and others that were elaborated into those of Ignatius Loyola and still practiced today in retreats led by Jesuits, forming the basis for a kind of self-conversion and self-renewal in which one comes to realise what is good and bad, and one's state of grace by examining the emotions one feels when doing the imagining. The fascinating salat exercises of the women are also reminiscent of the renaissance memory palace techniques taught in China by the Jesuit Matteo Ricci, in which an imagined palace becomes a way to mentally place and remember objects." I thank Fenella, Bill, and Bob for the many fruitful conversations I have had with them over the years.

CHAPTER THREE

1. See, for example, the website of Ayatollah Kadivar, Mohsen Kadivar Official Website, accessed April 2, 2018, http://kadivar.com.

2. Marshall and Mosher, *Prayer*, xvii.

3. See Robert Orsi's description of encouraging Catholic children to "chat informally with God about their daily concerns." Orsi, *Between Heaven and Earth*, 99.

4. Other hadis from the Prophet speak of do'a as the key to God's kindness (*kelid-e dar-e rahmat*), the protector of the believer, and a pillar of religion. See "Kelid-e dar-e rahmat," Wikifeqh, accessed April 5, 2018, http://www.wikifeqh.ir/%D8%AF%D8%B9%D8%A7_(%D9%86%DB%8C%D8%A7%DB%8C%D8%B4)#foot55.

5. See Travis Zadeh, "Ingestible Scripture."

6. *Monajat* as a term perhaps gained wider currency after Khajeh Abdullah Ansari (d. 1088) wrote his *Munajatnameh* [Book of monajat]. It has been translated into English as *Munajat: The Intimate Prayers of Khawjeh Abdullah Ansari*. Such writings greatly contributed to widening the scope of written Persian and making it acceptable as a language of religion and worship.

7. Some scholars suggest God has many more names. However, everyone agrees that He has at least ninety-nine.

8. See "Raz-o-Niyaz," YouTube, accessed March 1, 2012, https://www.youtube.com/watch?v=UtiSizyf-Eg. Another example is Hussein Alizadeh's "Raz u Niyaz," YouTube, October 19, 2012, https://www.youtube.com/watch?v=6emCh801ocw.

9. I thank Linell Smith for this suggestion.

10. The complete quotation is: "At its heart, this is the dilemma of all human knowledge. We reach out to grasp a world we know to be more complex than our capacity to understand it, and we choose to act despite our awareness that what we take to be true may be an illusion, a wispy misperception." Luhrmann, *When God Talks Back*, xvii.

11. Luhrmann speaks of "reality monitoring . . . that involves [the] basic decision

about whether the source of a momentary experience is internal to the mind or external to the world." She goes on to say, "From the reality monitoring perspective, our minds are always aware of our awareness, always separating out the cognitive events in the burbling stream of consciousness, distinguishing those that are externally generated from those that are not, those that are real from those that have been imagined." Luhrmann, *When God Talks Back*, 217–18.

12. In one of Maryam's many conversations with her Rumi teacher, he spoke of "preparing for namaz" as an essential part of the worship. He explained that preparing means that "you make your mind ready to receive, you are open to what may transpire once you start to pray. If you do not do that and simply stand to repeat the words, not much will happen to you." Perhaps readying oneself in this way is also something that requires time and practice. One may not be aware of one's own state at prayer time.

13. This foundational concept in 'erfan is the focus of a vast body of writing, beginning with the work of Ibn Arabi (1165–1240). In Iran, one of the main philosophers associated with it is Mulla Sadra (d. 1635). See Rizvi, "Mollā Sadrā Sirāzi," *Encyclopædia Iranica*, http://www.iranicaonline.org/articles/molla-sadra-sirazi.

14. We also saw each other when we got her grandson together with my son.

15. Luhrmann states: "Skeptics sometimes imagine that becoming a religious believer means acquiring a belief the way you acquire a piece of furniture . . . and once it's done it's done. . . . In fact, what I saw was that coming to a committed belief in God was more like learning *to do* something than *to think* something. I would describe what I saw as a theory of attentional learning—that the way you learn to pay attention determines your experience of God . . . people learn specific ways of attending to their minds and their emotions to find evidence of God." Luhrmann, *When God Talks Back*, xxi.

16. Maryam left Tehran during the Iran-Iraq war when the city began to be bombed by Iraqi forces. Her daughters were very scared and she was alone, as her husband had gone to the United States to find a job. She tried to live in the United States with her husband for a few years, but things proved difficult, and she went back to Iran. At that point, she had to decide what to do with her daughters. Her own sisters were in the United States, so she left the older daughter more or less in their care and took the other one back home with her.

17. Ata Anzali describes this process well and in great detail in *"Mysticism" in Iran*.

18. It takes time to learn to pray in this way—lengthy, intimate, free-flowing. Parvin laughed as she made fun of how she prayed when she was young: "This is how I prayed: '*Khodaya*, I hope I can now get my BA and MA in America and see what they say [learn their ways]. . . . Then when I grow old, I will read the Qur'an and things like that.' . . . That's how I prayed when I was young."

19. See Mahmood, *Politics of Piety*.

20. See Lewis, "Semiotic Horizon of Dawn in the Poetry of Hafiz," 213.

21. Translated by Schimmel, *I am the Wind, You Are the Fire*, 162.

22. "ādāb-e Do'a," Wikifeqh, accessed June 15, 2017,
http://www.wikifeqh.ir/%D8%A2%D8%AF%D8%A7%D8%A8_%D8%AF%D8%B9%D8%A7. My translation.

23. "Do'a (niyayesh)," Wikifeqh, accessed December 10, 2017,
http://www.wikifeqh.ir/%D8%AF%DB%8C%D8%A7_(%D9%86%DB%8C%D8%A7%DB%8C%D8%B4).

24. For an extended explanation of such caution, see "Ehtiyat," Wikifeqh, accessed

December 10, 2017, http://www.wikifeqh.ir/%D8%A7%D8%AD%D8%AA%DB%8C%D8%A7%D8%B7.

25. Ayatollah Mohsen Kadivar, communication in Persian by email on December 31, 2017.

26. Robert Orsi, *History and Presence*, 65.

27. Armenian, Jewish, and Zoroastrian Iranians are exempt from this requirement, as they are exempt from religion classes.

28. Dubois, "Am I Just Talking to Myself?"

CHAPTER FOUR

1. Social histories of prayer books in Iran are sorely lacking, but Constance Padwick's *Muslim Devotions* and William Chittick's introduction to his translation of *Sahifeh Sajjadieh* are helpful and illuminating. Also see Ibn al-Hysayn, *Psalms of Islam*.

2. The website masjed.ir is a central source that offers links to useful topics for sermons. The first two links that follow (a and b) access websites with prepared sermons in Persian, and those that are specifically for women are marked as such. The third link (c) leads to a related website that focuses on building cultural and artistic centers (*kānūn*) in mosques. The final link (d) accesses a free app designed for those who regularly give sermons, referred to here as *moballegh* (imam, sermon-giver, propagandist). (a) "Fiche Manbar-e Akaharin Rooz-e Mah-e Mobarak-e Ramazan Montasher Shod" [The pulpit memo of the last day of the blessed month of Ramadan has been published]," masjed.ir, accessed May 7, 2019. http://news.masjed.ir/fa/newsagency/32051/. (b) "Fich-e Manbar" [Pulpit memo], masjed.ir, accessed May 7, 2019, http://www.masjed.ir/fa/products/fishmenbar; (c) Masjed, accessed May 7, 2019, https://masajed.farhang.gov.ir/fa/home; (d) "Fichha-ye Manbar-e Amadeh va Marsieh" [Ready-made memos of the pulpit and eulogies], Café Bazaar, accessed May 2019, https://cafebazaar.ir/app/com.velayat.fish/?l=fa.

3. The historian of Islam Angelika Neuwirth finds that "the primarily liturgical purpose of the Qur'anic texts not only expresses itself in conventional liturgical forms, such as prayers and hymns, which are ubiquitous in the Qur'an, it also infuses the Qur'anic narratives with a highly stylized diction that serves to distinguish them from profane speech." Neuwirth, *Scripture, Poetry and the Making of a Community Qur'an*, xxx. Constance Padwick believes that "the Qur'an is the psalter as well as the lectionary of Muslim worship." Padwick, *Muslim Devotions*, xxii.

4. Michael Sells explains: "The Qur'anic experience is not the experience of reading a written text from beginning to end." He continues: "Rather, the themes, stories, hymns, and laws of the Qur'an are woven through the life stages of the individual, the key moments of the community, and the sensual world of the town and the village. Life is punctuated by the recitation of the Qur'an by trained reciters who speak from the minarets of mosques, on the radio, and from cassettes played by bus drivers, taxi drivers, and individuals. The experience is a nonlinear repetition through recitation." Sells, *Approaching the Qur'an*, 12.

5. I have modified the translation on Qur'an.com, accessed August 10, 2019, https://quran.com/2/255.

6. Perhaps the most famous rabbina is the recitation by the hugely popular veteran contemporary Iranian singer Mohammad Reza Shajarian. Some religious authorities dislike the fact that a not so outwardly religious singer has produced a rabbina that is extraordinarily powerful. Shajarian was also banned for years until recently because he opposed the broadcasting of his performance on regime-controlled national television.

See "Rabana Ostad Shajarian," YouTube video, August 3, 2012, https://www.youtube .com/watch?v=1ZBrqXEBj28.

7. For each of these, the website quran.com provides various translations. Accessed May 10, 2020. https://quran.com/59/10?translations=101,84,21,20,19,18,17,85,22,95.

8. Zadeh, "Touching and Ingesting."

9. *Ahl al-bayt* in Arabic.

10. "*Etrat*," Wikifeqh, accessed June 10, 2019, http://wikifeqh.ir/%D8%B9% D8%AA%D8%B1%D8%AA. My translation.

11. This is probably the case for Sunnis as well, but it seems more popular among Shi'a.

12. See Chittick, xvi.

13. See Shari'ati, *Niyayesh*; and Shari'ati, *Falsafeyeh Niyayesh*. These two works overlap as they both are based on a lecture Shari'ati presented.

14. According to Medoff: "Although Sunnites hold Zayn-al-'ābedin in high esteem as a pious *tābe'i* (successor of the companions) and one of the seven jurists (*faqīh*) of Medina, his do'a are practically unknown amongst them. The source of emulation (*marja' al-taqlīd*) and bibliophile Sehāb-al-Din Mar'aši Najafi (d. 1990) relates sending a copy of the *Ṣaḥifa* to the Egyptian mufti and exegete Jawhar al-Ṭanṭāwi, who replied that it was unfortunate that the Sunnites were unaware of its sublime eloquence and lofty teachings. The Zaydi Shi'ites, on the other hand, accept and venerate the *Ṣaḥifa* in much the same way as the Imami Shi'ites." See Medoff, "Ṣaḥifa al-Sajjādiya, al-," *Encyclopædia Iranica*, http://www.iranicaonline.org/articles/sahifa-al-sajjadiya.

15. In his translation of the original fifty-four prayers in *Sahifeh*, Chittick states: "According to Shi'ite tradition, Zayn al-Abidin had collected his supplications and taught them to his children, especially Muhammad al-Baqir and Zayd. In later times the text became widely disseminated among Shi'ites of all persuasions. The specialists in the science of hadith maintain that the text is *mutawatir*; in other words, it was generally known from earliest times and has been handed down by numerous chains of transmission, while its authenticity has never been questioned." Chittick mentions that Allameh Majlesi (d. 1699) gathered many Sahifeh manuscripts and edited them. Chittick, xviii.

16. The list contained on the seminary website has brief commentaries on the quality of various translations. One of the most famous editions is a translation by the late Javad Fazel, who was not a religious scholar but a writer of religious and nonreligious fiction. Of Fazel's translation, the website comments, "one cannot really call this translation. The unforgettable [*zendeh yād*] author says all that his heart desires under [the excuse of] translation, with a beautiful and valuable prose." It characterizes other translations as "difficult," and still others as using a contemporary and comprehensible language. See "Tarjomeha-ey Sahifeh Sajjadieh" [Translations of Sahifeh Sajjadieh], Wikifeqh, accessed August 10, 2019, http://www.wikifeqh.ir/%D8%AA%D8%B1%D8%AC%D9%85%D9% 87%E2%80%8C%D9%87%D8%A7%DB%8C_%D8%B5%D8%AD%DB%8C%D9%8 1%D9%87%D8%B3%D8%AC%D8%A7%D8%AF%DB%8C%D9%87.

17. Padwick mentions this prayer book but not *Mafatih al-Jinan* in her study *Muslim Devotions*, although this text was published long before her book appeared.

18. "*Sheikh Abbas Qomi*," Wikifeqh, accessed May 17, 2017, http://www.wikifeqh. ir/%D8%B4%DB%8C%D8%AE_%D8%B9%D8%A8%D8%A7%D8%B3_%D9%82% D9%85%DB%8C.

19. The WikiShia article "*Mafatih al-Jinan*" states that although Sheikh Abbas Qomi described his motivation as producing a more reliable prayer book, he did not achieve

that goal. The article concludes that his book has the same problem as its predecessor of reproducing prayers considered to lack authenticity—that is to say, the chain of attribution to an Imam is so far-fetched that someone other than an Imam could have penned the prayers. See "Mafatih al-Jinan (Book)," WikiShia, accessed August 10, 2019, http:// fa.wikishia.net/view/%D9%85%D9%81%D8%A7%D8%AA%DB%8C%D8%AD_%D 8%A7%D9%84%D8%AC%D9%86%D8%A7%D9%86_%28%DA%A9%D8%AA%D 8%A7%D8%A8%29.

20. Use of the terms *mafatih* (keys) and *miftah* (key) is an old tradition, signaling a particular genre of religious writing with specific aims. A fair number of pre-twentieth-century religious books have this term in their title.

21. Qomi, *Kolliyat Mafatih al-Jinan*.

22. See Rahnema, *Islamic Utopian*.

23. That this and other prayer books are produced to look "sacred," with titles in calligraphic fonts, and with geometric patterns associated with Islamic art, and so on, creates more ambivalence among some people. The history and debates surrounding the look of these books await further research.

24. Shari'ati, *Niyayesh*, 30. My translation.

25. Shari'ati, *Falsafeyeh Niyayesh* [Philosophy of prayer], 57–58.

26. Shari'ati, *Falsafeyeh Niyayesh* [Philosophy of prayer], 58–60. He delivered similar ideas in a lecture that begins with praise of Alexis Carrel (1873–1944), a French surgeon who, among other things, wrote a book on prayer. This book was translated into Persian by Shari'ati, who offered extensive quotes from it to develop his discussion. Also see Shari'ati's website, Bonyad-e Doctor Shari'ati (Dr. Shari'ati's Foundation), accessed on August 10, 2019, http://drshariati.org/?cat=24.

27. In order to get a clear idea of what a chain of transmission is, see Ibn al-Hysayn, *Psalms of Islam*, 2–3.

28. See Qomi, *Kolliyat Mafatih al-Jinan*, 1079–1082.

29. Ayatollah Kadivar, *Mohsen Kadivar Official Website*, accessed May 27, 2017, http://kadivar.com/?p=15399.

30. Padwick, *Muslim Devotions*, xi.

31. He also related the story of a well-known but controversial religious leader who published a prayer whose authenticity is famously in doubt. The leader eventually had to put out a retraction, and the booklets were taken off the store shelves under pressure from other ayatollahs. This religious leader is looked upon as someone who just wants to profit and increase his fame from publishing many books under his name, even when he has not done the research or compilation himself.

32. It is explained as "life in this world," rather than the paradise *Mafatih al-Jinan*'s name promises. Another relatively well-known recent prayer book is Ayatollah Yusefi Gharavi's *Minhaj al-Haya fil al-Ad'iya wa-l-Ziyara*.

33. This introduction is an allusion to the characterization of *Mafatih al-Jinan* by some as "Akhbari." Akhbaris are those Muslims who reject the idea that ordinary humans have the capacity to approach the Qur'an with their own unmediated reason. Believers must rely on the Prophet and the Imams. The group challenging them is the Usūlis, who do believe in individual *ijtihad* and reason—the best-known Usuli in contemporary Iran is Ayatollah Khomeini. This is an old historical division among Shi'a. The Islamic republic's leadership and institutions are dominated by Usulis, though one can see the influence of Akhabaris as well. When I asked a librarian in a Qom research center whether there were

histories of prayer books such as *Mafatih al-Jinan*, he seemed incredulous at the question and replied, "No, it is not worthwhile to do a history; it is an Akhbari work." See, for example, Newman, "The Nature of the Akhbari/Usuuli Dispute"; and Gleave, *Scripturalist Islam*. A source in Persian is "Ketabkhaneh Markaz Feqahat," accessed August 10, 2019, http://lib.eshia.ir/search/%D8%A7%D8%AE%D8%A8%D8%A7%D8%B1%DB%8C%D9%88%D9%86. Several other Persian-language sources are listed on this site.

34. Amoli, *Mafatih al-Hayat* [Keys to life], 1.

35. In the "Khatemeh" [Ending] the author devotes about twenty pages to what prayer books usually cover in terms of rites that should be carried out on particular days (in the lunar calendar). The selections are rather random, covering topics such as why one should pay alms, and why Nowruz (the New Year) is a good holiday.

36. For example: one must strive for knowledge that enlarges God and shrinks the world so that nothing worldly can attract his or her attention while doing *raz-o-niyaz* with the *ma'būd* (idol, divinity, the being one worships). One must choose the right location for praying—avoid praying in front of objects and things that may distract us because that is *makrūh* (disfavored)—the same with praying in front of open doors or where people come and go, or in front of mirrors and pictures. For this reason, according to Ayatollah Makarem Shirazi, mosques and other Muslim places should be simple and plain, without *zarq o barq* (glitter).

37. Shirazi, *Kolliyat Mafatih Novin*, 18–19. The two words in Persian are *rowhani* and *ma'navi*. Both can be translated as "spiritual" but also as "sacred," "inward," "moral," "incorporeal," "immaterial," and so on. Rowhani can also mean a cleric, a holy man.

38. Shirazi, *Kolliyat Mafatih Novin*, 16; emphasis added.

39. Ibid., 27; emphasis added.

40. A sample of the kinds of religious books they publish can be found on the Ketab-e Qom website, which displays books from the Ministry of Culture and Guidance, the Syndicate of Qom Publishers, and the Qom Internet Bookshop. Ketab-e Qom, accessed August 10, 2019, http://ketabeqom.com/fa/index. The well-known Hossein Elahi Qomshei, who lectures widely on mystic poetry and the Qur'an and appears on and off on television progams, also has a book with the title Connection with God. See Ghomshei, *Ertebat ba Khoda*.

41. Prayer books recommend that if one cannot go to the gravesite of an Imam, one can do a pilgrimage from afar: one can do ablutions, dress cleanly, and then go on the roof of a house or a high point somewhere, turn in the direction of that gravesite, and do a *ziyarat* namaz. See "Ziyarat: Ziyarat from Far way," Wikifeqh, accessed on June 13, 2019, http://wikifeqh.ir/%D8%B2%DB%8C%D8%A7%D8%B1%D8%AA#%D8%B2%DB%8C%D8%A7%D8%B1%D8%AA%20%D8%A7%D8%B2%20%D8%B1%D8%A7%D9%87%20%D8%AF%D9%88%D8%B1.

42. It is not easy to tell readers what this price means in terms of a foreign currency because due to sanctions and the economic situation in Iran, Iranian currency has lost much of its value. At the moment, about 12,000 toman is the equivalent of one dollar, more or less (before the revolution it was 7 toman to one dollar). Given the many hardships that most people are experiencing, 5,000 toman is the price of about five large pieces of flat bread, and so beyond middle-class consumers, few could afford to spend this amount on a prayer book. This is one of the reasons why mosques and shrines stock up on prayer books.

43. It also advertises, as do most prayer books these days, that the printed text has clear indications of all "pause marks" (*'alamateh vaqf*)—diacritical marks that show where the final vowel need not be pronounced or where the reciter can pause and take

a breath. Recall that the prayers are in Arabic, and most readers need some guidance in pronunciation as well as in translation. The diacritical marks are particularly important on occasions when one must recite aloud, as in vow gatherings. Such performances involve demonstrating knowledge of Arabic, the Qur'an, and recitation techniques. The shorter book in the series is in its twenty-ninth printing and is eighty pages in length; each printing produces 10,000 copies; and each book costs 1,500 toman, cheaper than the other one but still not easily affordable. It has five prayers: for Ashura (the tenth day of the lunar month of Muharram, when Imam Hussein was killed in the battle of Karbala in 680 CE); the Do'a of Kumail (Kumail was a companion of Imam Ali, to whom this prayer is said to have been taught by an Imam); the Do'a of Tavassol (intercession); the Do'a of Nudbeh (wailing, regret); and the Do'a of Faraj (relief). The last three prayers address God but also address the Prophet, Hazrat Ali, Imam Hasan, Fatima al-Zahra (the daughter of the Prophet and wife of Imam Ali), and other Imams to help the reciter in times of need.

44. One example is a do'a I own that was published by a charity devoted to orphans. The charity produces a series of such do'a, available on the website of the Fatemeh Zahra Charitable Organization, accessed August 10, 2019, http://www.fatemehzahra.org.

45. "Man va Ancheh Nemipasandam" [Me and what I do not like].

46. Ibid.; emphasis added.

47. This is reminiscent of "translations" of Hafez and Rumi into English where the translated poems often are almost unrecognizable to those who know the poems in Persian. However, the poets' names sell. Similarly, in Iran, a book that on the one hand claims to be based on the prayers of the Prophet and the Imams but on the other hand tries to evoke a contemporary sensibility is clearly aiming to maximize readership. One rarely comes across translation of popular American self-help authors such as Deepak Chopra in religious bookstores, yet their books do get instantly translated and distributed. These are also easily available, and due to satellite TV, their Persian-speaking counterparts residing outside Iran are accessible as well.

48. "Man va Ancheh Nemipasandam," back cover.

49. Nazar-Ahari, *Chai ba Ta'meh Khuda*. The book was favorably reviewed on the following weblog and many people have written in the comments section, admiring almost everything about it. The author of the weblog suggests the book presents a "simple mysticism." Kanoon News, website of Institute for the Intellectual Development of Children and Young Adults, accessed August 10, 2019, http://hormozgan.kanoonnews.ir/NSite/Service/News/?&Serv=133&SGr=191.

50. Ketab Ofogh, accessed August 10, 2019, http://ofoqbook.blogfa.com/tag/%DA%86%D8%A7%DB%8C-%D8%A8%D8%A7-%D8%B7%D8%B9%D9%85-%D8%AE%D8%AF%D8%A7.

51. Florence Scovel Shinn (1871–1940) wrote *The Game of Life and How to Play It*. See also the website devoted to her: "Florence Scovel Shinn," accessed August 10 2019, http://www.florence-scovel-shinn.com.

52. It is recommended that this prayer be recited on Friday nights (and in the middle of the lunar month of Sha'ban). Here are a few lines (I chose lines from various translations and I also changed some words, so this is neither entirely my own translation nor anyone else's, though many of those available on the Internet are similar to this one):

Prayer of Kumail (abridged)
In the Name of God, the Merciful, the Compassionate

Oh God, I ask you by your mercy that "encompasses all things" [Qur'an 7:156]
And by your strength that dominates all things,
And toward which all things are humble
And before which all things are lowly,
And by your invincibility through which you overwhelm all things,
And by your might that nothing can resist,
And by your grandness that has filled all things,
By your force that towers over all things

. . .

And by the light of your face, through which all things are illuminated,
Oh Light, oh Holy,
Oh first of those who are first
O Last of those who are last.
Oh God, forgive me those sins that tear apart safeguards,
Oh God, forgive me those sins that draw down adversities.

. . .

Oh God I seek closeness to you through remembrance of you.

53. Reinburg, *French Books of Hours*, 53. Reinburg states that women were the main readers of prayer books before 1400, and afterward they came to be used by the whole family.

54. Qomi, *Kolliyat Mafatih al-Jinan*, 1085.

55. Omm Davood is an actual historical figure who is said to have been taught a do'a by Imam Jafar Sadegh in order for her imprisoned son to be freed. Elaheh may or may not have been referring to this figure.

56. Reinburg, *French Books of Hours*, 92.

57. Azam Torab, *Performing Islam*.

58. Videos of Haideh Khadem are available on YouTube, and she seems to have Facebook and Instagram accounts.

59. See, for example, Anzali. *"Mysticism" in Iran*.

CONCLUSION

1. My translation.

Bibliography

Abu-Lughod, Lila. *Veiled Sentiments: Honor and Poetry in a Bedouin Society*. Berkeley: University of California Press, 1986.

Adelkhah, Fariba. *Being Modern in Iran*. New York: Columbia University Press, 2000.

Ahmed, Shahab. *What Is Islam? The Importance of Being Islamic*. Princeton, NJ: Princeton University Press, 2016.

Amin, Camron Michael. *The Making of the Modern Iranian Woman: Gender, State Policy, and Popular Culture, 1865–1946*. Gainesville: University Press of Florida, 2002.

Amanat, Abbas. *Iran: A Modern History*. New Haven, CT: Yale University Press. 2019.

Amoli, Ayatollah Javadi. *Mafatih al-Hayat* [Keys to life]. Tehran: Intisharat Sokhan, 2012 [1933].

Anzali, Ata. *"Mysticism" in Iran: The Safavid Roots of a Modern Concept*. Columbia: University of South Carolina Press, 2017.

Arasteh, Reza. *Rumi the Persian, the Sufi: Rebirth in Creativity and Love*. London: Routledge, 2008.

Asad, Talal. *Genealogies of Religion: Discipline and Reasons of Power in Christianity and Islam*. Baltimore: Johns Hopkins University Press, 1993.

———. "The Idea of an Anthropology of Islam." Occasional Paper Series 1. Washington, DC: Georgetown University, Center for Contemporary Arab Studies, 1986.

———. *Secular Translations: Nation-State, Modern Self, and Calculative Reason*. New York: Columbia University Press, 2018.

Atabaki, Touraj, ed. *Iran in the 20th Century: Historiography and Political Cutlure*. London: I. B. Taurus, 2009.

Atabaki, Touraj, and Erik J. Zurcher, eds. *Men of Order: Authoritarian Modernization under Ataturk and Reza Shah*. London: I. B. Tauris, 2003.

Avery, Peter. "Foreword: Hafiz of Shiraz." In *Hafez and the Religion of Love in Classical Persian Poetry*, edited by Leonard Lewisohn, xi–xx. London: I. B. Tauris, 2015 [2010].

Badi'i, Mohammad. *Hozūr-e Qalb dar Namaz: Az Didgah-e 'Aleman-e Rabbani va 'arefan-e Elahi ba Asari Az Imam Khomeini va Digaran* [Presence of the heart in name: Views of divine scholars and mystic, with works from Imam Khomeini and others]. Qom: Intisharat Tashayyo', 1999.

Bakhtin, Mikhael, "Discourse in the Novel." In *The Dialogic Imagination: Four Essays by M. M. Bakhtin*. Edited by Michael Holquist. Translated by Caryl Emerson and Michael Holquist. Austin: University of Texas Press, 1981 [1935].

Barthes, Roland. *Mourning Diary: October 26, 1977–September 15, 1979*. New York: Hill and Wang, 2010.

Bashir, Shahzad. *Sufi Bodies: Religion and Society in Medieval Islam*. New York: Columbia University Press, 2011.

Bauer, Patricia. "Marzieh." In *Encyclopaedia Britannica*. Published online January 21, 2019. https://www.britannica.com/biography/Marzieh.

Bayat, Asef. *Life as Politics: How Ordinary People Change the Middle East*. Stanford, CA: Stanford University Press, 2013 [2010]).

Benjamin, Walter. "The Storyteller: Reflections on the Work of Nikolai Leskov." In *The Storyteller Essays*. New York: New York Review of Books, 2019.

Benveniste, Emile. *Problems in General Linguistics*. Miami: University of Miami Press, 1973.

Birašk, Ahmad. "Education: x. Middle and Secondary Schools." In *Encyclopædia Iranica* online. December 15, 1997. http://www.iranicaonline.org/articles/education-x-middle-and-secondary-schools.

Bowen, John. *Muslims through Discourse: Religion and Ritual in Gayo Society*. Princeton, NJ: Princeton University Press, 1993.

———. "*Salat* in Indonesia: The Social Meanings of an Islamic Ritual." *Man*, n.s., 24 (1989): 600–619.

Breyley, G. J., and Sasan Fatemi. *Iranian Music and Popular Entertainment: From Motrebi to Losanjelesi and Beyond*. New York: Routledge, 2016.

Bush, Andrew J. "An Offer of Pleasure: Islam, Poetry, and the Ethics of Religious Difference in a Kurdish Home." *American Ethnologist* 44, no. 3 (2017): 516–27.

Cannell, Fenella. "How Does Ritual Matter?" In *Questions of Anthropology*, edited by Rita Astuti, Jonathan Parry, and Charles Stafford, 105–36. London School of Economics Monographs on Social Anthropology, no. 76. Oxford: Berg, 2007.

Caton, Steven. *"Peaks of Yemen I Summon": Poetry as Cultural Practice in a North Yemeni Tribe*. Berkeley: University of California Press, 1990.

Chehabi, Houshang. "The Imam as Dandy: The Case of Musa Sadr." *Harvard Middle Eastern and Islamic Review* 3 (1996): 20–41.

———. "Staging the Emperor's New Clothes: Dress Codes and Nation-Building under Reza Shah." *Iranian Studies* 26 (1993): 209–29.

Christian, William, and Amira Mittermaier. "Muslim Prayer on Picture Postcards of French Algeria, 1900–1960." *Material Religion* 13, no. 1 (2017), 23–51.

Culler, Jonathan. *On Deconstruction: Theory and Criticism after Structuralism*. Ithaca: Cornell University Press, 1983.

Dabashi, Hamid. *The World of Persian Literary Humanism*. Cambridge, MA: Harvard University Press, 2012.

Dastjerdi, Hossein Vahid. "Translation of Poetry: Sa'di's Oneness of Mankind Revisited." *Translation Directory* online. Accessed January 9, 2020. http://www.translationdirectory.com/article231.htm.

Davis, Dick. "Sufism and Poetry: A Marriage of Convenience?" *Edebiyat* 10, no. 2 (1999): 279–92.

de Blois, François. "Epics." In *Encyclopædia Iranica* online. Last modified December 15, 2011. http://www.iranicaonline.org/articles/epics.

Delkash: A Dream of Sound. Website. Accessed January 8, 2020. http://delkashmusic.tripod.com.

Derrida, Jacques. *The Ear of the Other: Otobiography, Transference, Translation: Texts and Discussions with Jacques Derrida*. Lincoln: University of Nebraska Press, 1985.

de Certeau, Michel. *The Practice of Everyday Life.* Berkeley: University of California Press, 1988.

Doostdar, Alireza. *The Iranian Metaphysicals: Explorations in Science, Islam, and the Uncanny.* Princeton, NJ: Princeton University Press, 2018.

Dubois, Joel. "'Am I Just Talking to Myself?' Extending Wittgenstein's Analysis of Language to Religious Forms of Thought and Inward Speech." *Harvard Theological Review* 94 (2001): 323–51.

Eliot, T. S. "The Love Song of J. Alfred Prufrock." The Poetry Foundation. Accessed January 20, 2020. https://www.poetryfoundation.org/poetrymagazine/poems/44212/the-love-song-of-j-alfred-prufrock.

Etesami, Parvin. *A Nightingale's Lament: Selections from the Poems and Fables of Parvin Etesami (1907–41).* Translated by Hershmat Moayyed and A. Margaret Arent Madelung. Santa Ana, CA: Mazda, 1985.

"Ezharat-e Dinani darbare-ye Raqs-e Arefaneh va Fatva-ye Maraji' Taqlid dar Radd va Takhta'e-ye ān" [What Dinani said about mystic dance and the fatwas of sources of emulation in their rejection]. *Maghreb News,* April 20, 2012. https://www.mashregh-news.ir/news/119654.

Farsani, Soheila Tarabi. *Asnadi az Madares Dukhtaran az Mashruteh ta Pahlavi.* Tehran: National Documents of Iran, 2000 [1378].

Farrokhzad, Forough. *A Literary Biography with Unpublished Letters.* Edited by Farzaneh Milani. Tehran: Persian Circle, 2016.

———. *Sin: Selected Poems of Forough Farrokhzad.* Edited and translated by Sholeh Wolpé. Fayetteville: University of Arkansas Press, 2010.

Farrell, Joseph. "The Latinate Tradition as a Point of Reference." In *Literacy in the Persianate World: Writing and the Social Order,* edited by Brian Spooner and William Hanaway, 360–87. Philadelphia: University of Pennsylvania Press, 2012.

Fischer, Michael, and Mehdi Abedi. *Debating Muslims: Cultural Dialogues in Postmodernity and Tradition.* Madison: University of Wisconsin Press, 2002 [1990].

Furey, Constance. "Body, Society, and Subjectivity in Religious Studies." *Journal of the American Academy of Religion* 80 (2012): 7–33.

Ghamari-Tabrizi, Behrooz. *Foucault in Iran: Islamic Revolution after the Enlightenment.* Minneapolis: University of Minnesota Press, 2016.

———. *Islam and Dissent in Postrevolutionary Iran.* New York: I. B. Tauris, 2008.

Gharavi, Ayatollah Yusefi. Minhaj al-Haya fil al-Ad'iya wa-l-Ziyara. Qom: Majma Jahani Ahl-Beyt, 2015 [1393].

Ghomshei, Ostad Elahi. *Ertebat ba Khuda.* Qom: Umm Abiha, 2013.

Gleave, Robert. *Scripturalist Islam: The History and Doctrines of the Akhbārī Shī'ī School.* Leiden: Brill, 2007.

Golestaneh, Seema. "The Social Life of Gnosis: Sufism in Post-Revolutionary Iran." PhD dissertation, Columbia University, 2014.

Gumbrecht, Hans Ulrich. *The Production of Presence: What Meaning Cannot Convey.* Stanford, CA: Stanford University Press, 2004.

Haeri, Niloofar. "The Private Performance of *Salat* Prayers: Time, Repetition and Meaning." *Anthropological Quarterly* 86 (2013): 5–34.

———. *Sacred Language, Ordinary People: Dilemmas of Culture and Politics in Egypt.* New York: Palgrave Macmillan, 2003.

———. "The Sincere Subject: Mediation and Interiority among a Group of Muslim

Women in Iran." *Hau: Journal of Ethnographic Theory* 7 (2017): 139–61.

Haeri, Shaykh Fadhlallah. "Prayer [*Salat*]." In *The Inner Meanings of Worship in Islam: A Personal Selection of Guidance for the Wayfarer*. Qom: Zahra, 2002.

"Hafez." In *Encyclopædia Iranica* online. Last modified March 1, 2012. http://www.iranicaonline.org/articles/hafez.

Hafez, Khatun, Jahan Malek, and Obayd-e Zakani. *Faces of Love: Hafez and the Poets of Shiraz*. Introduced and translated by Dick Davis. New York: Penguin Books, 2012.

Hanaway, W. L., Jr. "Amīr Arsalān." In *Encyclopædia Iranica* online. Last updated August 3, 2011. http://www.iranicaonline.org/articles/amir-arsalan-a-prose-romance-of-the-genre-dastanha-ye-ammiana-popular-tales.

Henkel, Heiko. "Between Belief and Unbelief Lies the Performance of *Salat*: Meaning and Efficacy of a Muslim Ritual." *Journal of the Royal Anthropological Institute* 11 (2005): 487–507.

Hillman, Michael. *A Lonely Woman: Forough Farrokhzad and Her Poetry*. Washington, DC: Three Continents Press, 1987.

al-Hujweri, Syed Ali Bin Uthman. *The Kashful Mahjub: Unveiling the Veiled*. Translated by Maulana Wahid Bakhsh Rabbani. Kuala Lumpur: A. S. Nordeen, 1997.

Ibn al-Hysayn, Zayn al-'Abidin Ali. *The Psalms of Islam: al-Sahifat al-Sajjadiyya*. Translated by William Chittick. Oxford: Oxford University Press, 1988.

Ilahi-Ghomshei, Husayn. "The Principles of the Religion of Love in Classical Persian Poetry." In *Hafez and the Religion of Love in Classical Persian Poetry*, edited by Leonard Lewisohn, 77–107. London: I. B. Tauris, 2015 [2010].

"Intiqad az Hazf-e Nam-e Bozorgan-e Adabiyat-e Iran" [Criticism of the elimination of the names of major literary figures]. BBC News Farsi, November 5, 2019. https://www.bbc.com/persian/iran-50311057.

Jackson, Michael. *The Palm at the End of the Mind: Relatedness, Religiosity, and the Real*. Durham, NC: Duke University Press, 2009.

Johnston, Barbara. *The Linguistic Individual: Self-Expression in Language and Linguistics*. New York: Oxford University Press, 1996.

Kadkani, Shafi'i. *Ba Cheraq va Ayne: Dar Jostejuyeh Rishehayeh Tahavvuleh Shi'reh Mosha'ereh Iran* [With light and mirror: In search of the roots of transformation in contemporary Persian poetry]. Tehran: Intisharat Sokhan, 2011.

Katouzian, Homa. *The Persians: Ancient, Medieval and Modern*. New Haven, CT: Yale University Press, 2010.

Katz, Marion. *Prayer in Islamic Thought and Practice*. Cambridge: Cambridge University Press, 2013.

Keane, Webb. *Christian Moderns: Freedom and Fetish in the Mission Encounter*. Berkeley: University of California Press, 2007.

Kermani, Navid. *God Is Beautiful: The Aesthetic Experience of the Quran*. Translated by Tony Crawford. Cambridge: Polity Press, 2015.

Khan, Naveeda. "The Acoustics of Muslim Striving: Use in Ritual Practice." *Comparative Studies in Society and History* 53 (2011): 571–94.

Khomeini, Ruhollah. *Adab As Salat* [The disciplines of the prayer]. Edited by Mohammad Jafar Khalili. Qom: Institute for Compilation and Publication of Imam Khomeini's Works, 1982 [1943].

———. *Sirr al-Salat: Mi'raj al-Salekin wa-Salat al-'Arifin*. Qom: Institute for Compilation and Publication of Imam Khomeini's Works, 2009 [1991].

Lambek, Michael. "Localising Islamic Performance in Mayotte." In *Islamic Prayer Across the Indian Ocean: Inside and Outside the Mosque*, edited by David Parkin and Stephen Headley. Surrey: Curzon Press, 2000: 63–98.

Khorramshahi, Baha'eddin. *Divan-e Hafez*, 4th ed. Tehran: Nahid, 2009.

Lewis, Franklin D. "The Semiotic Horizon of Dawn in the Poetry of Hafiz." In *Hafiz and the Religion of Love in Classical Persian Poetry*, edited by Leonard Lewisohn, 251–77. London: I. B. Tauris, 2015 [2010].

Lewisohn, Leonard, "The Religion of Love and the Puritans of Islam: Sufi Sources of Hafiz's Anti-Clericalism." In *Hafiz and the Religion of Love in Classical Persian Poetry*, edited by Leonard Lewisohn, 159–96. London: I. B. Tauris, 2015 [2010].

———, ed. *Hafiz and the Religion of Love in Classical Persian Poetry*. London: I. B. Tauris, 2015 [2010].

Lindisfarne-Tapper, Nancy, and Bruce Ingham, eds. *Languages of Dress in the Middle East*. Surrey: Curzon, 1997.

Losensky, Paul. "Sa'di." In *Encyclopædia Iranica* online. Last modified February 12, 2012. http://www.iranicaonline.org/articles/sadi-sirazi.

Luhrmann, Tanya. *When God Talks Back: Understanding the American Evangelical Relationship with God*. New York: Vintage Books, 2012.

Madigan, Daniel. "A Christian Perspective on Muslim Prayer." In *Prayer: Christian and Muslim Perspectives*, edited by David Marshall and Lucinda Mosher, 65–72. Washington, DC: Georgetown University Press, 2013.

Mahmood, Saba. *Politics of Piety: Islamic Revival and the Feminist Subject*. Princeton: Princeton University Press, 2005.

———. "Rehearsed Spontaneity and the Conventionality of Ritual: Disciplines of '*Salāt*.'" *American Ethnologist* 28 (2001): 827–53.

"Man va Ancheh Nemipasandam" [Me and what I do not like]. *Niyayeshha*, no. 12. Edited by Ali Baqerifar. Tehran: Boshraa, 2010.

Manoukian, Setrag. *City of Knowledge in Twentieth Century Iran: Shiraz, History and Poetry*. London: Routledge: 2012.

Marshall, David, and Lucina Mosher, eds. *Prayer: Christian and Muslim Perspectives*. Washington, DC: Georgetown University Press, 2013.

Mauss, Marcel. 2008. *On Prayer*. New York: Berghahn Books.

Medoff, Louis. "Ṣaḥifa al-Sajjādiya, al-." In *Encyclopædia Iranica* online. September 7, 2016. http://www.iranicaonline.org/articles/sahifa-al-sajjadiya.

Meskoob, Shahrokh. *Iranian National Identity and the Persian Language: Roles of the Court, Religion, and Sufism in Persian Prose Writing*. Washington, DC: Mage, 2015 [1992].

Metcalf, Barbara. *Moral Conduct and Authority: The Place of Adab in South Asian Islam*. Berkeley: University of California Press, 1984.

Mirhadi, Munir al-Sadat. *Ta'sir Madares Dokhtaraneh dar Towse'eh Ijtima'i Zanan dar Iran*. Tehran: Kavir, 2015 [1393].

Moayyed, Heshmat, ed. *Once a Dew Drop: Essays on the Poetry of Parvin E'tesami*. Santa Ana: Mazda, 1994.

Mojaddedi, Jawid. "Rumi, Jalāl-al-Din viii. Rumi's Teachings." *Encyclopædia Iranica*, online edition. Accessed September 8, 2014. http://www.iranicaonline.org/articles/rumi-jalal-al-din-teachings.

Moore, Brenna. "Friendship and the Cultivation of Religious Sensibilities." *Journal of the American Academy of Religion* 4 (2015): 1–27.

"Moosa va Shaban beh Qara'at-e Mohsen Qara'ati" [Moses and the Shepherd According to Mohsen Qara'ati]. BBC online, May 7, 2014. http://www.bbc.com/persian/blogs/2014/05/140507_l44_nazeran_gheraati_masnavi.

Najafian, Ahoo. "Poetic Nation: Iranian Soul and Historical Continuity." PhD dissertation, Stanford University, 2018.

Naficy, Hamid. *A Social History of Iran.* Vol. 2, *The Industrializing Years, 1941–1978.* Durham, NC: Duke University Press, 2011.

Nafisi, Saeed. "Introduction." In *Reading Persian and Grammar for Third Year of High School: According to the New Program of the Ministry of Culture.* [In Persian.] Tehran: Ministry of Education, 1959 [Iranian year 1338].

"Naqd-e Shi'r-e Mowlavi Tavasott-e Hojjat al-Islam Qara'ati" [Critique of Mowlavi's poem by Hojjat al-Islam Qara'ati]. Aparat. Accessed October 10, 2017. https://www.aparat.com/v/io8Zw/.

Nasr, Seyyed Hossein. *Islamic Philosophy from Its Origin to the Present: Philosophy in the Land of Prophecy.* Albany: SUNY Press, 2006.

———. *Three Muslim Sages: Avicenna, Suhrawardi, Ibn Arabi.* Delmar, NY: Caravan Books, 1976 [1964].

Nazar-Ahari, Irfan. *Chai ba Ta'meh Khuda* [Tea with a Taste of God]. Tehran: Ofoq, 2006.

Neuwirth, Angelika. *Scripture, Poetry, and the Making of a Community: Reading the Qur'an as a Literary Text.* Oxford: Oxford University Press, 2014.

Newman, Andrew J. "The Nature of the Akhbari/Usuuli Dispute in Late Safawid Iran. Part One: Abdallah al-Samahiji's 'Munyat al-Mumirisin.'" *Bulletin of the School of Oriental and African Studies* 55 (1992): 22–51.

Orsi, Robert A. *Between Heaven and Earth: The Religious Worlds People Make and the Scholars Who Study Them.* Princeton, NJ: Princeton University Press, 2005.

———. *History and Presence.* Cambridge, MA: Belknap Press, 2016.

Padwick, Constance. *Muslim Devotions: A Study of Prayer-Manuals in Common Use.* Oxford: Oneworld, 1996 [1961].

Parkin, David, and Stephen Headley, eds. *Islamic Prayer across the Indian Ocean: Inside and outside the Mosque.* Surrey: Curzon Press, 2000.

Perry, John. "New Persian: Expansion, Standardization, and Inclusivity." In *Literacy in the Persianate World: Writing and the Social Order,* edited by Brian Spooner and William L. Hanaway, 70–94. Philadelphia: University of Pennsylvania Press, 2012.

Pirnia, Daryush, with Erik Nakjavani. "Golhā, Barnāma-ye." In *Encyclopædia Iranica* online. Last updated February 14, 2012. http://www.iranicaonline.org/articles/golha-barnama-ye.

Pnina, Lahav. "Seeking Recognition: Women's Struggle for Full Citizenship in the Community of Religious Worship." In *Gendering Religion and Politics,* edited by Hanna Herzog and Ann Braude. New York: Palgrave Macmillan, 2009.

Prophet Moses (AS)—Part 1. Accessed January 9, 2020. http://eram.shirazu.ac.ir/www2/CD1/www.iua-net.org/Books/Stories_of_Prophets/moses1.htm.

Puett, Michael, and Christine Gross-Loh. *The Path: What Chinese Philosophers Can Teach Us about the Good Life.* New York: Simon & Schuster, 2016.

al-Qushayri, 'Abd al-Karim ibn Hawazin. *Epistle on Sufism: Al-Risala al-qushayriyya fi 'ilm al-tasawwuf.* Translated by Alexander D. Kaysh. Ithaca, NY: Garnet, 2007.

Qomi, Sheikh Abbas. *Kolliyat Mafatih al-Jinan.* Tehran: Saba, 2003 [1381].

Rahnema, Ali. *An Islamic Utopian: A Political Biography of Ali Shari'ati*. London: I. B. Tauris, 2000 [1998].

"Ravayat-e Mansoori Larijani Darbare-ye Dinani" [The story of Mansoori Larijani about Dinani]. *Philosophyar* (September 23, 2014). https://philosophyar.net/interview-with-mansoori-larijani.

"Raz-o-Niyaz." YouTube. March 1, 2012. https://www.youtube.com/watch?v=UtiSizyf-Eg.

Reinburg, Virginia. *French Books of Hours: Making an Archive of Prayer, c. 1400–1600*. Cambridge: Cambridge University Press, 2014 [2012].

Rizvi, Sajjad. "Mollā Sadrā Sirāzi." In *Encyclopædia Iranica* online. July 20, 2005. http://www.iranicaonline.org/articles/molla-sadra-sirazi.

———. "Mulla Sadra." In *The Stanford Encyclopedia of Philosophy*. Spring 2019 Edition. Edited by Edward N. Zalta. https://plato.stanford.edu/archives/spr2019/entries/mulla-sadra.

Rostam-Kolayi, Jasamin. "From Evangelizing to Modernizing Iranians: The American Presbyterian Mission and Its Iranian Students." *Iranian Studies* 41 (2008): 213–39.

———. "Origins of Iran's Modern Girls' Schools: From Private/National to Public/State." *Journal of Middle East Women's Studies* 4 (2008): 58–88.

Rumi, Jalal al-Din. *The Essential Rumi*. Translated by Coleman Barks. San Francisco: HarperOne, 2004, [1995].

———. *Rumi: Swallowing the Sun*. Translated by Franklin D. Lewis. Oxford: Oneworld, 2008.

———. *This Longing: Poetry, Teaching Stories and Letters of Rumi*. Translated by Coleman Barks and John Moyne. New York: Threshold Books, 1988.

"Rumi, Jalāl-al-Din." *Encyclopædia Iranica* online. Last modified August 14, 2017. http://www.iranicaonline.org/articles/rumi-jalal-al-din-parent.

Saadi, *Selections from Saadi's Gulistan*. Translated by Richard Jeffery Newman. New York: Global Scholarly Publications, 2004.

Schayegh, Cyrus. *Who Is Knowledgeable Is Strong: Science, Class, and the Formation of Modern Iranian Society, 1900–1950*. Berkeley: University of California Press, 2009.

Schimmel, Annemarie. *I Am the Wind, You Are the Fire: The Life and Work of Rumi*. Boulder: Shambhala, 1992.

Sells, Michael Anthony. *Approaching the Qur'an: The Early Revelations*. Ashland: White Cloud Press: 2007 [1999].

———, trans. and ed. *Early Islamic Mysticism: Sufi, Qur'an, Miraj, Poetic and Theological Writings*. Mahwah: Paulist Press, 1995.

Shabestari, Muhammad Mujtahid. *Naqd Bunyadha-eh Fiqh va Kalam*. Last modified 2018. http://mohammadmojtahedshabestari.com/1282-2.

Shari'ati, Ali. *Falsafeyeh Niyayesh* [Philosophy of prayer: Awareness, love, need, and jihad]. Tehran: Elham, 2010.

———. *Niyayesh*. Tehran: Sepidbavaran, 2011.

Shayegan, Dariush. *Panj Eqlim-e Huzur: Bahsi Darbari-ye Sha'eranegi-e Iranian* [Five realms of presence: A discussion of the poeticity of Iranians]. 7th ed. Tehran: Farhang Moaser, 2017 [Iranian year 1395].

Shinn, Florence Scovel. *The Game of Life and How to Play it*. Mansfield Centre, CT: Martino, 2011.

Shirazi, Nasser Makarem. *Kolliyat Mafatih Novin*. Qom: Imam Ali Ibn Abi Taleb, 2011.

Simms, Rob, and Amir Koushkani. *The Art of Avaz and Mohammad Reza Shajarian: Foundations and Contexts.* Lanham, MD: Lexington Press, 2012.

Simon, Gregory. "The Soul Freed of Cares? Islamic Prayer, Subjectivity, and the Contradictions of Moral Selfhood in Minangkabau Indonesia." *American Ethnologist* 36 (2009): 258–75.

Smith, Jonathan. "Religion, Religions, Religious." In *Relating Religion: Essays in the Study of Religion,* edited by Jonathan Z. Smith, chap. 8. Chicago: University of Chicago Press, 2004.

Soroush, Abdolkarim. *Masnavi Ma'navi.* Two vols. Tehran: Elmi & Farhangi, 1996.

Spooner, Brian, and William L. Hanaway, eds. *Literacy in the Persianate World: Writing and the Social Order.* Philadelphia: University of Pennsylvania Press, 2012.

Torab, Azam. *Performing Islam: Gender and Ritual in Iran.* Leiden: Brill, 2007.

Yarshater, Ehsan. "Ḡazal ii. Characteristics and Conventions." In *Encyclopædia Iranica* online. November 15, 2006. http://www.iranicaonline.org/articles/gazal-2.

———. "Ventures and Adventures of the Persian Language." In *Persian Language, Literature and Culture: New Leaves, Fresh Looks,* edited by Kamran Talattof, 195–215. London: Routledge, 2015.

"Younesi va Tada'i Ma'ani Sokhanan-e masha'i" [Younesi and the implications of the sectarian words of Masha'i]. Tasnim News Agency. May 7, 2014. https://www.tasnimnews.com/fa/news/1393/02/14/358505/.

Youssefzadeh, Ameneh. "The Situation of Music in Iran since the Revolution: The Role of Official Organizations." *British Journal of Ethnomusicology* 9 (2000): 35–61.

Zarrinkoub, Abdolhossein. *Jostejoo dar Tasavoff-e Iran.* Tehran: Amir Kabir, 1978.

———. *Two Centuries of Silence.* Edited by Paul Sprachman. Costa Mesa, CA: Mazda, 2017.

"Zabaneh Farsi" [The Persian language]. Wikifeqh. Accessed February 17, 2018. http://www.wikifeqh.ir/%D8%B2%D8%A8%D8%A7%D9%86_%D9%81%D8%A7%D8%B1%D8%B3%DB%8C.

Zadeh, Travis. "An Ingestible Scripture: Qur'ānic Erasure and the Limits of 'Popular' Religion." In *History and Material Culture in Asian Religions,* ed. Benjamin Fleming and Richard Mann, 97–119. New York: Routledge, 2014.

———. "Touching and Ingesting: Early Debates over the Material Qur'ān." *Journal of the American Oriental Society* 129, no. 3 (2009): 443–66.

———. *The Vernacular Qur'an: Translation and the Rise of Persian Exegesis.* Oxford: Oxford University Press in association with the Institute of Ismaili Studies, 2012.

Index